DEEP
VEGETARIANISM

In the series
America in Transition: Radical Perspectives,
edited by Gary L. Francione

DEEP
VEGETARIANISM

MICHAEL ALLEN FOX

TEMPLE UNIVERSITY PRESS

PHILADELPHIA

Temple University Press, Philadelphia 19122
Copyright © 1999 by Temple University,
except Foreword © 1999 by Gary L. Francione
All rights reserved
Published 1999
Printed in the United States of America

Library of Congress Cataloging-in-Publication Data

Fox, Michael Allen.
    Deep vegetarianism / Michael Allen Fox.
        p.   cm. — (America in transition: radical perspectives)
    Includes bibliographical references and index.
    ISBN 1-56639-704-9 (cloth : alk. paper). — ISBN 1-56639-705-7
(pbk. : alk. paper)
        1. Vegetarianism.   2. Vegetarianism—Moral and ethical aspects.
I. Title. II. Series.
TX392.F79   1999
613.2′62—dc21   98-54680

To Louise and Zoé,
who showed me the way

I suggest that vegetarianism should not be studied or adopted in isolation, but should be seen as part of a way (a more eclectic and eco-*logical* way) of life that may help our species to attain a higher level of physical and mental health than we have known before. . . . Not only do we owe it to ourselves to examine our eating habits, but also to our environment, to the species with whom we share that environment, and perhaps above all to our children and those future generations whose very existence will be determined by the path we choose to take today.

Jon Wynne-Tyson, *Food for a Future*, pp. 11, 12

Contents

Series Foreword

Gary L. Francione

Each day, those of us who are fortunate enough to have food consume that food in temporal rituals known as breakfast, lunch, and dinner. For many of us, these meals include the flesh of nonhuman animals and products that are derived from animals, such as eggs, cheese, butter, and milk.

In the United States alone, we consume approximately 8 billion animals a year for food: 38 million cows and calves, 95 million hogs, 5 million sheep and goats, 278 million turkeys, 20 million ducks, and over 7 billion chickens. Most of these animals are bred, raised, and killed on enormous mechanized farms that specialize in one species and house hundreds or thousands of animals at a time. This practice is known as "factory farming" and is defined by *The Agricultural Dictionary* as a "type of farming which is usually operated on a large scale according to modern business efficiency standards, solely for monetary profit." Factory farms are usually owned by large corporations and are operated on economies of scale. They are generally fully automated and enclosed, and the concepts of profit and efficiency that drive them require that animals be viewed as nothing more than economic commodities.

In practice, factory farming entails that animals be raised in the smallest possible space and cheapest facilities, and that they receive the least expensive food in a manner that requires the least handling by humans. For example, most cows raised for beef production are squeezed shoulder to shoulder in large dirt corrals called feedlots. Most other animals, including pigs and chickens, are housed in massive confinement buildings that resemble factory warehouses, and most of these animals never see the outdoors until they are sent for slaughter. The animals that we eat are branded, castrated, dehorned, and debeaked, all without pain relief. They are kept in cramped spaces in which they are often isolated from contact with other animals, and, as a general matter, are treated as things—as beings without any value except their value to us. Any interest that these animals have can be quantified and "sold away" as long as it benefits humans to do so. Although "free-range" animals may suffer to a lesser degree than those who are factory-farmed, they are still regarded as commodities, as resources, as our property.

Although most of us do not bother to think about the moral implications of our consumption of animal products, even a casual analysis reveals that our use of animals for food raises some important and troubling moral questions.

First, as a cultural matter, we claim to condemn the "unnecessary" suffering of animals as morally unacceptable. But our eating of animals and animal products cannot be regarded as "necessary." No one maintains any longer that humans must consume animal products in order to maintain optimal health. Although we in rich, Western nations are often unwilling to acknowledge it, many millions of people around the world now and throughout human history have functioned very well on diets that lack animal products altogether. Indeed, voices as mainstream as the U.S. Department of Agriculture and the American Dietetic Association have recognized that a plant-based diet can provide sufficient protein, vitamins, minerals, and other nutrients and is perfectly healthy for humans. Animal foods are coming under greater suspicion within the mainstream scientific community. The most conservative and traditional health care professionals are urging a reduction in the consumption of meat and other animal products, and some are even calling for the elimination of animal products from our diet.

It is uncontroverted that vegetarians have lower levels of cancer, heart disease, diabetes, hypertension, gallstones, and kidney stones, and evidence is mounting that animal fat is an important factor in the onset of these diseases and other physical conditions, such as obesity, that adversely affect human health. And we hear on an almost daily basis of illnesses—ranging from simple food poisoning to more exotic maladies such as Creutzfeldt-Jakob ("mad cow") disease—that are connected with meat-eating. So not only are animal foods unnecessary for human health; they may very well be detrimental to human health.

Second, a meat-based agriculture has devastating environmental consequences and condemns many of our fellow humans to starvation and malnutrition. Animal agriculture produces food inefficiently because animals consume more protein than they produce. We feed 41 million metric tons (2,200 pounds per metric ton) of plant protein to animals in order to produce 7 million metric tons of animal protein. Every day, we feed enough grain to American livestock to provide two loaves of bread to every human being on the earth.

Animal agriculture consumes other resources in alarming quantities: Approximately 90 percent of the cropland in the United States is losing topsoil at 13 times the sustainable rate under the pressure of producing crops to feed animals, the average amount of fossil energy used for animal agriculture is more than eight times the average for grain-protein production, and it takes many times the amount of water to produce a kilogram (2.2 pounds) of beef as compared with the amount required to produce a kilogram of wheat. Animal agriculture results in enormous amounts of water pollution—some factory farms produce as much animal waste as does an entire city, and animal waste, which emits methane, one of the "greenhouse gases," contributes to global warming.

Third, our eating of meat reflects a profound schizophrenia in our thinking about animals. On one hand, many of us live with dogs and cats and other animals as companions. We regard these animals as members of our family. We recognize that these animals are sentient and intelligent, and exhibit most of the emotions—from fear to joy to love—as do humans. We love our animal companions, and they love us back. We spend considerable amounts of money for veterinary care for them, and we are emotionally devastated when they die. On the other hand, we eat the bodies of animals that are indistinguishable in any relevant sense from the animals whom we regard as members of our family. Pigs, or cows, or chickens, like dogs and cats, are sentient, intelligent beings who possess interests. One animal we treat as a member of our family; the other we stick our forks into and consume.

In his fascinating book, *Deep Vegetarianism,* Professor Michael Allen Fox challenges us to rethink our attitudes about consuming animals and animal products. Fox argues that just as "deep ecology" required that we go beyond traditional environmental theory that sees all of nature as a human resource with only extrinsic value, "deep vegetarianism" requires that we recognize that vegetarianism involves far more than a dietary choice—it informs a way of life and represents a shift in human consciousness that "takes humans to be part of nature, not apart from nature."

For the most part, earlier books on the subject have been limited in focus to the history of vegetarianism, or the philosophy of vegetarianism, or on the health or environmental benefits of vegetarianism. Fox's book incorporates all of these approaches—and much more. Fox's approach is interdisciplinary: He draws on the scholarship and doctrines of philosophy and ethical theory, political theory, history, sociology, feminism, psychology, and environmentalism.

Fox is a philosopher, and his book certainly presents a discussion of vegetarianism from the point of view of moral theory. But unlike most others who have written on the subject from this perspective, Fox draws from a broad range of different ethical approaches and shows how diverse philosophical approaches all point in the same general direction: that our use of animals for food is not morally defensible.

Fox begins with a history of vegetarian arguments, and he demonstrates convincingly that the vegetarian position has long been accepted and promoted by many prominent Western thinkers. He then shifts to a discussion of the sociology and psychology of food choices and attitudes about food. First, Fox explores the cultural symbolism and meaning of our eating of animals, and he contrasts this with the symbolism and meaning of a vegetarian diet. Second, he shows how this symbolism shapes our resistance to vegetarianism. As part of this discussion, he presents an intriguing case study: the problem of the environmentalist who seeks to affirm the moral status of nature as a whole but who does not advocate or accept vegetarianism. Recently, I was having lunch with a friend who is an environmental lawyer. As he consumed his hamburger, I raised with him the moral and environmental consequences of meat. His reply was to dismiss my concern by declaring that meat-eating is "natural." His reply illustrated precisely the phenomenon that Fox identifies and analyzes so clearly when he discusses the failure of us supposedly rational beings to make some clearly rational connections. I responded by recounting for him the discussion in Fox's book in which he demonstrates that the environmental position is seriously flawed in a number of respects to the extent that it does not recognize vegetarianism as a baseline issue.

Fox then goes on to explore the arguments in favor of vegetarianism, and his survey includes arguments about health, the environment, the moral status of animals, the relationship between animal exploitation and various forms of human oppression (including racism and sexism), and spiritual and religious doctrine. He follows with a survey—and a very fair and complete one—of the arguments against vegetarianism. He concludes with a discussion of vegetarianism as a way of life and as representing a fundamental shift of human consciousness.

Although Fox develops and presents an interdisciplinary approach to the topic of vegetarianism, he does so in a way that is accessible and thoroughly engaging but that at the same time does not compromise the intellectual integrity of the material that he discusses. These qualities reflect not only Fox's considerable and admirable mastery of material of disciplines in addition to philosophy, but his acknowledged excellence as a teacher. I have had the pleasure of hearing Fox present papers at conferences, and I have long admired his ability to synthesize diverse and complicated materials and to present them in a way that does justice to the material but that also commands the attention of everyone in the room—from students to senior colleagues to members of the public. Fox brings precisely this combination of clarity, synthesis, and substance to his discussion throughout the book. When I first read Fox's manuscript, I was unable to put it down. From his opening discussion of the vegetarian views of Porphyry to his concluding observations about what he calls the "vegetarian conscience," Fox leads the reader through a thicket of some of the most daunting moral, religious, psychological, political, and sociological issues that we humans face, and the journey is a pleasure. A challenging pleasure to be sure—Fox's analysis, and particularly his discussion about the inconsistency and compartmentalization that characterize our present attitudes toward vegetarianism, require that we rethink some fundamental moral questions—but his engaging presentation facilitates our task and provides an opportunity for true moral reflection and moral growth.

Fox has succeeded in taking our thinking about vegetarianism to a different level. He is correct to say that vegetarianism is more than a diet; it represents a particular consciousness about fundamental issues involving violence, our various obligations to others (human and nonhuman), and the planet on which we live. Fox's theory of "deep vegetarianism" is truly an approach to the "deep structure" of the many different strands of thought that converge and find expression in our choice to reject violence and to embrace kinship with all sentient beings as part of our daily lives.

Fox's book—the first to really propose a unified theory of vegetarianism—will undoubtedly shape the debate about vegetarianism, and will become the standard reference book in the area for students, scholars, vegetarian advocates, and anyone interested in approaching the matter of vegetarianism from an informed and informative perspective.

Newark, New Jersey

Preface

Just as "deep ecology" (which inspired this book's title) calls for replacing the resource-oriented view of "shallow ecology" with one that highlights the intrinsic value of the biosphere, the aim of this text is to explore vegetarianism in considerable depth. My intention is to show that vegetarianism represents much more than an arbitrary or eccentric dietary preference, belief, or mind-set dictated by considerations of health or lifestyle alone. A full examination of the vegetarian outlook instead raises a broad range of philosophical issues connected with the moral, social, and political spheres of our existence. Thus it is proper to think of vegetarianism as helping to shape a way of life and to effect a shift in conscious awareness.

A philosophical examination of the foundations of vegetarian thought provides an opportunity to assess microscopically the macroscopic problems of the human relationship to nature and nonhumans. These issues are receiving considerable attention today because they compel us to reconsider such basic questions as the scope of ethics and the moral significance of someone or something.

The chapters that follow survey a spectrum of arguments that urge us toward the conclusion that vegetarianism is a commitment we ought to make in both theory and practice. I do not argue from the fixed perspective of a particular ethical theory but borrow instead from many diverse yet compatible approaches, as the context warrants. Such an eclectic procedure is intended to offer the refreshing opportunity to unite varying positions in support of a common cause. We shall thereby discover that the arguments for vegetarianism have a cumulative impact, as they mutually reinforce one another. In each chapter, I shall draw conclusions as we go along, indicating where the position under review is leading us. At the end, I shall weave a composite picture of the varied strands of the argument.

Chapter 1 examines the vital, colorful, and controversial history of vegetarian arguments. It takes a detailed look at the surprisingly modern opinions put forward by Porphyry, a third-century Greco-Roman philosopher who is credited with being the founder of Neoplatonism. In Chapter 2 the subject is the symbolic meaning of food and its social construction. The meanings of meat, in particular, are contrasted with vegetarian meanings of food. Chapter 3 discusses compartmentalization, or the tendency to separate beliefs, values, and attitudes from actions. Together Chapters 2 and 3 explain why so many people eat meat and have a strong resistance to vegetarianism. Chapter 4 classifies several kinds of vegetarianism and considers the motivations and grounds for becoming a vegetarian. Chapters 5 through 7 focus on the numerous arguments *for* vegetarianism, both Western and non-Western. A miscellaneous array of arguments *against* vegetarianism, including several that have not been dealt with previously, are discussed in Chapter 8. Finally, Chapter 9 summarizes the vegetarian outlook, addresses issues such as the choice between vegetarianism and veganism, and highlights vegetarianism as a way of life. A Select Bibliography that contains, among other things, a thorough listing of philosophical works on vegetarianism will be found at the back of the book.

My hope is that the reader will judge *Deep Vegetarianism* to be accessible, interesting, and informative, and that, whatever position he or she takes on the issues aired here, further reflection will result from a dialogue with the arguments and considerations I present. My goal will be achieved if I can assist those who are already vegetarians to clarify and consolidate their views, and those who are not to consider changing theirs. The guiding spirit of what I have written is my belief that vegetarianism can contribute to a better future for people and for our planet.

Acknowledgments

This book was begun during a 1995–96 sabbatical from Queen's University, which I spent in Australia. I would like to thank Queen's for providing me with both a University Research Grant and the necessary time to launch the project. I am grateful as well to the Australian National University (ANU) for naming me a Visiting Fellow, which helped me conduct preliminary research there. I wish to thank the Philosophy Department in the Faculty of Arts at ANU, and especially Paul Thom, Bruin Christensen, and Beverley Shallcross, for their hospitality and assistance during my enjoyable year in Canberra. Thanks are also due to other members of the Philosophy Seminar in the Faculty of Arts at ANU.

Several individuals have been generous with their time in reading and commenting upon manuscript drafts in whole or in part: Robin Fox, Eric Litwack, Milton Newman, Louise Noble, Ann Olovson, Evelyn Pluhar, and my undergraduate and graduate students at Queen's, especially Sung Kang, from whom I have learned a great deal. I appreciate their input very much. Louise Noble also supplied me with some important literary references. Robin Fox designed the book's front matter, and I am indebted to her for this. Corrie Reiman offered infectious enthusiasm and encouragement at a crucial point. My editors at Temple University Press, Gary Francione and Doris Braendel, have been extremely helpful and supportive all along, and I owe them a great deal. I would like to thank Andrea Maenza and the Animal Alliance of Canada for assistance in gathering research materials for parts of Chapters 5 and 6, Maxine Wilson for her help with the bibliography and with word-processing problems, and my colleagues Steve Leighton and Carlos Prado for computer advice. Finally, Sherry Babbitt greatly improved the manuscript by her intelligent and judicious copyediting.

Earlier versions of some portions of Chapters 3 and 5 first appeared in the journal *Between the Species* and in the anthology *Canadian Issues in Environmental Ethics*. I am grateful to the editors of these publications for encouraging me to write for them, and to the Schweitzer Center of the San Francisco Bay Institute/Congress of Cultures and Broadview Press for allowing me to draw upon these sources.

Some of the material in Chapters 5 and 7 was presented at a workshop on "The Ethics of Human Health and Ecosystem Health: Toward an Inclusive Understanding," held at McMaster University in October 1998.

CHAPTER

A Historical-Philosophical Overview

1. Learning from the History of Vegetarianism

Two approaches to the history of ideas have relevance to the topic of vegetarianism. One of these is the view, suggested by William James (1842–1910), that theories pass through three "classic" stages: "First, you know, a new theory is attacked as absurd; then it is admitted to be true, but obvious and insignificant; finally it is seen to be so important that its adversaries claim that they themselves discovered it."[1] James's metatheory about theories may be applied to ideas equally well. A catchy but oversimplified formula, it derives its force from the notions that the truth will triumph, and that a baptism by fire must first be endured by positions that initially defy conventional wisdom, human prejudices, or vested interests. Usual examples include such theories as the fundamental equality of all human beings, the heliocentric solar system, the evolution of species, and the nonexistence of absolute truth. While some

might contend that vegetarianism is an idea whose time has arrived, it seems unlikely that, even if this were so, such a claim
could be construed as implying that vegetarianism has passed
through all of these stages, let alone the first.

Vegetarianism—long well-established in the East—is no
longer being ignored in the West by such prominent portions
of society as opinion-makers, publishers, and the service sector,
but it is still frequently subject to ridicule and hostile/aggres-
sive or suspicious/skeptical interrogation. It is somewhat easier
to place attitudes toward vegetarianism on a scale of development or evolution if we acknowledge that the broader concept
of animals as beings having or deserving moral status—an important ground for vegetarianism—is itself in its infancy in
terms of social acceptance, normative affirmation, and public
advocacy. One could scarcely expect vegetarianism, when seen
as a specific implication of this moral status, to be any further
along in its journey toward general cultural endorsement.

The second way of perceiving the history of ideas that relates
to vegetarianism was put forward by Daniel A. Dombrowski,
and focuses on its "intermittent" or "phoenixlike" quality: "Often an idea is suggested, held to be true for a while, then ignored, finally to be rediscovered. But if the idea is ignored for
too long, the rediscoverers may consider themselves discover-
ers."[2] Dombrowski maintains that Western philosophical vegetarianism is properly viewed as "an idea with a history of nearly
1,000 years in ancient Greece. . . . Then the idea curiously died
out for almost seventeen hundred years. After such a long dor-
mancy, all that remained of the idea was ashes, out of which
blooms the phoenix of contemporary philosophical vegetarianism."[3] Arguments for vegetarianism are accordingly reaffirmed
in a way that is reminiscent of the cyclical manner in which the
history of Western thought has been peppered with such antimetaphysical views as Greek skepticism, medieval nominalism,
Humean skepticism, the "Scottish School" of common sense,
logical positivism, ordinary language philosophy, and the "end

of philosophy" theories. The difference, however, would appear to reside in the fact that in relation to vegetarianism—at least if we adopt Dombrowski's position—a process of reinventing the wheel is at work.

A certain amount of truth in the "phoenix" view of the history of ideas cannot be denied. For example, Søren Kierkegaard (1813–1855) pointedly suggested that there are those who forget "what it means to be a human being," adding that "the existing individual who forgets that he is existing will become more and more absentminded."[4] It is just as easy to forget what it means to exist as a *humane* being. And when we forget, we eventually have to remind ourselves of the meaning. Or, as G.W.F. Hegel (1770–1831) would observe, the history of ideas, like the history of anything else, reveals a dialectical process in which beliefs are initially championed, then scorned, then reaffirmed in an enriched, "higher" form. Hence some acquaintance with the historical sources of vegetarian thought not only generates an appropriate sense of humility but also imparts greater depth to our understanding of its contemporary manifestations.

The two perspectives on vegetarianism outlined above are neither incompatible nor exhaustive. We are not forced to choose between mutually antagonistic views about the history of ideas in general and of ideas about vegetarianism in particular. Perhaps vegetarianism has, in some meaningful sense, been rediscovered of late in the West. But the contrasting "baptism of fire" image also captures central features of the attempt to establish vegetarianism as a mainstream or socially normative idea. Indeed it might be argued that it is precisely because vegetarianism has not fully emerged as a guiding idea (or ideal) that it *can* be periodically rediscovered and relaunched.

Even when a particular idea is triumphant—and vegetarianism is far from being proclaimed victorious—it is not exempt from having to be rediscovered yet again, after an age of forgetfulness, at some future time. It seems to be the fate of Western and other nonindigenous peoples always to be recovering or unearthing the lessons of the past, many of which they themselves have intentionally buried or are actively erasing. And maybe this fateful condition of rediscovery, inasmuch as it is part of the dialectic of moral enlightenment, ought not to be despised. For perhaps it keeps vegetarianism vital and progressive as it gains ever-greater acceptance within new historical contexts.

Beyond the two theories concerning the history of ideas discussed above lies another perspective: that an idea such as vegetarianism may be percolating through the ages in a subterranean and subversive, countercultural manner. It is this position I shall adopt in the discussion that follows.

There are of course plenty of nay-sayers on the issue of whether we can learn from history. We all know the adage that "those who cannot remember the past are condemned to repeat it."[5] This may be perceived by some as a warning rather than as a pronouncement on the possibility of benefiting from a close scrutiny of the past. But other voices are even more negative. Hegel, for instance, opined that "what experience and history teach is that peoples and governments have never yet learned from history, let alone acted according to its lessons."[6] And Henry Ford (1863–1947) once notoriously declared that "history is more or less bunk."[7] Presumably Hegel would have exempted the history of ideas from his own censorious generalization, for otherwise he should be at a loss to explain why his approach to so many subjects, philosophy not least among them, was historically constructed in a painstaking and highly self-conscious manner. Sound ideas, for Hegel, grow organically out of a fertile seedbed of past hunches, inklings, insights, and partially correct attempts to understand; out of a process of trial and error in the search for knowledge. Perhaps, then, we may reasonably expect to be rewarded by an investigation into the ideas that lie behind modern vegetarianism.

And yet here too we find detractors. The author of an article on vegetarianism in the *Encyclopedia of Religion and Ethics* claims that "in this particular subject no sound inferences as to modern problems can possibly be drawn from any records of the past."[8] This seems an astounding statement from a scholar of religious studies, a field that is inevitably historical. And we would do well to ignore such counsel, for while it may be granted that knowing about vegetarian tendencies of the past cannot tell us all we need to know concerning the tendencies of the present, such historical knowledge is nevertheless instructive for several reasons. First, it demonstrates that vegetarianism is not merely an isolated or faddish aberration of our era or of any other. Second, it illuminates the origins of particular arguments as well as their various expressions and amplifications over time. Third, it explains how vegetarianism and its prominent proponents relate to certain historical contexts. Fourth, and most important for our purposes, it enables us to appreciate the complexity and power of vegetarianism by recognizing the diverse sources of the positions that support it. These different dimensions are best explored in their entirety within the framework of a comprehensive historical study of vegetarian theories and practices, which the reader is encouraged to seek in works such as those listed in the Bibliography.[9] My goals in this chapter are much more modest: to connect contemporary arguments in support of vegetarianism with important historical precursors, and to illustrate, by taking a careful look at the ancient philosopher Porphyry (c. 234–c. 305 CE), how "modern" certain early views about vegetarianism have been.

2. Antiquity and the Special Case of Porphyry

The most striking feature of the history of vegetarianism is its length. Some scholars suggest that prehistoric hominids were vegetarians and develop their case at considerable effort.[10] Perhaps more persuasively (or at least less speculatively), it has been claimed that from observations of present-day tribal groups our ancestors were basically omnivorous scavengers who were nonetheless "semivegetarians."[11] This seems scarcely very illuminating, however, both because the evidence is thin and because our interest is in vegetarianism as a product of modern critical reflection, not of sheer necessity. For these reasons I shall not discuss this debate further here (but see Chapter 7, Section 4).

Within recorded history, however, vegetarianism is evident as a common way of life well before the birth of Christ.[12] Many discussions begin with the ancient Greeks, but this Eurocentric approach neglects to acknowledge the much earlier appearance in India of ideas and practices centering on nonviolence toward living things. Aśoka, who was emperor of India in the third century BCE, was a convert to Buddhism who prohibited a number of cruel practices involving animals, including animal sacrifice. He adopted vegetarianism himself and strongly encouraged his subjects to do likewise.[13] Vegetarianism in fact still is a prominent aspect of Hinduism and Jainism, which both date from long before the Common Era (see Chapter 7, Sections 3 and 5).

In the West Pythagoras (c. 580–c. 500 BCE) is generally regarded as the first prominent thinker who prescribed vegetarianism for his followers. His views were influenced by many sources, including Orphic, Zoroastrian, and Egyptian religions and probably the writings of Hesiod (active c. 800 BCE), who relates that the gods feasted only on "the pure and bloodless food of Ambrosia."[14] Although none of Pythagoras's own writings has survived, his philosophy can be extracted from several works by other authors, among them the *Metamorphoses* by Ovid (43 BCE–17 CE), the *Lives of the Eminent Philosophers* by Diogenes Laertius (probably early third century CE), the *Moralia* by Plutarch (c. 46–after 119 CE), and *On Abstinence from Animal Food* by Porphyry.

Pythagoras's vegetarianism arose from his belief in the ensoulment of animals, the identical composition of human and animal souls, the transmigration of souls after death, obligatory nonviolence, and the natural and supernatural kinship of humans and animals. This form of vegetarianism (which also included abstinence from certain vegetables) thus had a spiritual and metaphysical foundation as well as ethical significance, inasmuch as kindness toward nonhumans became mandatory for the Pythagoreans, perhaps at least in part because of their belief that humanity and compassion are extinguished by cruel practices and reinforced by regular observance.[15] It is worth noting that this early vegetarian taught a doctrine that, two centuries later, Aristotle (384–322 BCE) made a central principle of his theory of moral education: that virtues are habits we instill in ourselves by repetition.[16] Aristotle, however, unlike Pythagoras, did not recognize that the compassionate treatment of animals should occupy a place in this process. (For more on Aristotle, see Chapter 5, Section 2.)

Other notable ancient Western vegetarian philosophers include Empedocles (c. 490–430 BCE), Theophrastus (c. 372–c. 287 BCE), Epicurus (341–270 BCE), Diogenes (died c. 320 BCE), Plutarch, Plotinus (205–270 CE), and Porphyry. Plato (c. 428–347 BCE), too, although he may not have been a practicing vegetarian, advocated a vegetarian diet for his utopian society both because he held it to be a more healthy alternative and because, remarkably, he was aware (as is commonly maintained today) that a vegetarian diet leads to greater economy of land usage.[17]

Among these illustrious figures the one who stands out is Porphyry, who authored a detailed treatise on the subject. Like his mentors Plutarch and Plotinus, he lived during the epoch described by Jon Gregerson as "the great pagan vegetarian revival in the Greco-Roman West," which was spurred by no less a personage than the Roman empress Julia Domna (c. 167–217 CE).[18] Porphyry wrote a critique of Christianity and many other works, most of which were destroyed in public book burnings ordered by the Roman emperors Constantine (died 337 CE) and Theodosius (347–395 CE).[19] One of his surviving works is the aforementioned *On Abstinence from*

Animal Food,[20] written to persuade a formerly vegetarian friend who had reverted to eating meat to reconsider his choice. This fact is significant because for Porphyry, as for many other vegetarians both past and present, vegetarianism is part of an overall worldview (see Chapter 9, Section 3). A number of his arguments in favor of vegetarianism are still relevant today, and are examples of those viewpoints that were once forgotten only to be rediscovered much later. To a significant extent his work on vegetarianism is a compendium of others' ideas, but Porphyry developed, extended, and re-presented them more systematically, adding many new insights of his own along the way.

Porphyry contends that vegetarianism is part of a frugal lifestyle that is virtuous in itself, and that has the advantage of depending on foodstuffs that are easily and inexpensively procured.[21] He also argues that it is more conducive to health and spiritual purification.[22] Like the Pythagoreans he looked back to an allegedly simpler, more peaceful, and more benevolent time before agriculture, enmity, and greed had entered human life, distorted our dietary perspective, and made meat seem indispensable.

Porphyry points out that the justifiable killing of animals for self-defense, religious sacrifice, or other reasons does not establish that they may or should be eaten. If it were equally justifiable to eat a being that one may, in given circumstances, be justified in killing, he reasons that cannibalism would also be defensible.[23] Here, as elsewhere, Porphyry argues that no moral distinction should be drawn between humans and animals, and that the slaughter of innocuous domesticated animals cannot be justified from a principle that sanctions the killing of wild animals for the protection of human interests.[24] Thus Porphyry clearly places the onus of proof upon those who would kill and eat animals, not on those who would oppose these practices, as has customarily been assumed within our anthropocentric and speciesist tradition.

Porphyry's reflections on animal sacrifice, a practice that preoccupied him and that he vehemently opposed,[25] led him to claim that it is preferable to kill plants rather than animals, since in killing animals we take their lives against their will, while this is not the case in killing plants.[26] We may also of course receive nourishment from plants—unlike receiving meat from animals—without killing them, by collecting fruits and vegetables that have fallen from them or that will do so in the natural course of events. Therefore, Porphyry concludes, less injury is caused by eating plant foods.[27]

Animals possess sensation, reason, and memory, according to Porphyry.[28] Sensation, or the capacity to experience pain and pleasure, and memory, he notes, are "naturally present" across a large spectrum of species to promote survival and the preservation of well-being, those who deny this and who caution against anthropomorphizing animal life merely distort the facts to suit their own preconceptions.[29] We cannot deny that animals possess reason, he continues, simply because they do not speak our language, for most of humankind would accordingly be subject to the same judgment. Animals do, argues Porphyry, vocalize in a manner appropriate to their natural physical constitution. They likewise understand the "speech" of members of their own kind perfectly well. In a prescient passage Porphyry remarks that it is *humans* who are unable to understand animal languages, not the animals who fail to master ours: "We only hear a sound, of the signification of which we are ignorant, because no one who has learnt our language, is able to teach us through ours the meaning of what is said by brutes."[30] Animals, for their part, would be equally entitled to declare humans deficient in communication skills because of the unintelligibility of our speech to them.[31] Animals' poor performance in typical human tasks is no indicator of their lesser worth, for the same shortcoming is to be found among many members of our own species.[32] Porphyry goes on to offer plentiful examples of humans (such as hunters, cowherds,

and shepherds) who *do* understand animal vocalizations because of their intimate association with them in the performance of certain tasks.[33]

Porphyry further puts forth anecdotal evidence of crows,
magpies, parrots, hyenas, and other animals who imitate human sounds and use them to obtain, through deception, what
they desire from us.[34] Domesticated animals know enough to
obey their master's voice and ignore that of others, to respond
to different tones and inflections, to solve problems, to learn
complicated performance routines, and to behave with prudence beyond that shown by humans.[35] Along with a number
of other early thinkers, Porphyry asserts, many centuries before
Darwin, that the presence of reason in animals and humans is
a matter of degree, not one of absolute presence or absence,
just as the same is true within the human species.[36] He points
out, a millennium before Descartes, that it is equally illogical
to deny that a particular species of bird can fly at all because another flies higher as to disclaim animal intelligence merely because humans excel in this regard.[37] Again he observes that our
lack of understanding of animal behavior does not warrant the
conclusion that they cannot possess reason.[38] The benefit of
the doubt, one might add, should be accorded to nonhumans
rather than allowing self-interested and species-chauvinistic
principles of parsimony (or economy of description and explanation) to override good sense and faithful observation.

According to Porphyry, domesticated animals and humans
exist in a relationship of "innate justice" toward each other,[39]
which is his way of describing the companionship, mutual protection, and caring husbandry that often characterize such associations. Even wild animals, he avers, would lose their "fe-
rociousness" if they had sufficient food to satisfy their needs.[40]
Porphyry hints that it does not matter whether any sort of social contract exists between humans and other animals, for
there are innate natural bonds that create a moral community
that includes animals.[41] Many contemporary philosophers

have either assumed or overtly proclaimed, with no reference to Porphyry's work and little awareness of animals' remarkable capacities, that in the absence of such a contractual social relationship between humans and animals, humans have no significant moral obligations to animals.[42] Porphyry develops his case by affirming that it does not matter that animals have no formal political, legal, or juridical institutions discernible to us,[43] since countless generations of our human ancestors lived quite happily and productively without one or more of these.[44] He suggests as well that tame animals display a thoroughgoing trust of humans that we frequently betray, especially when we slaughter them and deliberately place them in danger.[45]

Porphyry also argues that while humans may be permitted to cause the degree of injury to living things that is necessary to obtain essential nourishment, it is wrong to exceed this limit merely to experience "luxury" or "the enjoyment of pleasure."[46] In other words, neither sensory gratification, taste preferences, nor self-indulgence should override human obligations to show benevolence toward other life-forms (especially those that serve our needs) and to minimize the harm we inflict on nature in exercising our own right to live. We can best honor these duties by refraining from killing animals for food. In general terms there is no justification for using violence against other living beings beyond the minimum level required for our safety and survival, and it is a mistake to model our relationship with all nonhuman animals on the state of mutual hostility that supposedly exists between humans and wild creatures.[47] If we try to subvert this argument by appealing to purely utilitarian considerations, we shall find ourselves in trouble, for it will be seen that just as some animals may be said to exist to serve human needs, so do *we* exist to feed predatory animals known to attack humans.[48]

Porphyry elaborates on the theme of nonmaleficence, or the avoidance of causing harm, by arguing that cultivating a

sense of kinship with other species leads to a generalized attitude of benevolence:

> For he who abstains from every thing animated . . . will be much
> more careful not to injure those of his own species. For he who
> loves the genus, will not hate any species of animals; and by how
> much the greater his love of the genus is, by so much the more
> will he preserve justice towards a part of the genus, and that to
> which he is allied. He, therefore, who admits that he is allied to
> all animals, will not injure any animal. But he who confines justice
> to man alone, is prepared, like one enclosed in a narrow space, to
> hurl from him the prohibition of injustice.[49]

Here he is not merely claiming that cruelty to animals results
(or may result) in cruelty to other humans, but makes the
broader case that a person who cultivates what the contemporary evolutionary biologist E. O. Wilson calls "biophilia"[50] (see
Chapter 7, Section 2) will not wish to harm any living thing,
whether human or animal. That cruelty to animals is of no
moral concern *in and of itself* was argued, infamously and
much later, by Immanuel Kant (1724–1804), who claimed
that we have only "indirect duties" toward nonhuman animals,
which are derived from "direct duties" to other humans. Thus,
he held, we ought not to kill, harm, or cruelly treat animals if
and when (but *only* if and when) doing so either destroys or
damages animals that are human property, thereby causing
some material loss to another human; or serves as a bad example to other humans or adversely affects one's own behavior toward other humans.[51]

By sharp contrast the aim of developing in oneself a hu-
maneness toward nonhuman creatures, as Porphyry sees it, is
to transcend speciesism rather than to reinforce it, and to mit-
igate the violent tendencies that lie within us all (see Chapter
4, Section 2). Even a great thinker such as Kant suffered from
a narrowness of vision that totally buried this important lesson
from the past. (For more on Kant, see Chapter 5, Section 2.)

Porphyry's philosophical vegetarianism was clearly centuries ahead of its time. His writing reveals an overwhelmingly modern outlook, a sophisticated analysis that goes to the core of the moral issues, and compelling reflections on what we would call environmental ethics, the likes of which are not witnessed again until comparatively recently.

3. From Medieval Times to the Modern Era

As in the case of all other issues pertaining to the use and treatment of animals, the Western mind (with a few noteworthy exceptions) went into a state of suspended animation in regard to vegetarianism for a millennium and a half, as Dombrowski records.[52] Christianity built upon the Aristotelian and biblical conception that humans and animals occupy separate realms of being, and reinforced this position with the theological doctrine that only humans have immortal souls. Saint Thomas Aquinas (1225–1274) consolidated these teachings still further, and it was also he who first promulgated the notion of humans' indirect duty to nonhumans.[53] There are of course many other, generally less renowned saints whose kindness to animals is legendary. Saint Francis of Assisi (1181–1226) is merely the most celebrated of these, and as Richard D. Ryder comments, "the closeness of the relationship between St. Francis . . . and nonhumans, far from being unusual, marked the end of a long saintly tradition, not yet revived in the attitudes of the modern church."[54] Yet Saint Francis did not compel his followers to adhere to a vegetarian diet, nor is such a rule part of the Franciscan order even today.

Vegetarianism played a central role in heretical Christian movements that swept Europe and the Middle East, from the Gnostics and Manicheans in the first few centuries of the Common Era to the Paulicians, Massalians, Bogomils, and Cathars in the medieval period. Vegetarianism was repeatedly cited as one among many reasons for the Catholic Church's condemnation of such sects. Colin Spencer shows that vegetarianism

alone was sometimes sufficient cause for arrest and the inevitable persecution, torture, and death that followed.[55] The
Cathar movement in southern France and northern Italy,
which forbade meat-eating, grew so strong that in the early
thirteenth century Pope Innocent III (1161–1216) ordered a
Holy Crusade to stamp it out. Much of the energy that went
into these early Christians' maintenance of a strict vegetarian
diet revolved around their effort to triumph over the evils of
the flesh, and therefore had nothing to do with concern for animal suffering or reverence for other species.[56]

Other, isolated religious figures who were distinguished by
their attitude toward animals include the Hermit of Eskdale in
England. Known as both an early animal liberator and an environmentalist, in 1159 he rescued a wild boar from hunters
only to be killed by them for his interference.[57] The Italian
Saint Robert Bellarmine (1542–1621) argued that animals'
lack of an immortal soul made kindness rather than cruelty the
appropriate response to them.[58] This view challenged the pre-
disposition, which is still operative today, to legitimize the tendency of one who is superior in terms of strength, wealth,
power, or the like, to dominate, subordinate, exploit, and op-
press one who is "inferior" (see Chapter 6, Section 4). According to Bellarmine and those who share his view, however,
compassion and kindness toward those who are at our mercy—
whatever their species—are obligatory.[59]

Contrary to what one might suppose, the plight of nonhuman animals actually deteriorated as the medieval world gave
way to that of the Renaissance. As Ryder observes, "the influence of the saints faded and the growing anthropocentrism of
the Renaissance heralded several centuries of outstanding
cruelty."[60] Philosophically this anthropocentrism—and some
would say the cruelty as well—reached its apex with René
Descartes (1596–1650), who taught that animals are capable of
neither consciousness nor pain sensation.[61] Yet even in this
bleak period there were dissident voices in Europe. Michel

Eyquem de Montaigne (1533–1592) affirmed an intimate connection, or "mutual bond," between humans and nonhumans that requires the latter be shown "respect and affection."[62] While both human and nonhuman animals possess their various attributes and capacities to different degrees, Montaigne argued, there is neither a basis nor a justification for placing our species above all the rest in the order of creation. Jakob Boehme (1575–1624) taught that there exists a mystical union between humans and God of which "kinship with the universe was the basis." Killing or violence of any kind destroys this union and places "barriers between the soul and God."[63] Saint Thomas More (1478–1535) condemned hunting in his *Utopia* (1516), Leonardo da Vinci (1452–1519) was a vegetarian, and Henry More (1614–1687) argued vigorously against Descartes that animals have not only consciousness but also immortal souls.[64] Thomas Tryon (1634–1703), another vegetarian, was the first to refer in writing (c. 1683) to the "natural rights" of animals,[65] and in *Some Thoughts Concerning Education* (1693) John Locke (1632–1704) urged that compassion is a natural human disposition, whereas cruelty is a learned behavior and state of character.[66] Locke's view, unfortunately, marked only a limited advance, for he regarded animals as mere property of humans owing to our species's divinely granted dominion over nature.

Thomas Paine (1737–1809) spread the ideals of democracy and universal human rights through powerful writings that were widely influential in the newly formed United States and across the world. Without such concepts that so effectively validate and enshrine the principles of equality, justice, and dignity, Spencer believes that "human beings could not begin to allow the concept of animal rights room to seed itself, much less grow."[67]

Other philosophers of note who contributed to this ongoing debate were Gottfried von Leibniz (1646–1716), David Hume (1711–1776) and Jean-Jacques Rousseau (1712–1778). Leibniz affirmed that differences between humans and other animals are ones of degree only and that animals possess immortal souls. Hume, while denying that equality and justice pertain to animals, nonetheless ascribed to them psychological traits readily identified as human: will, passion, reason, pride, humility, love, hate, and sociability. Rousseau maintained that animals have the right to protection against abuse by humans on the grounds of sentience rather than reason.

From the late Enlightenment onward a gradually increasing number of individuals and groups have openly and demonstratively declared their compassion for nonhuman animals and their advocacy of vegetarianism, or have at least explored these issues, often in quite modern ways. For example, in 1791 John Oswald (1730–1793), a British soldier who had studied Hinduism and who fought and died in the French Revolution, produced what James Turner calls "the first published protest on nonreligious grounds against the 'murder' of animals for food."[68] In 1797 George Nicholson (1760–1825), a writer, printer and crusader against popular prejudices, offered a multifaceted and extended argument for vegetarianism that featured considerations of justice and compassion, and referred to animal slaughter as "murder."[69] Joseph Ritson (1752–1803), a well-known champion of scholarly accuracy, was often caricatured for his staunch vegetarianism.[70] In 1785 the theologian William Paley (1743–1805), author of the celebrated "Great Watchmaker" argument for God's existence, noted that land is used more efficiently by raising vegetable crops rather than grazing livestock.[71] Unfortunately Paley, like Locke, defended meat-eating on the grounds of humans' divinely bestowed dominion over nature. His contemporary Oliver Goldsmith (1730–1774) reiterated an insight first expressed by the ancients: that it is deeply inconsistent to claim to be compassionate toward animals yet dine on them.[72] The Dorrilites, an American religious sect founded in 1790 in Vermont, embraced vegetarianism and proscribed clothing made from animal products.

Meanwhile some philosophers in this period began to formulate more considered pro-animal positions. Jeremy Bentham (1748–1832), from whose thinking flow nineteenth- and twentieth-century utilitarian ethical and political theories, proposed that issues of rationality and language are irrelevant in deciding whether animals belong to the moral community; in such deliberations only sentience (and specifically the capacity to suffer) should be considered, for where sentience exists, so likewise is our moral concern appropriate.[73] Arthur Schopenhauer (1788–1860) posited that all living entities manifest an identical underlying metaphysical will, and drew close parallels between his own thought and that of Buddhism, both of which teach compassion in the face of universal suffering. Because of the metaphysical and ethical unity of all living beings, animals are to be treated with compassion; they also have basic rights that dictate corresponding obligations from humans. In spite of all this, and notwithstanding his clearly expressed disgust for "European systems of morality" that are "revoltingly crude" in regard to animals, Schopenhauer was able to state blithely that humans are justified in eating animals because the pleasure they derive from doing so outweighs the suffering experienced by the animals eaten.[74] (For more on Schopenhauer, see Chapter 7, Section 2.)

In the first decade of the nineteenth century William Cowherd (1763–1816) founded the Bible Christian Church in Manchester, England, with vegetarianism as one of its doctrinal pillars. Ryder refers to this as "the start of the organized modern vegetarian movement,"[75] which appears to be a fair assessment. As Paul R. Amato and Sonia A. Partridge point out, "members of [Cowherd's] group later formed the Vegetarian Society in England in 1847—the first secular vegetarian organization in the West."[76] It was cofounded by members of the Alcott House Concordium, which took its name from Amos Bronson Alcott (1799–1888), father of the writer Louisa May Alcott, after his visit in 1842.[77] (The word "vegetarian," incidentally, had first been coined five years earlier, and soon secured a place in both the language and the common consciousness of the period.)[78] A follower of Cowherd's, William Metcalfe (1788–1862), founded the American Vegetarian Society soon afterward, in 1850. Other Western religious and spiritual movements containing powerful vegetarian currents, including the Theosophists, the Society of Friends, and the Seventh-Day Adventists, also contributed to the spread of vegetarianism. During the 1870s vegetarianism became firmly connected with the animal welfare movement and antivivisectionism via the idea that a healthy diet should make remedial medical treatments unnecessary.[79]

The acceptance of vegetarianism in the nineteenth century—at least among certain segments of society—was enhanced by such social, historical, and cultural developments as the passage of early animal welfare legislation in England and Germany; the founding of animal protection societies in England, Switzerland, and Scandinavia; the respectful and sensitive attitudes toward nature that had been projected by naturalist writers since the seventeenth century;[80] the work of Charles Darwin (1809–1882), which breached the species barrier so dramatically; and the influence of vegetarian writers including Percy Bysshe Shelley (1792–1822),[81] Mary Wollstonecraft Godwin Shelley (1797–1851), and George Bernard Shaw (1856–1950). Mary Shelley's *Frankenstein; or, The Modern Prometheus,*[82] for example, although generally distorted within our contemporary culture, features a vegetarian monster whom Shelley utilizes to explore important themes concerning humans' relationship to nature and hierarchical ethics.[83] Sarah Trimmer (1741–1810) and Dorothy Kilner (1755–1836) were among the numerous authors of children's books teaching kindness to animals.[84] The British social activist Frances Power Cobbe (1822–1904) was a very outspoken feminist antivivisectionist, the poet Christina Rossetti (1830–1894) was also an antivivisectionist, John Ruskin (1819–1900) and Lewis Carroll (1832–1898) both crusaded against animal experimentation, and Henry Salt (1851–1939) tirelessly produced tracts on vegetarianism and other animal issues. In 1899 Salt was "probably the first to publish an essay on animal rights in a philosophical journal," according to Charles R. Magel, the chief bibliographer on this topic.[85] Salt had previously published a book on the subject (in 1892), and as Magel notes, his works are "amazingly modern in concept and argument, and are historically of great importance."[86] Salt's works were widely influential; Mohandas Karamchand Gandhi (1869–1948), for one, although raised from childhood as a vegetarian, reported that Salt's writing first made him "become a vegetarian by choice."[87] (For more on Gandhi, see Chapter 7, Section 3.)

In the early twentieth century few thinkers stand out as dedicated to reexamining the nature of animals, and especially their moral status, in a way that would prove instrumental to advancing the case for vegetarianism. Among those worth mentioning are L. T. Hobhouse (1864–1929), Albert Schweitzer (1875–1965), and Leonard Nelson (1882–1927). Hobhouse, in *Mind in Evolution* (1901), not only explored animals' mental life but also postulated that mind propels evolutionary development in general. Schweitzer has inspired many with his reverence for life, expressed in several works published from 1923 onward. Profoundly influenced by Schopenhauer, he is a pivotal figure in the rapprochement between Eastern and Western philosophical approaches to humans' relationship to nonhuman animals and to nature as a whole. (For more on Schweitzer, see Chapter 7, Section 2.) Nelson delivered a lecture entitled "Duties to Animals," composed sometime before 1927 and published posthumously in his *System of Ethics,*[88] that Magel designates as "probably the first systematic essay by a professional philosopher defending animal rights."[89] It is still occasionally cited by today's philosophers who debate this issue. Nelson argued that conflicts of interest involving humans and animals must be evaluated case by case, and that "in no event is it permissible to regard the animal's interest as inferior without good reason, and to proceed to injure it."[90] Since animals have an interest of the first order in living, human dietary preference is not a sufficient reason for killing them. Although a case may be made in favor of killing nonhumans for food, this is limited to situations "when our interest in our own life or in the preservation of our own mental or physical powers can be safeguarded only by the destruction of an animal."[91] Nelson insists that this choice must not be taken lightly, however, for "each time we are confronted with a conflict between a man's and an animal's interest in life, we must weigh the interests involved before deciding which of them deserves to be given preference."[92]

During the middle part of the twentieth century philosophical attention was turned elsewhere and it is not until the 1970s that animals again become a focus of ethical theorizing. With the appearance of Australian philosopher Peter Singer's *Animal Liberation* in 1975,[93] a revolutionary shift occurred. As Singer recounts in his book, conversations with fellow students that took place during his period of graduate studies at Oxford University in the early 1970s persuaded him of the philosophical merits of vegetarian thinking and of animals' systematic oppression by humans.[94] Most influential among this group was Roslind Godlovitch, who was co-editing (with Stanley Godlovitch and John Harris) a collection of writings on animal issues published under the title *Animals, Men and Morals: An Enquiry into the Maltreatment of Non-Humans*.[95] Positive response to the review article on this work that Singer wrote for the *New York Review of Books*[96] encouraged him to write *Animal Liberation*, so it is fair to say that *Animals, Men and Morals* was the catalyst for a new generation of pro-animal literature. The whole question of moral considerability, which had been brewing in the background of ethics, was now opened to intense scrutiny. Who or what has moral status or is an object of moral concern? Why? What level of concern is appropriate to the type of entity under consideration? These and other matters became pressing issues for analysis in relation not only to nonhuman animals but also to human fetuses and humans who are either congenitally or circumstantially incapacitated (so-called marginal humans or human nonpersons). This sort of inquiry was further stimulated by Tom Regan's 1983 book *The Case for Animal Rights,*[97] which argued for a much higher estimation of animals' capacities and for the recognition that many nonhuman animals are individual "subjects-of-a-life" that has "inherent value" that belongs to them "categorically," not according to a scale of degrees. Both of these works staunchly defend vegetarianism on moral grounds.

Initially, professional philosophers greeted Singer's and Regan's ideas with general disbelief, derision and a superior, dismissive air, and it was quite some time before these new perspectives could receive a serious hearing. But fortunately this initial resistance was overcome; eventually these two theories came to have unprecedented influence, and have largely shaped the discourse and set the agenda for debate in the 1980s, 1990s, and beyond. In fact, almost all of the voluminous recent literature in the area of ethics and animals begins where Singer and Regan leave off. That is, contemporary discussions are generally concerned with either extending their views, exploring their implications, finding their inconsistencies and conceptual problems, or offering alternative perspectives designed to surmount their alleged shortcomings.

One recent work that deserves special mention is Carol J. Adams's *The Sexual Politics of Meat,*[98] a landmark of postmodern philosophy and critical theory. In a strikingly original and productive way that does not derive directly from anything published before, Adams delves into the connections between the oppression of women and animals and attempts to create an opening for vegetarian discourse within patriarchal culture. (A detailed discussion of Adams's views can be found in Chapter 2, Section 3.)

Our brief historical overview has shown that, notwithstanding a dominant and apparently unshakable anthropocentrism rooted in Western thought, strong strands of vegetarianism, and of a reasoning that promotes a more generous and realistic understanding of animals' moral status leading to vegetarian conclusions, are present throughout our tradition. Often ridiculed and sometimes even persecuted, many of these countervailing and neglected tendencies cycle through history, and their prominence in today's world—in both intellectual and practical life—signals for the future the possibility of major changes in thinking about animals as well as dietary habits. Vegetarianism remains today, as in the past, part of the persistent undercurrent of minority ethical discourse that energizes the evolution of personal and social morality.

CHAPTER

*You Are What
You Eat (Almost):
The Meaning of Food*

1. Food Symbolism

Eating is a basic need, and because it is so central to our existence, procuring, preparing, and consuming food have universally been made the subject of much ritual and ceremony, and items of food have themselves been endowed with rich cultural symbolism. Mealtimes are generally (and even under less than ideal external conditions) times of togetherness, cultural self-affirmation, and often celebration. In early human cultures the gathering of the foodstuffs that supplied most of the dietary requirements of the social group, which was the women's task, and the hunting, which was usually but not always the men's activity, took up a great deal of people's time. There was therefore a natural human inclination to rejoice and give thanks for bountiful and life-sustaining yields of the land. Many of these celebratory acts occurred at or in close association with meals, and quite early in our species's history they became associated

23

or even identified with reverential attitudes toward spirits and deities as well as with ritual and prayer. As cultures developed and humans engaged in methodical agriculture and the domestication of animals, food procuring relied less on luck and more on planning, scientific principles, and good environmental management. The symbolism of food evolved too, although many of the old values were retained. Here we shall consider the contrasting meanings that have come to be associated with both meat and vegetation as food in order to appreciate fully the difficulty many have in abandoning meat-eating and the often hostile opposition to vegetarianism.

The German philosopher Ludwig Feuerbach (1804–1872) made the famous declaration that "a human being is what he eats,"[1] meaning that the material conditions of human life are paramount. Karl Marx (1818–1883) was deeply indebted to this view and applied it to good effect in his early attempts to move European thought away from the prevailing influence of Hegelian idealist philosophy. In his early, so-called humanistic writings, Marx argued that "nature is the *inorganic body* of man."[2] Here he used "inorganic" to describe that which is other than the human organism proper, but that has the potential to become part of the body and bears an essential relationship to it.[3] Nature is us, and we are nature. The same basic notion is to be found in the spiritual beliefs of aboriginal peoples throughout the world and in the ancient traditions of the East. Eagle Man, an Oglala Sioux lawyer and writer, expresses it as follows: "Every particle of our bodies comes from the good things Mother Earth has put forth. Mother Earth is our real mother, because every bit of us truly comes from her, and daily she takes care of us."[4] No one can deny the truth of this insight, but we must also realize that we are likewise formed by the symbolism we have projected onto the food we eat. Thus, we are what we eat in a dual sense: because our corporeal selves would not exist without it, and because what we are is due to the meaning we superimpose on our food. In short, the symbolic meaning of food is an important aspect of the social construction of our self-identity. This is in no way intended to imply that symbolic meanings are any less "real" than physical things, for what people are willing to stake their identities and sometimes their lives on is often either impossible to detach from the symbolism that defines these things (e.g. one's ancestral territory or a uniquely important cultural artifact), or else purely symbolic (e.g. national flags or religious icons).

2. The Meaning of Meat

The symbolic significance of meat is complexly intertwined with myths about human nature. Until fairly recently a commonplace of anthropological theorizing as well as ordinary opinion has been the image of "man as hunter." This and related forms of self-definition not only identified the entire species with the male half, but also elevated the concept of humans as aggressive, warlike, and predatory to the status of a permanent essence.[5] In the past two or three decades a new generation of anthropologists, many of whom are women, has rewritten the story of *Homo sapiens* and predecessor species, arguing that our hominid ancestors were originally vegetarians who only later developed omnivorous habits as they adapted to fresh environmental challenges and opportunities. Because hominids and prehistoric humans were more reliant on gathering than on the unreliable yields of hunting, women were therefore more characteristic guardians of the food economy in early societies than were men.[6] Other anthropologists have postulated that a golden age of peace prevailed before the invention of war.[7] These viewpoints tend to undermine the arguments that "aggressive" humans are "natural" meat-eaters and that our need to hunt or otherwise kill animals for food is part of our genetic inheritance.

Freeing ourselves from the old-fashioned masculinist assumptions about human nature is liberating in several respects, but especially because it permits us to look more critically at food symbolism. We can now see that many of the attributes attached to meat have no legitimacy apart from the context generated by endless talk of "man as hunter." Once the links between meat-eating and manliness, power, and adequate nutrition are thus broken, decisions about what we ought to eat can be examined with a greater degree of objectivity. We can even construct new ways of thinking about ourselves and our relations with others as a result. In freeing ourselves from the male-centered model of eating, we help advance the larger goal of seeking sexual equality and reshaping society and its prevalent values. Equally importantly, our species's self-identity need no longer rest upon the systematic infliction of suffering and death on sentient nonhumans.

Anthropologist Nick Fiddes, who has studied the issue most extensively, contends that meat and meat-eating possess profound cultural significance, and that the institutions surrounding them encapsulate and affirm the ideology governing our species's relationship to nature. He writes that "meat is the flesh of what were once living animals; it is destined for our physical consumption. This makes it an exceptionally well suited exemplification of our ability to control and vanquish the non-human world—a goal . . . upon which we have . . . placed great emphasis."[8] Elsewhere, Fiddes adds that the "belief in human dominion does not merely legitimate meat-eating—the reverse is also true: meat reinforces that presumption. Killing, cooking, and eating other animals' flesh provides perhaps the ultimate authentication of human superiority over the rest of nature, with the spilling of their blood a vibrant motif."[9] By virtue of killing animals for their meat, we make their subservience and death instrumental to our own flourishing; we reassert our claim to be the dominant species at the same time as we satisfy our basic need for food. We also, to a degree at least, assume the right to wield power over life and death and to annihilate the alien other. With the domestication of food animals we transform them into beings at our mercy, whose sole purpose in living is to serve our needs, both when they are alive and when they are dead. Bloodletting, in addition to possessing the obvious significance of vanquishing, is also connected in interesting ways with ancient attitudes about ritualized animal sacrifice to appease the gods and the drinking of blood to gain the strength of an animal or human foe.

In accordance with these symbolic links, meat or its accessibility has been invested, in our own culture and others, with a number of properties, including strength, aggression, high social status, and identification "with the very idea of food itself."[10] Noëlie Vialles notes that both the French and Italian words for meat (*viande* and *vivanda*, respectively) were used for *all* foodstuffs until the seventeenth century.[11] As I have implied, meat is a highly visible reminder and reinforcer of patriarchal control in all of its manifestations, from the exercise of political and economic power to the definition of gender roles. Meat is masculine food, powerful food; to be a "real man" in our culture is to eat meat—lots of it, and the redder the better. And to be a "real man" is to be what our current form of society holds up as the most valid and valuable kind of being. The message here is that if you don't eat meat you must be effeminate; your sexual identity is called into question because vegetables are "women's food" and meat is "men's food." We may fancy that we aren't so simple-minded or biased as to fall for such crude associations of images, ideas, and emotions. But in a sociocultural context like ours it is difficult to be sure, especially if we haven't thought about the matter with any depth. Without engaging in a process of critical self-examination, no one can be completely confident of immunity from influences of this sort.

Meat and meat-eating play similar symbolic roles across a wide and ethnically diverse spectrum of human cultural and social groups in addition to our own. Contemporary British philosopher Mary Midgley comments that "meat-eating indicates success and prosperity, therefore hospitality."[12] This holds true in many cultures, notwithstanding their degree of "primitiveness" or "civilization." Colin Spencer observes that in early tribal societies "meat which was shared became a token of the group itself, of its identity, unity and power. . . . Meat still performs this very first ritual role of unifying a family and being the focal point of a feast or celebration."[13] Classical scholar James Davidson reports that in ancient Greece, animals sacrificed at religious festivals were cut into equal shares for the participating citizens to consume once the ceremonies were finished. He advances the intriguing claim that "this principle might be considered the true foundation of Athenian democracy, since we hear of *isonomia,* 'fair shares,' some time before we start hearing the ideology of *demokratia,* 'people power.' "[14]

Cross-culturally, it may be observed that those who have enough meat for both themselves and others possess the kind of social wealth needed to gain and maintain status. And, as might be expected, males often demand the best meat and the largest portions for themselves, while women and children receive what, if anything, is left over.

According to Frans de Waal, "in proportion to its nutritional value, the importance attached to meat is actually quite excessive—and [among humans] universally so. . . . It is the kind of food most often subject to special privileges and religious taboos."[15] Based on his and others' primate studies, de Waal conjectures that sharing among animals and humans had its origin in the eating of meat acquired through hunting. He then comments that "if carnivory was indeed the catalyst for the evolution of sharing, it is hard to escape the conclusion that human morality is steeped in animal blood."[16] However, by highlighting hunting as a paradigm of sharing and cooperation, de Waal has accepted the masculinist myth of "man as hunter" and neglects the major contribution of female gatherers to the development of our species's communal life. De Waal goes on to argue that, given the scenario he has sketched whereby hunting incubated the sharing impulse, which led to morality, "it is profoundly ironic that its [morality's] expansion should culminate in a plea for vegetarianism."[17] Perhaps this is so; but the distant origin of ideas or practices bears little (if any) relationship to the process of establishing the validity of present-day arguments in their defense. As individuals we may have been conditioned by fear of the unknown to believe in God, for example, but this settles nothing about the justification of religious beliefs as judged from the standpoint of reflective adulthood. Similarly, the inequalities taken for granted in many human societies of the past do not in any way delegitimize today's quest for human rights and social equality. Nor does the conjectured role of hunting and meat-eating in developing the human moral community negate today's vegetarian arguments against killing animals for food. Studying the social evolution and intellectual maturation of *Homo sapiens* doubtless uncovers many incongruities, but that these exist is simply a fact about our kind that we have to accept and move beyond when our evolving collective conscience propels us to do so.

Given the social values attached to meat, it is no wonder that, as Fiddes points out, "children have traditionally been brought up to regard consuming the flesh of other animals as both normal and desirable." It is therefore not surprising that "meat eating is . . . a principle unquestioned by most people."[18] When a practice or attitude is tied in with the system of beliefs that constitutes our picture of reality, such as those that revolve around our exploitation of animals for food, then it becomes simply the way things are done. Many accordingly accept that animals are food just as they believe that civilization resides in the West, everyone wants to be like us, and God is on our side. For these reasons the ideas symbolically associated with meat-eating "need seldom, if ever, be directly thought in order to be significantly influential. They can operate at a level of cultural consensus rather than individual awareness, and may be all the more powerful for that."[19] Meat symbolism, then, forms part of the silent backdrop of our everyday life to such an extent that pleasant and naively bucolic visions of farm animals cannot deter us from serving them up for dinner, and advertisements with cartoon animals who speak to us about their ultimate ambition to sacrifice themselves in order to feed us do not repel us.

It may reasonably be suspected that such associations readily nourish the weakness of will, self-deception, and rationalization that block moral resolve when it comes to examining and changing one's diet. What happens when the meat-eater's intricate mental set *is* confronted and brought into question? As part of the structure of humans' power over nature, meat-eating is a political act. Therefore, taking issue with this practice is in fact a subversive political act. Any challenge to meat-eating can be expected to face considerable resistance, with corresponding attempts to undermine, discredit, marginalize, ridicule, silence, and intimidate those who have breached the assumed common ideology of human domination of nature. Sometimes it is sufficient for a known vegetarian simply to be present among meat-eaters, who, apparently feeling threatened, begin to close ranks and interrogate the vegetarian abrasively, even if the issue of dietary choice hasn't been raised. Anthropologist Mary Douglas argues that "the ordered system which is a meal represents all the ordered systems associated with it. Hence the strong arousal power of a threat to weaken or confuse that category."[20] A challenge to established social eating patterns is thus experienced as not only odd, eccentric and antisocial but also radical and deeply unsettling.

Strong, vested economic interests will also predictably reinforce these responses, particularly when an outspoken individual with command of the media advocates vegetarianism. An instructive example of this sort of backlash is provided by the case of Canadian country music performer k. d. lang. Although she was a highly successful international entertainer, lang in the early 1990s became the target of numerous vituperations as a result of what came to be known as her "Meat Stinks" advertising campaign, sponsored by the animal rights group People for the Ethical Treatment of Animals (PETA). She was picketed by cattlemen and denounced as "anti-agriculture" by an official of the province of Alberta; her mother received harassing phone calls and had to leave town; and radio stations in Canada and the United States stopped playing her recordings. (One station elected to keep airing her music but gave away filet mignons to "lucky listeners" with each selection in a crude attempt to counteract her message about meat.) Because of such reactions, lang was forced to cancel concerts for fear of inciting hostile behavior, and her self-avowed lesbianism was predictably singled-out as a way of discrediting her. (The sign welcoming visitors to her hometown of Consort, Alberta, for example, was spray-painted with "Eat Beef Dyke.")[21] Perhaps it is understandable that people associated with the beef industry felt offended by lang's public stance, and that their responses turned readily into anger. However, the reaction went far beyond this to demonstrate that a challenge to the culturally prevalent practice of meat-eating has the potential to undermine not only social norms of sexuality but also the accepted notion of human supremacy over nature (see Chapter 6, Sections 2 and 4). It is this factor, as much as any, that made lang into a lightning rod to attract bolts of antivegetarian sentiment. Countercultural eating can be a danger to your health.

On a personal level there can also be considerable resistance to changing dietary habits, which for each of us have become enmeshed in a complex network of meanings surrounding cultural practices, rituals, expressions of friendship, modes of self-recognition, and sexual self-identification. Sharon Bloyd-Peshkin observes that

> diet is one of the most personal of habits. People have a long-standing and deep emotional attachment to the foods they eat. What a person ate as a child will always spell comfort, and for

many people, the foods they eat express the culture they come from or the class [one could add the race and sex] they belong to. . . . In addition, people who change their diets find their relationships with their colleagues, family and friends affected. . . . Other habits don't carry this emotional weight. . . . Giving up the foods you were raised on is a very large sacrifice—if you can do it at all.[22]

Obstacles to be overcome before adopting a vegetarian diet, then, are not only cultural-political but also cultural-personal, interwoven as they are with socialization patterns and intimate behaviors that shape our self-identities. These can render such a change quite difficult and often impossible, even in those who recognize in themselves a need for the change.

3. Vegetarian Meanings

This book is, in effect, entirely about the meaning of being or becoming a vegetarian. Certain specific insights into the meaning of food for vegetarians help illuminate this outlook. We will start with the signification of meat. The most profound statement on this subject was made by Midgley, who writes that "the symbolism of meat-eating is never neutral. To himself, the meat-eater seems to be eating life. To the vegetarian, he seems to be eating death. There is a kind of gestalt-shift between the two positions which makes it hard to change, and hard to raise questions on the matter at all without becoming embattled."[23] We have all (or nearly all) been raised according to the belief that meat is a healthy, natural food and a central, essential component of our daily meals. Since nutrition is life and meat is indispensable to nutrition, it follows (according to the prevailing ideology) that eating meat is "eating life." The vegetarian, by contrast, understands the death and suffering that meat represents. She or he appreciates that "meat" is not some kind of manna that miraculously appears on our plates, but instead is the dead flesh of previously alive, sentient beings. We try to hide this from ourselves by removing stockyards and slaughterhouses from highly visible, populated locations and by packaging, renaming, and displaying animal parts so that their true identity is erased. As Carol J. Adams points out, "by speaking of meat rather than slaughtered, butchered, bleeding pigs, lambs, cows, and calves, we participate in language that masks reality."[24] But however we disguise it, in eating meat we are consuming sentient life that has been rendered painfully dead for our palates' preference. We are implicated in the process of producing this death. Of course we cannot escape participating in the process that produces plants' death if we are vegetarians. But the latter lacks the literal as well as the symbolic significance of the former, given that we are not implicated in acts of terminating conscious, sentient life—life that we endow with value of a different and higher order than we do vegetative life.

Adams suggests that vegetarians symbolically equate eating meat with eating death in the additional sense that they take seriously the "association between meat consumption and disease."[25] Since they are usually motivated to make the "gestalt-shift" of which Midgley speaks at least in part for health reasons, the idea remains that while illness and earlier death accrue to meat diets, vegetarianism opens the door to improvements in well-being and greater longevity.[26]

A further set of meanings of meat has been explored by Adams, who argues that in our society there is a close connection between the oppression of animals and the oppression of women, which can be sharply discerned by an analysis and deconstruction of meat and meat-eating. Adams points out that (as we have seen) "meat's . . . meaning recurs within a fixed gender system."[27] In other words, meat is associated with the alleged superiority of being men, and its meaning is embedded in a system that features the domination of men over nature and women. Adams's presentation is richly textured, subtle, and controversial, and it is difficult to reproduce her argument briefly without doing it an injustice. But we may glimpse the drift of her thought by attending to her concept of the "absent referent."[28] She tells us that "there are actually three ways by which animals become absent referents. One is literally: . . . through meat eating they are literally absent because they are dead. Another is definitional: when we eat animals we change the way we talk about them. . . . The third way is metaphorical. Animals become metaphors for describing people's experiences. In this metaphorical sense, the meaning of the absent referent derives from its application or reference to something else."[29] It is in relation to this third element that the link between women and animals is most directly established, in that women whose personhood has been degraded by misogynist violence or sexual harassment not uncommonly report feeling as if they had been treated like an animal or like "a piece of meat." But the first and second senses of absent referent also apply, for women are all too frequently the subjects of fatal assaults, and women (or their body parts) are often referred to in derogatory and demeaning terms usually applied to animals (e.g. "bitch," "vixen," "bird," "chick," "pussy," "beaver"). Furthermore, Adams contends, the oppression of women is sometimes appropriated and distanced from them and from its source when we invoke it metaphorically, as in talk about the "rape of nature."[30]

In the second stage of her account, Adams firmly establishes the connections she has postulated between women and animals by introducing terminology that has been pivotal in feminist social critiques:

> What we require is a theory that traces parallel trajectories: the common oppressions of women and animals, and the problems of metaphor and the absent referent. I propose a cycle of objectification, fragmentation, and consumption, which links butchering and sexual violence in our culture. Objectification permits an oppressor to view another being as an object. The oppressor then violates this being by object-like treatment. . . .

Consumption is the fulfillment of oppression, the annihilation of
will, of separate identity. So too with language: a subject first is
viewed, or objectified, through metaphor. Through
fragmentation the object is severed from its ontological meaning.
Finally, consumed, it exists only through what it represents. The
consumption of the referent reiterates its annihilation as a subject
of importance in itself.[31]

Both butchering and sexual violence are assisted, made possible, and rendered acceptable within the sort of framework
Adams describes. Objectification makes animals and women
into things. Animals are perceived as merely human food on
the hoof, women as sources of sexual gratification for men,
whose desires define their female counterparts. Just as objectification deprives animals of independent life, so does it deprive
women of agency and distinct personhood. Fragmentation, in
the case of animals, has a clear meaning: being chopped up and
transformed into cuts of meat or meat by-products. Women's
bodies are similarly fragmented all the time as advertising,
pornography, and other types of cultural image-making focus
attention on body parts and superficial traits in order to promote everything from harmful commercial products to the sexual possession and sadistic subservience of female human beings. Finally, as Adams correctly indicates, these images are
constantly *consumed* by everyone who is exposed to them.
Women, like animals, and their bodies, like those of animals,
are commodities on the market, and in both cases their repre-
sentational images, metaphorically transformed through language, caricature, and associations of ideas, are readily available
for perceptual ingestion. These images of women are often
served up free of charge too, as in advertisements and Internet
pornography. Language and graphic depictions are used to
identify women as animals, thus strengthening the oppressive
structures that act at all levels of society to impede the movement toward greater equality.

Some may regard Adams's hypotheses as too extreme. But

it is important to realize that our society is in serious inner tur-
moil about its values. At the same time as demands for greater
equality for groups traditionally discriminated against are beginning to be heard and acted upon, governments are cutting
back on programs designed to achieve equality, and reac-
tionary forces are promoting this evasion of responsibility. Progressive trends that have been established over many years are
sliding into reversal. The less circumscribed, more generous
images of men and women we have become accustomed to
now face an unpredictable future. Adams did not invent this
situation but simply taps into formative contemporary worldviews in ways that are sometimes painful to witness. What she
provides is a complex model for understanding and explaining
how viewing animals as meat and women as second-class human beings are related. This yields a further tool for analyzing,
deconstructing, and altering the societal outlook that legit-
imizes the inferior status of both animals and women, and in
turn opens up a cultural space within which vegetarianism can
receive endorsement and validation. For without a diagnosis of
social problems, we are at a loss to know how we should frame
and effect a cure. In short, Adams infuses the push for equality with fresh vitality.

We may now consider some aspects of emerging vegetarian
meanings of food. Vegetarianism, so far as it represents a constructive and thoughtful engagement with issues concerning
basic dietary needs, allows and even encourages philosophical
and emotional connections between oneself and the world to
develop. Vegetarians often have a heightened awareness of the
ecological consequences of food production as well as of the
toll exacted upon nonhuman animals by factory farming, large-
scale slaughtering, and related industries. A sense of social responsibility to end these abuses becomes linked with the evolution of a new outlook that focuses on taking charge of one's
nourishment through more careful and deliberate choices, as
well as on developing a deeper understanding of our depen-

dence on nature. It is not uncommon for vegetarians to get involved in their own or others' organic gardening or at least to seek the best sources of fresh produce in the alternative (that is, small-scale) food economy. Many accordingly gain a new and finer appreciation of the seasons and of the crops they yield.

Vegetarianism need not leave us without rituals, ceremonies, symbols, and meaningful forms of togetherness, as those rich cultures that are predominantly or exclusively vegetarian, such as many within the Hindu and Buddhist traditions, demonstrate. Western vegetarians too have found that it is just as easy to celebrate important occasions with gourmet dishes that are not built upon animal suffering and death. (Step back and consider how strange it is that we celebrate memorable and joyous occasions, even times of rebirth like Easter, by killing sentient beings in order to fill our plates.) Various forms of plant life have always had symbolic significance associated with their nourishing, healing, empowering, stimulating, relaxing, therapeutic, or other powers. And the meanings of food can also be connected to the vibrant self-growth and reproduction of nature rather than with the short but miserable lives of enslaved animal artifacts. Vegetarians, like everyone else in our society, can scarcely avoid supporting some forms of oppression, as we shall see (Chapter 3, Section 2). But if Adams is right, they not only make an important personal step in the direction of mitigating the human oppression of animals, but also have the opportunity to help weaken other links in the chain of oppressions. (Adams encourages the extension of her theory to the analysis of racism as well.)[32]

Furthermore, by eating at the bottom of the food pyramid, vegetarians can feel that they are doing something good for the world around them. They are striving to attain better health and well-being at the same time as they lighten their impact on the support systems of life. This can enable them to experience a sense of "rootedness" or "at-homeness" in nature. Mark

Mathew Braunstein expresses this idea of greater relatedness to nature in a somewhat quirky manner, but many will find it easy to grasp and relate to his point: "If we are what we eat, then we must ask: What do we eat? And from where does what we eat come? Our food either comes directly from plants, or from animals who come from plants. In either case we indirectly come from what plants directly come from, so we are really eating the sun, the earth, the stars, and the moon. Most of all, plants depend upon the sun—so the sun is most of all that which we really come from. . . . As far as we can see, the sun is the one source to which we owe existence."[33] This is said not to advise us to become sun worshipers but rather to realize that a better understanding of our eating function potentially leads to a much more profound insight into where we stand in the universe, an insight that may appropriately evoke in us a response of gratitude and humility.

We return here to the thought with which this chapter began, namely that we are what we eat. But the phrase has acquired vastly enriched significance due to our explorations and will continue to stay with us as a catalyst for further efforts of collective and individual self-knowledge. We are what we eat, but we are—each of us—much more than this, and there is in what we eat much more meaning than we have ever expected.

CHAPTER

Compartmentalization of Thought and Feeling— and the Burden of Proof

1. The Compartmentalization Phenomenon

Why do thoughtful people continue to be carnivores (or more accurately omnivores)? This happens, I submit, at least in part because they fail to apprehend and/or appreciate the significance of certain considerations that should have an important bearing on their dietary choices. In other words they do not make inferences and see connections that point in the direction of vegetarianism, and hence do not feel morally compelled to change their eating habits. The arguments for vegetarianism will be taken up in Chapters 5 to 7. Here, however, the issue is why individuals who are reasonably intelligent and caring, and not insensitive or thoughtless, do not more frequently and readily become vegetarians. We have seen in Chapter 2 that meat, as an important cultural symbol and coveted commodity, exercises a strong hold on our imagination, emotions, and desire. This is a major obstacle to the vegetarian choice. I propose that in addition to this factor, and in part because of it, we often fail to draw connections that might otherwise move us along the pathway to vegetarianism. Instead we create various divisions within thought, and separations between thought and feeling, that then function to block out or keep at a distance concepts that bear important relations to one another. For example, we know that the animals we eat are subjected to many kinds of suffering in factory farming, but we choose not to think about this and go on eating them. We know that billions upon billions of animals are slaughtered and shudder at the idea of visiting a slaughterhouse, yet we still center at least one meal a day around meat. We would never dream of eating our companion animals or of subjecting them to what food animals routinely endure, but we seldom give a thought to the fate of the cattle, sheep, pigs, and chickens that populate our dinner plates.

Compartmentalization, an admittedly ugly-sounding word that is also clumsy on the tongue, is the most accurate label for the phenomenon I wish to discuss. A concrete example will illustrate the meaning of this term. Before me on the table as I write lies a recent issue of a local newspaper. On the front page is a tasteless photograph of two actual police constables bringing a pretend prisoner (in a striped suit and handcuffs) before someone impersonating a judge. One of the constables brandishes a club over the "prisoner's" head, while the "judge" appears to be striking her on the temple with his gavel. All the participants are smiling broadly as they advertise the Cancer Society's "Jail 'n' Bail" event in which "you can put someone in jail (for a good cause)." Directly below this feature is an article headlined "Inmates Wreck and Burn Friday," which describes how thirty men in an area penitentiary rioted over an apparently minor grievance, with the incident resulting in major damage to the facility and the treatment of several inmates for smoke and gas inhalation.[1] While those on the outside play prisoner games to raise money for charity, those on the inside, whom society would rather forget, suffer the real consequences of the demeaning and dangerous condition in which they live. A more revealing instance of compartmentalization is difficult to imagine: both the juxtaposition of these two stories on the page and the implications of their contents demonstrate both our ability and our tendency to hold apart, intellectually or emotionally, those things that we do not want to compare or investigate too closely.

Compartmentalization and several related concepts have gained a certain amount of currency via studies of the motivational aspects of war preparedness and war-making. Psychologists and others have pointed out, for example, that the mental and physical distancing of oneself from the devastating results of one's weapons that occurs in modern warfare assists in or is even essential to creating a willingness to use them in the first place, and to do so without remorse.[2] In general it seems that the less one knows and the further one is removed from the outcome of weapons of destruction, the more prepared one is to "push the button." Today's technology maximizes this distance, since the doer can be separated from the deed by computers, robotics, remote sensing equipment, satellite technology, and the like, so that the only evidence of one's actions may be a numerical display, a blip on a screen, or some other symbolic sort of electronic feedback. Alienation of the doer from the deed is enhanced by other psychological processes, such as rationalization; objectification; the use of stereotyping of enemies, euphemisms, or double-talk; and even, in some cases, denial that an act took the form that it did or that it was committed at all.

It is this complex of underlying factors that explains—to the extent that it is possible to do so—how the Nazi elite could manifest an appreciation for high culture and a loving concern for family and friends, on the one hand, and a thoroughly vicious, pitiless cruelty and relentless destructiveness, on the other. The notion of compartmentalization also sheds light on the Allied firebombing of German and Japanese cities during

World War II, the use of nuclear weapons on Hiroshima and Nagasaki at the end of that conflict, and the ecologically destructive American military campaign against the Vietnamese people just two decades later.

Similar motivational elements are present in everyday dietary preference and practice, and they are consolidated by both culture and the food industry. Compartmentalization in some form is employed by all of us in our efforts to cope with things that we find unpleasant or threatening, or that for some reason or other we cannot or will not deal with at the moment. My intention here, however, is not to try to show that eating meat is like being a Nazi or like dropping napalm on Vietnamese peasants.[3] These latter acts represent deeply flawed moral thinking. Perhaps it dignifies them too much to describe them as issuing from *any* type of moral thinking at all, rather than as merely being the outgrowth of mindsets that are bereft of objectivity and rotten to the core. Whatever may be the case in this regard, I believe that, by offering insight into why people do or do not engage in harmful acts, the compartmentalization phenomenon helps us understand resistance to vegetarianism.

It may be useful to begin by observing that at all times and all places animals have been the objects of atrocious acts of wanton cruelty, often accompanied by the loftiest declarations and most solemn social endorsements, by persons otherwise renowned either for their fair and just treatment of fellow humans or for their kindly sentiments toward favored companion animals. In ancient Rome, according to E. S. Turner, "emperors with a reputation for humanity and enlightenment followed the bloody tradition" of spectacles involving wholesale animal slaughter in the amphitheaters. He adds that "Commodus, the infinitely corrupt, himself descended into the arena and led the slaughter." Likewise "even Nero was fond of animals, in his fashion, and Commodus ordered that a favourite horse should be buried in holy ground. Indeed the list of tyrants who were pet lovers is embarrassingly long."[4] But the matter is more com-

plicated than this, for as Richard D. Ryder notes, "there has always been a strange [human] ambivalence towards nonhumans;
a tendency to exploit them mercilessly combined with a common respect for some, but not all, things natural."[5] As a species,
then, humans are habituated to compartmentalization where
animals are concerned. This is, of course, but one dimension of
the much larger, self-generated problem facing our species today—or at least the part of it that deems itself "advanced"—
namely, alienation from and domination over nature, which is
accordingly defined as "other," "threatening," "strange,"
"waiting to be conquered," "needing the imprint of humanity," and the like.

Even those who have risen to the defense of animals,
sometimes at personal or professional risk to themselves, may
practice compartmentalization. For instance, Richard Martin
(1754–1834), one of "the first people, anywhere in the world,
to succeed in legislating against cruelty to animals by means
of parliamentary procedure,"[6] was nevertheless a hunter. Nor
was "Humanity Dick," as he came to be called, alone in this:
both Charles Darwin, who has perhaps done more than anyone else in Western history to point up the kinship between
humans and nonhumans, and Aldo Leopold (1886–1948),
the founder of contemporary Western holistic environmental
ethics, were avid sport hunters. Leopold even kept hunting
journals throughout his life containing, along with naturalis-
tic observations, "a careful record of his hunts: the date,
weather conditions, bag, weights, sexes, shots fired, cripples,
etc."[7] Frances Power Cobbe, feminist, philosopher, and for-
midable Victorian antivivisectionist, showed little interest in
animal use in areas other than scientific research. And in *The
New Vegetarians*, Paul R. Amato and Sonia A. Partridge cite
an unidentified animal rights activist who, although she maintained a very strong commitment to the cause of animals, un-
derwent what they label a "not atypical" transition phase that
she described as follows:

> For the past two years, I had been heavily involved in the Animal Rights Movement. In April, 1984, I was one of the first fifteen people ever arrested in the United States during an act of civil disobedience on behalf of animals. I had been arrested, brought to trial, and convicted. I had been in demonstrations, on the picket line, and had written letters until worn out. But it took me a full two years before I stopped eating dead animals. I wonder sometimes why it took me a while, particularly since I knew the truth about where the flesh came from.[8]

Daniel A. Dombrowski, building upon the Neoplatonist precept that "often spirit is divided against itself," reflects on "some meat eaters' appreciation of pastoral painting and poetry, where The Bird, The Fish, et al., are painted or described with an archetypal, reverential awe, while individual birds or fish in reality are easily killed and eaten."[9] Les Brown summarizes the matter straightforwardly by stating that "animals may be walled off as inferior in many human perceptions."[10]

Meanwhile the life sciences, like evolutionary biology and genetics, reveal ever more amazing and close similarities between humans and nonhumans, making it increasingly unreasonable for us to treat animals as if they were intellectually, emotionally, and morally worlds apart from us and therefore subordinate.[11]

2. Inconsistency

Inconsistency may be of a logical sort, as when one asserts two incompatible propositions. In formal terms these are either contraries (statements that cannot both be true but may both be false) or contradictories (statements that cannot both be true and cannot both be false). But inconsistency may also be less clear-cut in the sense that it can arise from some kind of blind spot in our thinking, from a misalignment of thought and behavior or of thought and feeling, or from a failure to apply principles that we willingly follow in one context to relevantly similar or even identical circumstances.[12]

The examples we looked at above reveal more than merely trivial or minor inconsistencies, and they certainly exhibit not just the behaviors of abnormal people; rather, they represent voluntary choices resulting from the bifurcation of human from nonhuman in either general or specific areas of consciousness and action. Sometimes compartmentalization is absolute, as when humans are said to be a totally different sort of entity from nonhumans and to possess the only lives on the planet with intrinsic value. Other times the division between humans and nonhumans is understood to be relative, as when the former are considered simply *more* valuable, worthy of moral concern, or superior in terms of some specified scale of assessment such as feeling, language, or reasoning capacity. The notion of "mere inconsistency" should be queried in any case, suggesting as it does that perhaps only nitpicking logicians and saints worry about discrepancies in their moral thoughts and behaviors. Consistency is not a supreme value or an end in itself. But nor is it to be dismissed as a purely abstract concept, lacking in normative significance. It is an important and desirable attribute of our character and conduct as well as of our moral assessments of both, and a significant lack of consistency should be a signal that something is awry in our outlook upon life and the world around us.

Philosophers are just as prone as anyone else to the compartmentalization of thought and feeling in regard to animals and to the resulting inconsistency. While many still see nothing wrong with eating meat, many others confess to having serious qualms about it, yet also admit they lack the will to stop. Some admit that they ought to stop, but claim they find the arguments for vegetarianism unconvincing. Evidently their emotions and good sense also fail to persuade them. Habit, fear of change, the cultural significance of meat, and other factors no doubt play their part here. Considering the arguments for vegetarianism more carefully may or may not help; everyone has to work through the issues in his or her own time and fashion. (We will return to the matter of philosophers and meat-eating in Section 4, and to the issue of consistency in Chapter 8, Section 11.)

3. Failing to See Connections

What sorts of examples illustrate a "significant lack" of consistency in our moral lives? Note that I am talking here about *major forms of dissonant moral thinking,* each of which embodies a *failure to see connections.* Thus focus will not be on relatively minor incongruities in our moral life that are readily observable by ourselves and/or by others.

Lack of consistency in the moral sphere may be the product of carelessness or unawareness, of the failure to think clearly or deeply about what we do and why, or of unfocused attention and lack of circumspection. In such cases the remedy is, if not easy to implement, at least ready-to-hand in the exercise of the opposite behaviors. However, lack of consistency may also arise from dishonesty with oneself, self-aggrandizement, or indifference instead of compassion. These latter dynamics are at work when we fail to see connections.

Although all the forms of inconsistency we have considered are involved in the compartmentalization of thought and feeling in relation to animals, the failure to apply appropriate ethical principles is especially implicated. This disposition can be illustrated in several ways: by those who are fully committed to human welfare causes but give little or no thought to animal welfare, or profess to see no important connection between the two; by those who tenderly enjoy the companionship of pets while showing no interest in or concern for the plight of animals reared and killed for either their own or their pet's food; by those who obsess about the cruelties of animal experimentation but marginalize the far greater suffering caused by factory farming and allied activities; by those who romanticize the image of dewy-eyed deer prancing in an unspoiled meadow at dawn but conveniently forget the atrocities committed against animals that their eating and other consumer preferences support; and by those who are deceived by meat industry images of smiling, anthropomorphized animals virtually begging humans to kill and eat them. These are just a few of the abundant everyday examples of the failure to see connections where harm to animals is at issue. Vegetarians who are "single-issue candidates," so to speak, may fall into the same trap—for example, by neglecting to address other areas of animal abuse and exploitation, such as vivisection or consumer-product testing, or pressing social concerns such as child abuse and world hunger. But this type of individual seems to be the exception rather than the norm. As Susan Sperling observes, "a high degree of concern about pollution and technological manipulation of the environment and living organisms is expressed by most adherents of the modern animal rights movement." She adds that their "goal is, ultimately, the restoration of harmony between humans and nature through the achievement of animal rights."[13] For vegetarians, then, connections of this kind tend *not* to be left invisible, unaccounted for, and unattended to.

In sum, vegetarianism entails seeing connections that others miss or disregard and that vegetarians themselves had previously overlooked or ignored; and taking responsibility for a larger sphere of personal actions, namely, dietary choices and their consequences. In the case of meat this includes acknowledging, first, that what is eaten comes from factory farms and/or involves the infliction of suffering and death on sentient creatures; and, second, that the meat-eater perpetuates certain practices that, if immoral, ought to be opposed.

4. A Brief Case Study: Environmental Ethicists and Meat-Eating

We can better understand the moral failure to see connections by examining a specific context in which this occurs and where, one might suppose, such connections ought to be readily grasped. The case study is provided by the writings of J. Baird Callicott and Holmes Rolston III, who are among the foremost contemporary environmental ethical theorists. Environmental ethics exists in many variants, but common to all of them is a concern to extend or refashion the moral community and to acknowledge and affirm the moral status of nature as a whole, or in part, in a way that has previously been denied. It seems that in the works of Callicott and Rolston, if anywhere, we should discover the making of connections that exhibit caring concern and relatedness—at the very least in regard to other sentient beings.

Disappointingly, such is not the case. Callicott is probably the most ardent and prolific exponent of Leopold's "land ethic," the view that conduct is right or wrong depending on how it affects the ecosystem—that life-community to which we undeniably belong. Actions that promote ecological health are good; those that degrade it are bad. Notwithstanding the apparent generosity and inclusiveness of this outlook, Leopold maintained an ardent dedication to hunting and showed a lack of concern over meat-eating and the treatment of domesticated food animals. Callicott rationalizes these traits as arising from a "different theoretical foundation," "cosmic vision," or "substratum of thought and value" that stands in opposition to the values shared by animal liberationists.[14] According to Callicott, the land ethic is not incompatible with these acts and attitudes. But such special pleading constitutes little more than an attempt to disguise and neutralize an embarrassing lack of ability to make connections residing at the heart of a theory that in many other respects serves as a paradigm of how one ought to frame connections. To link the perception of nature's intrinsic value with nonviolent action toward animals would seem to be an obvious step in the development of a land ethic of the type Leopold proposes, wherein humans become "plain members and citizens" of the "land-community" who "respect . . . fellow-members."[15] Although it may be argued that the holistic environmental ethicist is concerned for the fate of ecosystems and species, not that of individuals, this explanation is not sufficient. Thinking holistically should not blind us to the palpable suffering of sentient beings with which we have strong ecological ties as well as close evolutionary and psychological affinities.

Callicott tries to shore up his argument by asserting that "the important thing . . . is not to eat vegetables as opposed to animal flesh, but to resist factory farming" of both animals and plants. He supports this position by observing that "the land ethic . . . helps us to recognize and affirm the organic integrity of self and the untenability of a firm distinction between self and environment."[16] Unfortunately this line of reasoning completely sidesteps the problem of animals' suffering and dying in the service of human dietary preferences, whether our meat comes from factory farms, hunting, or personally slaughtered livestock. These things, one reasonably supposes, might trouble the conscience of a self dedicated to maintaining its own integrity and to experiencing connectedness with all forms of life. If there is no "firm distinction between self and environment," then there is likewise no firm distinction between one's own suffering and dying and those of any other creature.

A similarly blinkered view can be found in the writings of Rolston, who begins a discussion of the treatment of domesticated food animals by declaring that while there is a weak link between them, "animal agriculture is tangential to an environmental ethic."[17] He says this because, he claims, "although food animals are taken out of nature and transformed by culture, they remain uncultured in their sentient life, cultural objects that cannot become cultural subjects."[18] What follows from this bit of gobbledygook? Rolston, who prides himself on defeating the "sentiment" and "logically attractive . . . charitable egalitarianism"[19] of vegetarian arguments, calculates in an emotionally detached manner that "they [food animals] ought to be treated . . . with no more suffering than might have been their lot in the wild, on average, adjusting for their modified capacities to care for themselves. . . . Domestic animals ought to be spared pointless suffering but they have no claim to be spared innocent suffering."[20] How does the "failure" of animals to resemble their "cultured" captors infuse substance into these startlingly dogmatic non sequiturs? Rolston explains that "the killing and the eating of animals, when they occur in culture, are still events in nature; they are ecological events, no matter how superimposed by culture. . . . Humans eat meat, and meat-eating is a natural component of ecosystems, one to which we do not object in nature nor try to eliminate from our cultural interactions with nature."[21] This is an interesting observation from one who had asserted only a page earlier that "domestic animals are breeds, no longer natural kinds."[22] Also worthy of note is his pronouncement that "we" do not try to eliminate meat-eating from our relationship with nature. Some of us do, and those who do not should perhaps start asking themselves why they don't, instead of just assuming that it's "natural" to behave in this way. Even if most of us do not refrain from eating animals or question our motives for not doing so, what happens to be the case in the present never provides infallible guidance as to what ought to be or might be in the future.

Since Rolston maintains that humans have no duty not to eat sentient nonhuman animals because they would do so in a state of nature, to locate a duty where there isn't one, he claims, is to confuse human ethics with environmental ethics, or to "see ourselves in fur." It is wrong, he writes, to "see ourselves in fur" when it comes to the question of eating animals because animals suffer less than humans: "they do not suffer the *affliction* . . . that humans would if bred to be eaten."[23] This argument—that humans may eat animals because they are capable of greater suffering than animals and would suffer more if raised for food than animals do in fact—seems merely bizarre. Perhaps, then, adult humans may also eat their children if the latter were found to suffer less! (Rolston makes an additionally confounding and question–begging claim a few pages later, when he asserts that food animals suffer only "instrumental pain," which serves a higher good and is not as bad as the "intrinsic pain" humans experience, which is "a bad thing, absolutely."[24] In any event, even if we could make sense of this peculiar argument, there seems little justice in comparing real animal pain with hypothetical human suffering so as to minimize the moral implications of the former.[25]

But evidently more is involved here than considerations about pain and suffering, for Rolston claims that more "value destruction"[26] would result from killing humans for food than from killing animals for food. Leaving aside the puzzling eccentricity of tying this whole discussion to the possible consequences of cannibalism, a reasonable reply would be that if we are going to worry about value destruction, it seems plain that less of it will be caused by eating plants and plant products than by eating sentient and even intelligent animals. (For more on this point, see Chapter 8, Section 1.)

5. Reversing the Burden of Proof

Compartmentalization plays a large role in human life, for better or worse. With respect to animals, it is endemic in our society. It is the underlying factor in the dissonant moral thinking—the failure to see connections—that allows meat-eating to assume the proportions it has. Carol J. Adams contends that the same process of objectification by which some humans turn others into things to be manipulated and oppressed also "converts animals from living breathing beings into dead objects."[27] Once dead, she notes, the way is clear for "fragmentation" (i.e., butchering) and finally consumption to occur. The same chain of events is reproduced by language: We objectify animals by, among other mechanisms, affirming our difference from them and our right to dominate them, referring to them impersonally, and designating them as "meat on the hoof."[28] When we think and speak of animals as "meat" or as various "cuts," "preparations," or "by-products" of meat, Adams argues, we fragment these creatures in order to make way for consuming them, and at the same time distance ourselves from the reality of animals and what we are doing to them: "Through language we apply to animals' names the principles we have already enacted on their bodies."[29]

As indicated vegetarians, through their dietary choices, do a great deal to lessen the suffering and harm done to sentient, living beings. This remains indisputable whether as a result of their diet they experience an enhanced closeness to other species, appreciate the subtleties of philosophical arguments in favor of vegetarianism, or exhibit minor inconsistencies in their behavior. On the other hand meat-eaters choose *not* to attack the major cause of animal suffering and harm by changing their diets. They could vote with their forks, but they fail to exercise this franchise. I conclude, therefore, that the burden of proof rests upon meat-eaters and not upon vegetarians. From an ethical standpoint, this implies that those who wish to defend meat-eating must demonstrate that they are doing nothing wrong or that the suffering and harm they either are indifferent to or acquiesce in can be mitigated or canceled out in some convincing way. Given the manifest cruelties and excesses attributable to the meat economy (see Chapter 5), there is a very strong prima facie moral case against meat-eating, which indicates where the responsibility for providing arguments lies.

In the West, vegetarians are considered to be out of step with the rest of society. The expectation is always that such a minority must justify and defend its position, and that it may legitimately be called upon at all times and places to do so. We never ask this of those who identify with majority groups, who unreflectively assume that they have the right to control the discourse and the prerogatives of interrogation in society (which they do quite effectively, for the most part). However,

I am arguing that this situation is incorrect and that, in the case of food, at any rate, a reverse onus exists.[30]

Having said this, some vegetarian readers may believe that our work is done. But this is far from the truth, for vegetarians are not exempted from the need to develop arguments to support their position just because their opponents have a weaker or nonexistent case to present. It is only with the aid of such arguments that one can clarify for oneself why vegetarianism is the right course to follow. Furthermore, most people still need to be persuaded that vegetarianism *is* morally obligatory. I shall consequently devote considerable attention to setting forth the provegetarian arguments in Chapters 5 to 7, after we have had a chance to examine, in Chapter 4, some basic ideas about vegetarianism and its philosophy.

CHAPTER

Vegetarian Outlooks

1. Types of Vegetarianism

Why does someone become a vegetarian? To answer this question properly and fully requires all of the material assembled in this book, as there is no simple recipe or formula that can be offered in response. The reasons why people are vegetarians are as diverse as the people are themselves. However, in this chapter I would like to consider some of the major explanations and then use them to frame arguments for vegetarianism throughout the rest of the book.

To begin, let us distinguish between *types of* vegetarianism and *grounds for* vegetarianism. The former refers to the classification of vegetarian practices or, so to speak, the taxonomy of vegetarianism. The latter designates the various foundations of, or bases for, vegetarian commitments. As I shall indicate, examining both helps us understand why vegetarians think and act as they do and why they advocate that others think and act likewise.

In *The New Vegetarians,* Paul R. Amato and Sonia A. Partridge offer a useful way of sorting through the types of vegetarianism that exist today: (1) *Lacto-ovo vegetarians* eat eggs and dairy products but no meat; (2) *lacto-vegetarians* consume dairy products but no eggs or meat; (3) *ovo-vegetarians* eat eggs but exclude dairy products and meat; (4) *vegans* eat no meat, dairy products, or eggs (and generally forgo honey as well); (5) *macrobiotic vegetarians* live on whole grains, sea and land vegetables, beans, and miso (a high-protein paste made from fermented grain and soybeans); (6) *natural hygienists* eat plant foods, combine foods in certain ways, and believe in periodic fasting; (7) *raw foodists* eat only uncooked nonmeat foods; (8) *fruitarians* consume fruits, nuts, seeds, and certain vegetables; and (9) *semivegetarians* include small amounts of fish and/or chicken in their diet.[1] Fruitarians comprise those whom we may label *noninterventionist vegetarians,* a small body of individuals who take no living things for food but rely for sustenance instead on fallen nuts, fruits, and vegetables, and on seeds that can be harvested without killing their host plant.

As Amato and Partridge point out, these forms of vegetarian practice are not necessarily observed with exceptionless rigidity, but are upheld for the most part. Nor does everyone who subscribes to one kind of practice do so unswervingly. Sometimes other dietary regimes are tried as an experiment. It will be noticed as well that some who lean toward vegetarianism (i.e., semivegetarians) actually consume the flesh of animals occasionally. Many vegans (of whom macrobiotic vegetarians, natural hygienists, raw foodists, and fruitarians are or may be variants) contend that they alone are the true, fully consistent vegetarians, a judgment that would be contested by numbers of nonvegan vegetarians. Vegans' claim to occupy the moral high ground, it must be noted, rests on their adopting a diet that does not exploit animals in any way. The point in making these observations, though, is not to assist us in refereeing internecine squabbles, but only to draw from our list a few pivotal similar-

ities, differences, and interesting interrelationships. Vegetarianism is often complex, in terms not only of formative outlooks,
but also of food inclusions and exclusions. (On vegetarianism
and veganism, see Chapter 9, Section 2.)

2.   Experiences, Emotions, and Vegetarianism

Commitments to and arguments for vegetarianism spring from
many sources, including experiences, emotional responses, and
rational thought processes. Sometimes, indeed, these are mixed
together in such a manner that they become inseparable corre-
lates. As an example of the first of these, one may cite the revul-
sion some experience upon visiting or learning about events that
take place in slaughterhouses, or upon seeing food animals kept
under abominable conditions. These are commonplace enough
to need little elaboration. A more interesting and less discussed
phenomenon is what Amato and Partridge call "meat insight experiences," which, they say, are "usually generated by particular
events."[2] Some people have disturbing images of living animals,
perhaps even of pets, while eating meat; others simply make personally meaningful connections while eating meat, seeing meat
being prepared, or viewing animal parts on display for sale. A few
brief examples will place these experiences in focus:

> I had been eating tongue when I saw a cow in my mind's eye.
> The cow was whole. I couldn't finish the food. I quit eating all
> flesh.

> I was 12 when I stopped eating meat. I didn't like it. My friend
> stuck a fork into a leg of lamb and said, "Baaa, Baaa." I quit
> eating all flesh after that.

> I first seriously decided to do without meat when my mother
> cooked my pet rabbit in a stew and I ate it without knowing it.
> [Needless to say, he/she found out soon after.][3]

Novelist Alice Walker describes a similar experience in her essay
"Am I Blue?," which she ends with these words: "As we talked

of freedom and justice one day for all, we sat down to steaks. I am eating misery, I thought, as I took the first bite. And spit it out."[4]

Amato and Partridge find it "curious that meat insight experiences are not more common than they are. . . . Perhaps individuals who are disgusted by meat simply have 'weak' stomachs."[5] But they quickly dismiss this explanation as facile, proposing instead an account centering upon the dynamic of compartmentalization (which we have investigated in Chapter 3). However, I believe these authors give short shrift to something quite significant, namely, the possibility that disgust, or what they casually refer to as a "weak stomach," indicates the presence and functioning of our second source of vegetarian commitments and arguments—emotional responses or more plainly, moral emotions, which I take to be inborn ways of reacting.

Richard D. Ryder, a former psychologist turned animal activist and historian of speciesism (a word he invented), illuminates this response, which he refers to as "squeamishness." While we often regard squeamishness as an immature, "sissified," or borderline abnormal reaction, Ryder suggests that it may actually have survival value, since (for example) it helps prevent people from contacting bodily fluids and excretions of others and from entering situations that may be of danger to them.[6] At a deeper level, he advances the following analysis:

> Putting young adults through ordeals of blood and injury is culturally widespread. Once through the gate of initiation there is no coming back, the intense sense of pride in the conquering of fear and squeamishness is a powerful part of the process of maturity, especially, perhaps, in warlike groups. Yet because of our shame at our squeamishness, because it does not conform with our macho culture's view of what is mature and manly, we try to pretend that it does not exist. But it *does exist,* and surely the lesson we should learn is that instinctively we are not

programmed to destroy other living things cold-bloodedly; and that possibly we cause emotional damage when we force ourselves to do so. Above all it suggests we can care *innately*.[7]

There is considerable insight packed into this paragraph. Within patriarchal cultures like ours, male-centered values prevail, and along with them come specific masculinist judgments about character traits, virtues, and vices. These tend, in the course of events, to establish themselves as the norms of attitude and conduct for everyone, regardless of sex. They likewise tend to determine emotional responses, especially those overtly displayed. Courage, honor, and the rational dispensation of justice have been charted as "masculine" virtues within the biblical tradition and from Homeric times (eighth century BCE) within the Greek. The development of morality, both as a way of life shaped by certain socially sanctioned emotions and as a theoretically based outlook, has been governed until recent times by the androcentric (male-centered) momentum of our cultural heritage. And the curious fact, from the standpoint of this inquiry, is that animals have often served as the vehicles for testing and honing morality, and hence too, for achieving personal worth and stature among one's social group, as well as "masculinity."

Ryder is correct: The masculinization of certain virtues, inculcated and promoted at the cost of animals' suffering and lives, has played a large role in the unfolding of warlike cultures, which is to say patriarchal cultures generally.[8] As practiced by such a diverse lot as the adolescent who undergoes a rite of passage, the priest who appeases the gods by means of animal sacrifice, the fearless prehistoric hunter, the conqueror of savage beasts in the Roman amphitheater or the bullring, the vivisectionist, the wild animal tamer, and the rodeo champion, the subduing of animals has advanced and underwritten the claims of humans (read: men) to maturity and great accomplishment. The commitment to toughness rather than compromise or pacifism, the resolve to advance and never retreat, the willingness to inflict deadly violence when called upon to do so, the ability to suppress emotion in the face of physical or psychological hardship and pain, and the show of valor in battle are all much heralded, admired, and emulated qualities in warlike societies, and are often viewed as the ultimate criteria of arrival at manhood.

Crucial to this process of maturation is the ability to overcome squeamishness, which we teach to our children so that they can enjoy and participate in fishing, hunting, farming, meat-eating, and—if we think necessary—waging war. Furthermore, we put animals in their place in no uncertain terms, so that we can know our own by comparison. Ryder maintains that we customarily condition our young (and ourselves) to hold in check certain inborn responses that would, if cultivated, connect us to other animals and develop in us a gentler, more compassionate nature. The implicit message here is that as a culture we might choose to capitalize on this tendency within our makeup instead of heightening those tendencies that set us apart from other beings (nonhuman *and* human), and that encourage violence and bloodletting. This hypothesis is surely worthy of further contemplation in our age of "ethnic cleansing," schoolyard massacres, and sexual abuse. For, as Jon Wynne-Tyson observes:

> If we think about it—and not many of us do—there are two main nightmares in our world—what men do to each other and what they do to other species. The connection between the two has as yet gone almost unrecognised. . . . One does not need to be a seer, a scientist, a sectarian or even a sociologist . . . to work out the simple but generally ignored fact that the total world situation is not going to be improved if evolution's leading animal imagines that its only moral obligation is towards its own kind. Bible or no bible, cruelty begets cruelty, violence breeds violence, and the exploitation and greed of which man is so uniquely capable cannot simply be switched off like a light when he turns from his rape of the animal world to the difficult problems of social relationships within his own species.[9]

Once again, when one begins to see connections, things come together and begin to make sense as a pattern emerges. One can't *prove* that all the complex processes that revolve around the production, preparation, and eating of meat contribute to the culture of violence in which humans find themselves steeped, but such a hypothesis cannot be dismissed out of hand and indeed gains in plausibility the more deeply we enter into our topic.

3.   Grounds for Vegetarianism

Experiential states and emotions obviously contribute to the genesis and construction of arguments for vegetarianism, and they may help explain why certain persons have become vegetarians. But interesting though they may be, reports of one's experiential states and displays of emotion rarely, if ever, convince others of a particular point of view. For this we need to examine *arguments,* such as those included in the next three chapters.

Arguments for vegetarianism may be ordered according to a number of patterns. Donna Maurer, for example, speaks of "vegetarian discourse" and locates within it "two key rhetorical idioms," namely those of "entitlement" and "endangerment."[10] As her terminology indicates, she is more interested in presentational strategies utilized in the arena of public opinion than in the nature of arguments, but her division of approaches is of interest nonetheless. "The rhetoric of entitlement," she informs us, "emphasizes freedom, choice, and liberation, while it condemns attitudes and actions that are discriminatory and unjust."[11] The rhetoric of endangerment, by contrast, addresses threats to health and well-being, ecological balance, and adequate food supplies, or in short, "to human beings and their social and physical environment."[12] As we shall see, this perspective, while helpful, contains part of the story but by no means all of it.

I shall adopt a different schema for categorizing the arguments for vegetarianism. In brief, it contains the following divisions:

1. Health
2. Animal suffering and death
3. Impartiality or disinterested moral concern
4. Environmental concerns
5. The manipulation of nature
6. World hunger and social injustice
7. Interconnected forms of oppression
8. Interspecies kinship and compassion
9. Universal nonviolence (*ahimsa*)
10. Spiritual and religious arguments

Each of the above in turn will serve as the theme that gives shape to a particular argument. Three observations are important at this point. First, this list comprises arguments generally understood to be philosophical or ethical in character, as well as some that are neither (or at least not conspicuously so). Second, although the arguments will be treated as separable, they are frequently interwoven in the literature. Third, the arguments are to be viewed as converging and mutually reinforcing.[13] This means that the arguments dovetail toward the same conclusion: meat-eating contributes to a less desirable way of life and the vegetarian option is preferable on many counts; and the overall force of the vegetarian position need not rest upon any single argument or member of an argument group. This is fortunate, since not everyone is convinced by a given appeal, but many—perhaps most— will find something persuasive along this spectrum of arguments.

4. The Moral Status of Animals

Because many of the arguments for vegetarianism hinge in one fashion or another on the moral status of animals, it will be useful to record some thoughts on this issue before we proceed. We need to note immediately that the word "animal" is often employed rather carelessly to cover any and all biological types ranging from microorganisms to primates. Among the most serious problems inherent in such an approach is the tendency to blur the highly significant distinction between sentient and nonsentient life-forms. Generally when I refer to animals I shall be talking about sentient beings, that is, those capable of consciously experiencing states that we usually denote as pleasurable or painful (including states of suffering). In addition, I shall usually be speaking of humans *and* animals. We all are notionally aware that humans *are* animals, but we let this awareness slip away from us in both the way we frame our attitudes toward the world and the way we speak. From time to time, therefore, I shall refer to "humans and nonhuman animals" to remind the reader that we are inseparably related to other sentient and nonsentient varieties of fauna.

Recent studies of animal behavior, both in the laboratory and in natural settings, as well as continuing advances in biological knowledge are eroding traditional barriers to the admission of animals to the moral community. Many animals experience pain and even suffering (a more complex experience of pain, which is either protracted or amplified by psychological awarenesses of various sorts). The so-called higher animals (mammals and especially cetaceans and nonhuman primates) exhibit rationality, concept formation, purposive behavior, symbolic communication, and even rudimentary self-consciousness. Moral behavior, including lifelong pair-bonding, altruistic acts, peacemaking, caregiving, sympathizing, and reciprocity, has been observed to one extent or another among dogs, dolphins, whales, and the great apes (chimpanzees, gorillas, orangutans, and gibbons). A number of characteristics have also been attributed to birds. A wide range of animals apparently possess forms of cognition and an emotional life.[14] These discoveries (or perhaps we should say these openings of previously closed human minds) support

Charles Darwin's contention that "the difference in mind between man and the higher animals, great as it is, certainly is one
of degree and not of kind."[15] On the basis of a very comprehensive survey of the work in the field (including his own landmark research), Donald R. Griffin urges "tentatively considering
animals as conscious, mindful creatures with their own points of
view," and notes that "it seems likely that a considerable amount
of animal behavior results from an animal's doing something
rather than being a passive object that is simply affected by the
world around it."[16]

What follows from all this is not altogether evident, nor is
it easy to sort through the empirical and conceptual issues that
separate different investigators and often lead them to divergent conclusions—a task I shall not attempt to undertake here.
It *is* clear, however, that animals' moral status must be taken
more seriously than it was hitherto, and that they are owed far
greater moral consideration than humans have accorded them.
We have, collectively, erected many barriers that prevent us
from acknowledging this insight. Humans stand to forfeit a
great deal if they give up their self-defined species supremacy.
Barbara Noske has shown in some detail how an implicit
awareness of this fact infects our empirical, social, and cultural
outlooks on animals.[17] Gary Francione has demonstrated that
our long tradition of defining animals as property under the
law plays a crucial role in preserving the human advantage by
effectively undermining a significant rethinking of nonhumans' moral status.[18] These authors have helped point us in
the right direction.

Animals have exercised a formative influence on the shaping of human culture,[19] and they are more like us than we
would have believed or even would have been able to concep-
tualize a few centuries ago, although there have always been a
few who could see this pretty clearly (see Chapter 1). As a
thought experiment we might ask ourselves questions of the
following sort: Does a cow think? How like us does it (or any

other animal) have to be in order to be morally worthy, for its life and interests to count for something? But in the end, maybe this inevitable comparison misses the point. For animals have to be valued for what they are, not for what they partly are and partly aren't as measured by standards appropriate to humans alone. As Mark Mathew Braunstein muses: "Do not even the smallest of animals with even the smallest of brains also think, though these be even the smallest of thoughts? . . . Who are so blind they cannot see that the rabbit also sees, and who so dull not to think the rabbit also thinks? It stares at you out of rabbit eyes just as you stare at it out of human eyes, and thinks of you through a rabbit mind just as you think of it through a human mind. The hawk too sees the rabbit out of hungry hawk eyes, and so on."[20] It takes strong, self-confident, open-minded, generous-spirited, gentle human beings to master these thoughts and assimilate them into their lives. We all need to try to do this for the world of the future. As never before in our species's history, we are challenged to mature ethically in a number of respects, and the way in which we choose to develop our relationship to animals—those others who are so like us—will be crucial to our survival and our ability to respond creatively and constructively to further moral tests, such as living in peace with fellow humans, encountering extraterrestrial beings, and coping with virtual reality artifacts and other forms of artificial intelligence.

CHAPTER

Arguments for Vegetarianism: I

1. An Overview

In Chapter 4 we saw that there are numerous motivations for becoming a vegetarian as well as varied grounds from which vegetarian practice might grow. Not every motivation corresponds to a ground, for a "ground," in the sense in which I use the term here, is the point of departure for constructing a persuasive account of one's reasons for being a vegetarian. As we have seen, Paul R. Amato and Sonia A. Partridge identified in their research interviews numerous sorts of "'meat insight' experiences" that spring from basic emotional reactions and evidently bypass any conscious thinking process that could transform them into reasons for the agents concerned (although we—and they—might retrospectively so identify them).[1] In these cases a decision has already been made to give up meat, apparently very directly and quite independently of the sort of logical deliberation and choice that, for philosophers at any rate, generally serves as a model of self-consciously rational behavior.

To appreciate that there are many kinds of vegetarianism is to understand that their corresponding grounds and motivations are equally diverse. Since vegetarianism is not a one-dimensional viewpoint, no individual argument can do justice to all the reasons why people choose to be herbivores or establish the entire case for vegetarianism. I hold, however, that the arguments presented in this chapter and the next two *do* show that vegetarianism is morally obligatory by offering solid, compelling reasons for being or becoming a vegetarian. Each fills in part of a complete picture, and the arguments have a cumulative weight, force, and value that can only be appreciated when one ponders them together: The whole is greater than the sum of the parts. That the arguments are many and varied is, then, not a weakness but a strength, for this fact demonstrates the large number of angles from which we can approach the issues surrounding our dietary choices.

Following the schema presented in Chapter 4, we will examine below arguments grounded in concerns related to health, animal suffering and death, and impartiality or disinterested moral concern. In Chapter 6 environmental concerns, the manipulation of nature, world hunger and social injustice, and interconnected forms of oppression will be our focus. Finally, interspecies kinship and compassion, universal nonviolence (*ahimsa*), and spiritual and religious arguments will be explored in Chapter 7. The point of emphasis throughout, as indicated, will be the *moral* foundations and implications of vegetarian thinking.

2.   Good Health

I shall begin by assuming that a vegetarian—even a vegan—diet is at least as nutritionally healthy as, and in all probability is healthier than, one that centers on or includes meat. Scientific evidence supporting this claim is beginning to accumulate.[2] There is abundant material for those who are interested in pursuing this aspect of the debate over food, and I shall not attempt to summarize it here. Every good bookshop has several vegetarian and/or vegan cookbooks, and many contain excellent chapters on the fundamentals of vegetarian nutrition as well as references to contemporary nutritional research. It may be wondered, then, why I have included the topic of health in this chapter at all. It is easy to view good health as a matter of purely personal and prudential concern, since one's health seems to fall fairly clearly under the heading of self-interest. Hence there may be a corresponding tendency not to credit good health as an *ethical* argument for vegetarianism. On closer examination, however, such a judgment is found to be mistaken. Let us see why.

To begin, it is obvious that on an intellectual level most of us care about our health and would prefer to be well rather than less well or ill. Yet many of us smoke, overeat, drink too much, eat excessive amounts of junk food, and do other things we know are bad for our health. And many of us have very little awareness of the essentials of nutrition. It would seem that if we cared about our health, and that if our health mattered to others, we would educate ourselves about nutritional matters and always choose to maintain and enhance our well-being in the best way we could. But since a large percentage of the population doesn't make healthy choices, an argument showing that good health is *morally obligatory* is worth examining. There is no guarantee that it will convince people to look after themselves, but it may help.

Now it may make sense to assert that one has duties to oneself, and if this is so, then the duty to pursue good health might well be one of these. Indeed it is hard to see how it could fail to be a central duty, since good health is so important to each of us and is a condition without which our ability to carry out duties owed to others is likely to be severely compromised.

The philosopher who is best known for positing a doctrine

of duties to oneself is Immanuel Kant, who "regarded the negative duties not to commit suicide or to indulge in drink, drugs,
gluttony, unnatural sex, cruelty to animals, or wanton destruction of nature, and the positive duties to cultivate physical, intellectual, and moral perfection, as duties to oneself."[3] There is
much here that is controversial, including the idea that cruelty
to animals is an offense to humans rather than to the animals.
Let us leave such matters aside for now, and consider another
approach to Kant's thought that permits us to appropriate his
ethical position in a constructive way. Kant argued that the
"supreme practical principle" of morality, the "observance of
which is obligatory for all rational beings," is to "act in such a
way that you always treat humanity, whether in your own person or in the person of any other, never simply as a means, but
always at the same time as an end."[4] (This is the so-called principle of respect for persons.) According to him each rational being is an end in itself, a being of independent or intrinsic value,
that is always to be respected and treated well. Within the de-
ontic (duty-based) framework of Kantian ethics, it would seem
to follow straightforwardly that aiming for good health in oneself is part of the process by which each person acknowledges
and adheres to this supreme principle. To neglect one's health
is to treat oneself as a thing, that is, without the respect that a
person should receive. Furthermore, without good health one
will be unable to participate fully in the life of the moral community, because one's powers of agency will be weakened and
restricted.[5]

The claim that there are duties to oneself refuses to go away
in spite of the fact that it has been "refuted" repeatedly in the
history of modern philosophy. The utilitarian thinker John
Stuart Mill (1806–1873), for example, maintained that "what
are called duties to ourselves are not socially obligatory, unless
circumstances render them at the same time duties to others."[6]
More recently, Marcus G. Singer has argued that there are certain logical peculiarities concerning the concept of duties to

oneself that make the whole notion contradictory. In having a duty to myself I am both the bearer of the obligation and the holder of the legitimate claim to have this obligation met. Therefore, I have a claim against myself to have the duty of good health enacted, which sounds odd to say the least. But the matter is even more complicated, since someone to whom a duty is owed may normally waive fulfillment of the obligation if he or she so wishes. Thus I both have a duty toward myself and am free to waive it. This structure, Singer believes, collapses into absurdity and even incoherence. He goes on to assert that what looks like a duty to oneself—as when one says, "I owe it to myself after all my hard work to go out and have some fun"—is really "an appeal to self-interest disguised in the language of duty."[7]

This is not the place to go into all the intricacies of duties and rights, including the issues of what kinds of duties and rights there are or may be, whether duties and rights are always correlated, and whether all duties to someone may be waived at will by that person. But it is worth observing that there are many situations in which each of us is both subject and object of our own actions, as in the case of reflexive self-criticism and of physical or psychological self-abuse. Indeed there is nothing at all peculiar about looking at and speaking of ourselves in this twofold way; we cannot avoid doing so. But it has also been argued that the concept of duties to oneself is, in some sense, the crucial link between self-interest and other-regarding interest that moral theory generally tries to capture. Thus, for example, Warner Wick, responding to Singer's argument summarized above, alleges that in the moral (as opposed to the legal) context, others cannot be obligated to me, nor I to them, unless each of us at a deeper level obligates him- or herself: "the essential thing is that I bind *myself*; for to be obligated wholly by another's act is nonsense."[8] Wick contends that "all duties, morally considered, are self-regarding, so that to deny self-regarding moral duties is to deny what is characteristic of morality."[9] In other words, all obligations have to be grounded in duties to oneself such that each of us owes it to him- or herself to act morally and to participate in the communal moral life in a spirit of self-imposed commitment. Wick maintains, further, that statements like "I owe it to myself after all my hard work to go out and have some fun" are fully recognized in everyday language as expressing a duty to oneself. If his argument has validity, it follows that the way is clear for viewing good health (and hence, I maintain, vegetarianism) as one's moral obligation to oneself.

Taking a somewhat different tack, William Neblett urges that, far from occupying separate conceptual realms, prudential and moral concerns often coincide.[10] It may appear obvious that what is to my own advantage may also be what I ought to do, and that what I ought not to do may also be to my personal disadvantage, but Neblett wishes to convey that these conjunctions are not merely fortuitous, especially where one's "dignity and self-respect are at stake."[11] Prudence and moral obligation reinforce one another and may be impossible to separate in the case of oneself. In more general terms, he states that: "I have obligations 'to human beings', and vis-à-vis these obligations that I have, I also count as a human being. I am as morally constrained from treating myself with disrespect and unconcern as I am constrained from treating any other human being with disrespect and unconcern—even, yes even, were I to find myself isolated on a desert isle."[12] This passage suggests that, like dignity and justice, attitudes such as caring, and feelings such as empathy and compassion, all of which play a large role in our moral life, are grounded in self-regard and give rise to self-obligation.

Oddly enough, in spite of Mill's critique of duties to oneself, classical utilitarianism affirms a convergence of the self-regarding and other-regarding aspects of morality. Mill observes that Jeremy "Bentham's dictum, 'everybody to count for one, nobody for more than one,' might be written under the principle of utility as an explanatory commentary."[13] But if nobody counts for *more* than one in our ethical deliberations, then nobody counts for *less* than one either. "Bentham's dictum" thus does not call for moral agents to be exclusively altruistic or to be self-abnegating. On the contrary: a central feature of utilitarian moral obligation is that it is directed to one's own self-fulfillment, which, for Bentham and Mill at least, means the promotion of one's personal happiness and all that that entails.

Finally, Mary Midgley suggests that there are "duties of integrity, autonomy, self-knowledge, [and] self-respect . . . [that are] not duties *to* someone in the ordinary sense" but rather to someone in an unusual sense, namely, oneself. "Duties to oneself, in fact, are duties with a different *form*," she maintains.[14] Duties one owes to others are generally of a sort that would be owed interchangeably to whoever stood in a sufficiently similar relationship to oneself. If I am obligated to tell the truth to those who trust and depend on me for their safety, then it doesn't matter who these others are; all things being equal, the obligation remains the same. But in the case of duties to oneself, the person to whom they are owed makes all the difference in the world; indeed it is essential to the very character of such duties. (See also the discussion of *ahimsa* on pp. 127–29.)

The notion of duties to oneself, some would say, is too controversial and precarious for the purpose of grounding other arguments. Others might cast it aside because it is often found wedded to a morality of duty that they reject. But I believe there is much to be said for thinking of duties to oneself as a way of expressing our sense of ourselves as beings who, in addition to having social responsibilities, also have our own needs and aspirations that deserve our care. Attending to these needs and aspirations is something *we ought to do* for our own sakes because we are beings of intrinsic value; making it possible for us to do so is something *other people ought to attempt* on our behalf, just as each of us should try to enhance the same opportunity for everyone else.

A second approach to viewing health as a moral issue has an

Aristotelian origin, and expresses the moral perspective on personal well-being in a somewhat different way. According to this view the good life for a human being is one of happiness. But happiness is not to be equated straightforwardly with pleasure or even with a durable state of contentment. Rather, "happiness" (or, for Aristotle, *eudaimonia*) refers to the overall quality of a life led as an attempt to realize fully the specifically human form of excellence. Every species has a good of its kind, an indwelling tendency, or *telos,* a characteristic type of activity in which its members engage and that, under optimal conditions, causes them to flourish.[15] We may think that for a "lower" animal, such as a spider, an armadillo, or a cat, the good of its kind is relatively simple and easy to determine (although in fact it may not be, and we seldom consider its ethical implications for ourselves at all seriously, except in the case of our domesticated pets). We may suppose that, by contrast, the good of human beings can be more straightforwardly defined. But a little knowledge of the history of philosophy shows that the good of our own kind, our "proper end" as a species, has remained embroiled in controversy since the beginning of serious reflection on human nature.

For Aristotle, the most influential virtue theorist in the Western tradition, the good of our kind, or the uniquely human form of excellence, consists of the right and able exercise of our rational powers. A life led in this way is a virtuous life, and we ought to lead a virtuous life in order to achieve the highest good attainable for a human being. We should seek to lead a life of virtue not merely because we would like to be happy, for happiness is assumed to be the goal of human life, and many routes to happiness are available. The real reason we should let virtue be our guide is that we ought to pursue happiness *in a certain way*. In other words, we should follow the path of the desirable, not merely the desired. Virtue, then, is seen as a means to an end, not as an end in itself.[16]

It should be clear where good health fits into this picture.

Aristotle does caution us to avoid extreme conditions such as self-indulgence and self-deprivation or excessive pleasure or pain.[17] Now while seeking "a mean between excess and deficiency," as Aristotle advised,[18] may be important, this is only a practical guideline; the link with health is more basic still. Actualizing one's happiness depends on securing the optimum state of well-being for a member of our species, and this process most certainly is contingent upon maintaining good health. But more is involved, for good health is not just a condition of realizing human excellence, it is part of the very meaning of that notion.

This insight is perhaps more directly captured by non-Western virtue theories such as those found in Confucianism and Buddhism. These ancient wisdoms likewise feature a conception of the good life that is attainable if one follows a specific and clearly outlined path to enlightenment. Confucius (551–479 BCE) taught that a virtuous life is one of learning from experience and practicing the art of living harmoniously with others. Moderation in all things and respectful adherence to tradition are essential.[19] The "Four Noble Truths" of Buddhism contain the essence of its teachings, and that part known as the "Eightfold Path," or the "Middle Way," lays out the vision and code of practice leading to nirvana, or the release from the cycle of desire and suffering that characterizes life on earth.[20] Central to the attainment of self-cultivation and enlightenment in both Confucianism and Buddhism are healthy living, self-discipline, and other forms of everyday conduct that avoid extremes that might upset one's physical and mental equilibrium. (In Buddhism, it is worth remarking, universal compassion is obligatory, and the killing of animals is to be avoided. For more on Buddhism, see Chapter 7, Section 2.)

Contemporary virtue theorists have dropped some of the Aristotelian trappings of their philosophy and tend to concentrate on such issues as "how one ought to live in shaping one's own character" and "what a 'good person' would do in real life situations."[21] Good health is connected to this ethical outlook in two ways. First, modern virtue theories examine what makes a good person, or "anyone regarded as having admirable moral character,"[22] a suitable model to follow. Surely part of the answer is that this person strives to look after him- or herself physically, psychologically, and spiritually. Second, as before, good health is considered both pervasively instrumental to and part of the meaning of the kind of life that one tries to shape for oneself.

We are now in a position to see an interesting point emerge. Virtue theories express the germ of truth embedded within the soil of theories that espouse duties to oneself. Thus we can build into a virtue theory the idea of good health as an aspect of the person we aspire to be if we wish to promote certain values through our lives, or if we dedicate ourselves to realizing a desirable form of enlightenment. And at the same time, theories of duties to oneself illuminate virtue theories. We should live virtuously not only because we ought to act "in accordance with nature" but also because we owe it to ourselves to be the best, most fully realized human beings we can be. The two views mutually reinforce one another.

Even apart from the foregoing positions, which focus on duties to oneself and virtuous self-betterment, it is possible to argue ethically that one has a moral obligation to strive for good health, for as Mill observed, there are others whose welfare directly hinges on our health or who otherwise have a stake in it. These may be "significant others," family members, or dependents, but they might also, if we adopt a utilitarian outlook, include members of society at large, all of whom have an interest in maintaining individual and collective productivity, controlling health-care costs, seeing that everyone sets a good example, and so on.

It is well known that particular kinds of meat-eating are unhealthy. The statistical correlation between high levels of meat consumption and increased probability of colon, breast, and other cancers, heart disease, and atherosclerosis—far and away the leading causes of death in North America—has been well established by many independent researchers.[23] This realization prompted Health and Welfare Canada (a federal department) to issue a new version of *Canada's Food Guide to Healthy Eating* in 1992. Alternatives to meat (such as tofu and legumes) are accentuated, as well as 5–10 servings of vegetables and fruits and 5–12 servings of grain products per day. Critics maintain that an even greater shift toward a vegetarian diet might have been endorsed in the *Guide* had it not been for the extraordinary (and entirely predictable) behind-the-scenes lobbying of the livestock industry.[24]

While evidence continues to mount linking meat-eating with serious health problems, vegetarian diets are coming to be seen as providing better health and greater longevity.[25] People tend to think of animal fat as the major issue here, but numerous other risk factors are associated with eating meat. These include the presence of parasites (such as microorganisms of many sorts, roundworms, and tapeworms) that cause trichinellosis, toxoplasmosis, helminthic diseases (anemia, infections, cysts, etc.), "Legionnaire's disease," salmonellosis, "mad cow disease," "Hong Kong bird flu," and other food-borne illnesses; hormone and antibiotic additives; and toxins (such as pesticides and herbicides that concentrate as they move up the food chain).[26] Mindful of these health threats, many have begun to accept that a shift in diet is not only prudent, and therefore sanctioned by self-interest, but also reflects a new vision of how our lives ought to be led. This includes an awareness that the good life entails good health, that good health in turn rests upon a carefully chosen diet, and that our diet in part reflects as well as determines our species's impact on the biosphere. Many are learning that the amount of meat we consume collectively has a profound effect upon how we use and manage natural resources—forests, land, water, and fossil fuels. To put it simply, the greater our dependence on meat and other animal products, the more we commit these resources to satisfying this demand; and if (as we shall see in the next chapter) the prevailing form of agroindustry abuses the environment in ways that are detrimental to our health, then the more animal products we consume, the more our well-being will suffer. All of this leaves us with an intriguing question: If good health *is* part of both the meaning and practice of virtue, and as such is a moral obligation, then to what extent is it possible to realize virtue, so understood, in a society that does not promote good health and even denies the conditions on which it materially depends? What dawns here is the awareness that the dietary orientation of an unhealthy society must be changed for the good of each of its members, and that this concern must therefore be at the core of the thinking and activist agenda of vegetarians.

3.   Animal Suffering and Death

The modern agribusiness industry, with its tendency toward fewer and larger farms and intensive rearing methods, is the source of the greatest amount of animal suffering and death of any human activity involving species other than our own. Animals are taken off the land and restricted to narrow pens and crates or crowded cages. The Government of Canada, a typical highly industrialized, meat-eating nation, reports that "total confinement of dairy cattle, pigs, and poultry is now common practice."[27] According to the Ontario Egg Producers' Marketing Board, "well over 90%" of eggs in Canada are produced using confinement methods.[28] Excesses are well documented.[29] The scale on which animals are "processed" for food beggars the imagination. In Canada alone over half a billion food animals are slaughtered a year, or nearly 1.5 million per day. An additional 29 million chicks are annually destroyed for various profit-dictated reasons.[30] In the United States 100,000 cattle are slaughtered every day.[31]

The huge scale of slaughtering and the economics of the

meat industry lead to illegal practices that cause untold animal misery. Recent authoritative eyewitness accounts indicate that "some U.S. slaughterhouses routinely skin live cattle, immerse squealing pigs in scalding water and abuse still-conscious animals in other ways to keep production lines moving quickly."[32] The alienation and dehumanization of slaughterhouse workers are extreme, as is the pressure placed on them to perform dangerous jobs at high speed; people working with animals under normal conditions would not commit such acts of atrocity.

For some people the suffering of the animals is the central or even the only issue. Utilitarian ethicists customarily regard animals as fully replaceable one by another; it is not the life of an animal per se that counts but rather the quality of that life, the comparative amounts of pleasure and pain it contains. Anyone who follows this line of thinking will find the issue of concern to be the heavy price animals actually pay for human dietary satisfaction. For him or her, the special wrongfulness of factory farming lies in its typically brutal procedures, which include lifelong confinement in artificial, stultifying, and barren environments; forced impregnation; debeaking to prevent stress-induced cannibalism; separation of veal calves and piglets from their mothers in early infancy; crowded caging; social deprivation; suppression of grooming and other species-specific behaviors; and cruel transportation, holding, and slaughtering methods. If, however, the pain and suffering caused by these practices could be eliminated, then it would seem no ethical quandary remains. Painless, instantaneous slaughter following a reasonably decent, if short, domesticated life would be an acceptable outcome.[33] (For further related discussion, see Chapter 8, Sections 3 and 9.)

Others see animals as irreplaceable individuals, or "subjects-of-a-life," in Tom Regan's sense.[34] Such individuals are bearers of rights, preeminent among them being the right not to be harmed and, most importantly, the right to life. Anyone who endorses this line of reasoning will find more to be concerned about than animal suffering, namely, animal death.

It is not my purpose here to try to settle this dispute but rather to indicate that, regardless of our ethical persuasion, we cannot ignore the vast amounts of pain and suffering that arise from current food animal rearing and marketing methods.[35] There are still a few philosophers prepared to argue that animals do not really experience pain and suffering, or that if they do, these states of consciousness in animals are not comparable to those in humans.[36] Such views are retrograde, and I believe they need not be taken seriously, since all the available evidence clearly indicates otherwise.[37] But it is fair to say that a great many people do believe (or at any rate act and talk as if they believe) either that colossal amounts of animal suffering and death have no moral significance at all; or that if they do have such significance, it is offset or even neutralized by the human enjoyment of animal products and the economic gain generated by providing such pleasure.

It would seem that only a distorted, desensitized form of consciousness could declare that human-caused animal pain, suffering, and death on a very great scale do not matter or are easily mitigated by aggregated, generally minor benefits to humans. And it is difficult to see how widely practiced, institutionalized cruelty of *any* kind can be in the best interest of a society that aspires to call itself decent. In any event, the human enjoyment derived from eating meat and the economic gains accruing to those in the meat, egg, and dairy industries could be realized just as well by alternatives available in a vegetarian economy. (People still have to eat, so some will always stand to gain from producing edibles for everyone.) And because far less pain and suffering would be generated in a vegetarian economy, its overall utility, one reasonably assumes, would be greater, and therefore the system itself would be morally preferable (see Chapter 8, Section 1).

Judging from their expressed attitudes and behaviors as consumers, most people sadly do not care very much, if at all, about these issues. However, this apparent lack of caring may indicate a self-serving and self-protective blind spot in their moral consciousness, an unwillingness to know too much or think too carefully about the fate of domesticated food animals (an example of the compartmentalization phenomenon considered in Chapter 3). But it is wrong not to care enough and not to develop the awareness needed to meet such ethical challenges. Bentham pointed out long ago,[38] and many others have since reaffirmed, that animal pain and suffering ought to concern us because *all forms of pain and suffering ought to concern us*—or at the very least those forms that are comparable in kind and degree to ones with which we are familiar at firsthand. A diet that depends on massive, mechanized carnage should at least give us pause to consider what we are doing to satisfy our palates. As Carol J. Adams contends, "meat eating is the most oppressive and extensive institutionalized violence against animals."[39] So even if we don't subscribe to the very strong view that "meat is murder," we should still be appalled at the cruelty and death-dealing in which we acquiesce by being meat-eaters. It is difficult to evade the conclusion that each of us must face up to the fact that our choices as consumers materially affect the amount of animal pain, suffering, and death in the world. Either we opt to be a part of the animal agony system or we opt to get out of it. If we do not reflect too carefully or critically upon our diets, we can easily overlook the consequences they have; but this is also a choice, namely one of omission. We are no less responsible for it than for any other choice we make. And if we *are* informed about the misery created by factory farming and related activities, yet still knowingly elect to eat meat, we are even more culpable.

This type of ethical neglect may also be seen as springing from culturally conditioned perceptions of our food (such as we examined in Chapter 2), and from the manner in which we as individuals choose, more or less consciously, to affirm these in our everyday lives. Each of us sees animal flesh in a supermarket or on a plate in one of two modes: as meat (or some cut thereof); or as body parts of a once living, now dead animal, perhaps even related to us as a natural kin. It is obvious that the former mode tends to evoke thoughts and feelings of pleasure, comfort, hunger, nourishment, well-being, and the like, while the latter may be accompanied by thoughts and feelings such as sadness, horror, disgust, displeasure, uneasiness, and perhaps even guilt. The basis for each set of reactions is neither purely subjective nor unique to us as individuals, for both are grounded in meaningful interactions with the world and shared attitudes toward it. The main point is simply that ethical responses here, as elsewhere, are contingent upon how we choose to apprehend the world and relevant items in it. If, as I believe, we do actually choose how we perceive animal flesh offered for food, or at any rate if we ought to become aware of how we do in fact perceive our food and why, then it follows again that we are responsible for our actions that proceed from our ways of seeing and taking (or "ingesting") the world.

4. Impartiality, or Disinterested Moral Concern

In *Cruelty to Animals: The Moral Debt*,[40] Les Brown argues that the moral viewpoint must be backed by a commitment to the principle that interests should be assessed impartially. Many contemporary ethical theorists have reservations concerning this formulation, which they associate with traditional rationalistic views, such as the Kantian theory that to act morally is to behave in accordance with a rational, exceptionless, abstract principle regardless of the consequences for oneself or others. For centuries Western philosophers have intoned the mantra that the ideal moral agent is a detached, objective, dispassionate, impersonal, uninvolved observer. Recent correctives, such as feminist theories of ethics, and more generally ethical systems based on love, care, compassion, or trust, point up the deficiencies in the traditional view. But even if such factors as emotions and special ties have often been excluded from refined thinking about the nature of ethics and moral decision-making, it does not follow that impartiality of a certain sort plays an insignificant role therein. Nor do all theorists who part company with the "rational man" approach to ethics deny this. Indeed impartiality may be particularly pertinent in deciding how we ought to treat *non-human animals*.

The merit of Brown's work is to be found precisely in the manner in which it demonstrates the element of truth in this claim. Let us allow that at least one possible way of looking at ethics is as a viewpoint that requires us to adopt a disinterested stance (what used to be routinely referred to as the "moral point of view"). We may take this to mean (among other things) that, in the absence of special considerations, it is inappropriate to assign greater worth to some persons' lives or happiness than to others'. Note too that "disinterested" does not mean "uninterested," in the sense of having no concern for or interest in something or someone. On the contrary, one may approach moral decision-making (for example, as a disinterested arbitrator) with a passionate commitment to doing what is right and fair for all parties involved. With these qualifications in the background, the business of deciding what range of interests we need to assess when we deliberate takes the spotlight. The question that now arises is this: Whose interests shall be allowed to count? It may seem that this question has already been answered by our theory of the moment, namely everyone's, equally. However, we need to remember that throughout most of the history of Western ethics, only *humans'* interests have been counted. And, shameful as it is to recall, for the most part only *certain classes of humans* were represented as having interests at all, in the morally relevant sense. Indeed, the idea of impartiality has served importantly as a way of attacking biases of this sort, even if some architects of the impartialist viewpoint, such as Kant (who was overtly both a sexist and a racist), failed to realize its egalitarian potential. In theory, as a species we have moved beyond the inferiorization of identifiable groups of our own kind. Shall we also now move beyond speciesism and count nonhuman animals among those beings who have morally relevant interests?

Brown observes that "rational persons do understand that animals have interests which contribute to their satisfactions in living, or to their wellbeing, which if frustrated by either natural forces or human intervention lead to their suffering."[41] He adds that "in many instances it is necessary to understand the needs of particular species before their wellbeing can be comprehended fully."[42] The result is that both the denial that animals have interests in a weighty, morally relevant sense and the simple, thoughtless unawareness of the whole issue stem from an ignorance about animals that should be remedied. That animals' natures and needs are commonly different from our own goes without saying. Consequently their specific interests will also vary from ours. As a general point, however, the existence of differences between individuals does not by itself justify differential treatment of them, especially if this runs to one party's disadvantage. In like manner the observation of differences between humans and nonhumans does not by itself justify discriminatory treatment of animals. Nor are the differences absolute; for we share with all sentient beings the capacity to experience pain, and with some the capacity to suffer, and hence with all an interest in not being caused to do either or both. If we bear these things in mind, Brown contends, "it is not difficult to move to the view that all animal interests are to be considered equally."[43] He concludes that "the three dimensions of our respect for animals, analogous to respect for persons, are benevolence, the utmost impartiality of which we are capable, and knowledge."[44] A further suggestion that flows from all of this, according to Brown, is that anthropocentrism (and we may say speciesism in particular) is egoism in disguise—the pursuit of collective human self-interest in which little or no species self-sacrifice or morally induced restraint is present. But egoism is the opposite of disinterestedness and is repugnant to the moral viewpoint as outlined above.

The conclusion to be reached by applying these thoughts to our issue is now quite straightforward: Animals have a morally significant interest in not being made to experience pain or to suffer. Using them for food causes them needlessly to experience pain and to suffer, and is therefore wrong. We neglect to acknowledge this insight only out of ignorance or deliberately egocentric choice.

CHAPTER

Arguments for Vegetarianism: II

1. The Environmental Impact of Meat Production

We live in a society that promotes individuality, self-reliance, self-development, and the cultivation of personal taste. We are bombarded all the time by messages that encourage us to pursue the construction of selfhood by means of consumer preferences, that is, by acting out self-centered desires and fantasies as more or less powerful purchasers within the global marketplace. We are well conditioned in the mode of thinking that interprets our consumer choices as expressions of personal freedom that are primarily, if not exclusively, of consequence to ourselves. And there are numerous vested interests that energetically promote this outlook: business leaders, industry spokespersons, the media, politicians, advertisers, and image-makers, to name a few. It therefore takes a major effort to develop a contrasting form of awareness, namely one that acknowledges that all our choices

have wider consequences, such as an impact on the environment. When we begin to appreciate these connections, we
can also start questioning our choices and the influences that
have helped shape them, a process some might label radical
or subversive but others might simply call an exercise in
healthy common sense. Being sensitized to ecological issues,
as an increasing number of citizens are today, opens our
minds to the possibility of change through the formation of
new values.[1] Vegetarianism may be and often is a part of this
creative ferment.

The ecodestructive side of the meat industry's operations
have been summarized concisely, with ample documentation
from both government and nongovernment sources, by John
Robbins in *Diet for a New America*.[2] His findings are substan-
tiated by many other authors as well.[3] These negative effects
include toxic chemical residues in the food chain; pharmaceu-
tical additives in animal feeds; polluting chemicals and animal
wastes from feedlot runoff in waterways and underground
aquifers; topsoil loss from relentless grazing; deforestation and
desertification from the clearing of land for grazing and for cultivating feed; threatened habitats of wild species of plants and
animals; intensive exploitation of water and energy supplies;
and ozone depletion from the extensive use of fossil fuels and
the significant production of methane gas by cattle. Sharon
Bloyd-Peshkin summarizes this sorry state of affairs in these
simple terms: "meat production is a major source of environmental damage."[4]

Some specific data will place these complex problems in
context so that we can analyze them more meaningfully. In
Canada, since the time of white settlement, expanding agriculture has been the major factor in an 85 percent reduction
of wetlands.[5] Agricultural acreage has increased fourfold since
1900, and the total area under irrigation more than doubled
between 1970 and 1988.[6] It must be inferred that the consumption of meat is a powerful force in producing these

trends, since in North America some 95 percent of oats and 80 percent of corn produced are used as livestock feed.[7] David Pimentel, a scientist who has been studying the environmental impact of modern American agricultural methods for over two decades, reports that 240 million tonnes (264.5 million tons) of grain are fed to livestock in the United States each year—enough to feed approximately 800 million people a vegetarian diet.[8] In Canada, a country with one-tenth the population of the United States, farm animals produce 322 million liters (85 million gallons) of manure *daily*, an overwhelming proportion of which comes from cattle. Each marketed kilogram (0.45 pound) of edible beef generates at least 40 kilograms (88 pounds) of manure, and each marketed kilogram of pork 15 kilograms (33 pounds) of manure. These wastes, plus the runoff of water used to clean farm buildings and equipment as well as pesticide residues and other agricultural chemicals, are often poorly handled and pollute waterways, soil, and the air.[9] Finally, it is calculated that 100,000 liters (26,425 gallons) of water are required in the process by which one kilogram (2.2 pounds) of beef is produced;[10] by contrast, a pound (0.45 kilogram) of wheat requires only 254 liters (60 gallons).[11]

Obviously not all of the environmentally hostile effects of today's unsound agricultural practices can be attributed to the production of animals for food. And it is clear that some of the abuses could be mitigated by, for example, a more dedicated approach to recycling animal manure (and human waste) into crop fertilizer, greater reliance on natural means of pest control instead of harmful chemicals; and the like. So it has been argued frequently that the proper target of criticism is not meat production per se, but rather the intensive rearing methods used by contemporary agribusiness. There is some point to this rejoinder, and surely those who obtain their meat from their own or others' free-range operations dedicated to organic methods of animal husbandry contribute less to the environmental toll exacted by human life. But given the appalling rate at which smaller-scale family farms are being absorbed by larger operations driven by the worst dynamics of capitalist concentration of wealth,[12] the opportunities for obtaining "environmentally friendly" meat are extremely rare in practice. Only a tiny fraction of the population *could* exercise this option, given current agricultural trends, and an even tinier group *desires* to do so in the first place. In any event, vegetarians—who *do* find environmental considerations important factors motivating their dietary choices—are able to live even more lightly on the land than are meat-eaters of any description. (For further discussion, see Chapter 8, Section 10.)

I have no doubt that there is sufficient evidence to support this assertion. Consider the following observation, for instance: "All the grain fed to livestock could feed five times as many people. *(Proponents of intensive animal agriculture claim that we only put animals on land that could not support plant production. But we could grow more than enough plant food for human consumption if we used even a fraction of the land that is now used to grow plant food for livestock consumption.)*"[13] If one of the guiding ideals of ecologically informed ethical thinking is that we ought to minimize the harmful impact of our lives—individually and collectively—upon the biosphere, then it follows that we ought to make those lifestyle choices that help achieve this objective. The principle of nonmaleficence (avoiding or minimizing harm) certainly seems to be about as basic a moral precept as can be imagined. Even if we added to the "do no harm" rule the qualifier "all things being equal," the obligation to choose the vegetarian option would still remain, for it has been shown by many nutritionists that a vegetarian diet lacks nothing people need; meat, in short, is not necessary for good health. And it is highly questionable, as I have pointed out, whether a diet that relied on only free-range, organically farmed animals, or even one that featured a significantly reduced component of meat, would enable most North Americans to maintain the kind of diet they have come to take for granted. Plainly neither could sustain high, North American–style levels of meat consumption worldwide.[14] A diet that relies heavily on meat only appears affordable and environmentally sustainable to those who are unaware of its larger ecological costs; who assume that such costs do not have to be factored into our choices and their consequences; or who believe that the costs can be passed on to others, such as people in developing nations and our children. We all have to eat, and some appreciable impact on the planet is inevitable as we pursue this natural end. But we should aim to minimize the environmental harm and degradation caused by humans' quest for nourishment. A commitment to vegetarianism seems clearly to be the best way to do this, and for this reason should be a choice made by each of us.

2. The Manipulation of Nature

Many authors, as we have seen, draw attention to the serious global environmental consequences of the meat production system. What hasn't been subjected to as much scrutiny are its effects on planetary biodiversity and on our attitudes toward nature as a whole. Let us look at these issues in turn.

There are many causes of species extinction, both human and natural. With respect to human factors, no single activity accounts totally for the sort of ecocide that undermines species viability. We should not expect, therefore, that the process whereby the flesh of animals appears on our tables by itself explains why certain ecosystems and the life-forms they support are either under threat or compromised beyond recovery.

We need to begin by getting some idea of the scope of

species eradication by humans. According to Edward O. Wilson, who has conducted one of the most detailed studies of the problem, "Ninety-nine percent of all the species that ever lived are now extinct."[15] Most of this carnage is due to natural causes (evolutionary, geological, atmospheric, and astronomical events being the principal agencies). However, Wilson projects that the rain forest extinctions for which humans are responsible are occurring at a pace that is between 1,000 and 10,000 times the natural rate.[16] What does this mean in terms of numbers of species lost? Anita Gordon and David Suzuki tell us that 20,000 species are driven into extinction annually.[17] Richard Swift offers a still graver statistic: "We are pushing a hundred species a day, four species an hour, into evolutionary oblivion."[18] Wilson's "maximally optimistic" approximation of 27,000 species per year (74 per day, 3 per hour) is a mean between these extremes.[19] A twenty-year study by the World Conservation Union shows that "at least one in eight plant species in the world—and nearly one in three in the United States—are under threat of extinction."[20]

Whatever the most accurate figures may be, this horrendous pace of destruction stems from several major sources, including the clearing of foreign and domestic forests for agricultural purposes and development, the drainage and filling in of wetlands, the damming of rivers, the use and abuse of coral reefs, and relentless, high-tech ocean fishing. Among these, deforestation and overfishing are the areas in which the relationship between human diet and species extinction is the strongest. Approximately 70 percent of ocean fish stocks are said to be in imminent danger of collapse.[21] Even more worrisome is the devastation of the earth's forests, particularly its irreplaceable rain forests. For this reason we shall concentrate our attention here.

Most people who follow the news are aware that global rain forests perform unique functions within the regulative cycles of the biosphere by helping to maintain global temperature, providing fresh supplies of oxygen and water, and sheltering the most complex web of life imaginable. It is reported that "there are more different species of birds in each square mile of the Amazon than exist in all of North America."[22] Up to 300 species of trees per hectare (2.47 acres) and 2,200 plant species per square kilometer (0.37 square mile) have been identified in neotropical (Latin American) rain forests.[23] A survey of a mere 19 trees in Panama yielded 955 species of beetles, while in Peru *one* sample tree housed 43 species of ants.[24] In all, 40 to 50 percent of the world's plant and animal species dwell in the rain forests.[25] This superabundance of life-forms yields a wide range of raw materials used in the manufacture of all manner of consumer goods and pharmaceuticals upon which the quality of human life crucially depends. Products of great value include hardwoods, rattan, natural rubber, waxes, essential oils, fruits, and nuts. One-quarter of all drug compounds obtained from pharmacies contain rain forest ingredients, while for most of the world's people, traditional medicines extracted from plants are used exclusively to treat ailments.[26] A "habitat holocaust"[27] continues around the clock, however, with an estimated 142,000 square kilometers (54,000 square miles) of rain forest being sacrificed to human need and greed annually.[28] Sadly, "fewer than one percent of tropical rain forest plants have been chemically screened for useful medicinal properties."[29] Meanwhile, "studies in Peru, the Brazilian Amazon, the Philippines and Indonesia suggest that harvesting forest products sustainably is at least twice as profitable as clearing them [the forests] for timber or to provide land for agriculture."[30]

That the rain forests are the earth's pivotal sustainers of species diversity seems unarguable. But why is species diversity so important? Thomas E. Lovejoy, a conservation biologist, places the matter in perspective:

> Assuming that the [earth's] biota contains ten million species, they then represent ten million successful sets of solutions to a series of biological problems, any one of which could be immensely valuable to us in a number of ways. . . .

> The point . . . is not that the "worth" of an obscure species is that it may someday produce a cure for cancer. The point is that the biota as a whole is continually providing us with new ways to improve our biological lot, and that species that may be unimportant on our current assessment of what may be directly useful may be important tomorrow.[31]

In more general terms, Wilson has commented that "biodiversity is our most valuable but least appreciated resource."[32] Quite simply, it has often been greatly to human advantage to be able to draw upon this precious resource, and therefore it is likely to be so in the future. Our own chances of survival as a species depend upon the rich variety of other life-forms that abound, and the rain forests comprise a unique "genetic library" of virtually untapped information.[33]

The assumption, of course, is that global biodiversity belongs to everyone. And perhaps it does, or should. But there is also an important sense in which those who live in developing nations and who are often caught in the middle of large-scale assaults on biodiversity have special interests at stake. Vandana Shiva points out that "biodiversity is a people's resource. While the industrialized world and affluent societies turned their backs to biodiversity, the poor in the Third World have continued to depend on biological resources for food and nutrition, for health care, for energy, for fiber, and for housing. . . . Biodiversity is fast becoming the primary site of conflict between worldviews based on diversity and nonviolence and those based on monocultures and violence."[34] Thus, where biodiversity is under threat, so too is cultural diversity, for the human lives sustained by a rich environment of life-forms are intimately interwoven with it.

Solid, human-centered reasons for preserving biological diversity are to be found in these reflections. But might there not be additional good reasons for promoting species diversity? We encounter little difficulty in valuing other species instrumentally, in terms of what they can do for us. Perhaps we can also value them for their own sakes, that is, for having marvelous ways of being that are worthy of celebrating quite independently of any actual or potential use we might make of them. All valuations of nature are human-centered to the extent that it is humans who make them and human experience that encompasses both the departure point for, and the end state of reflection upon, the valuation process. While this conclusion seems inescapable, it does not negate our ability to value otherness for its own sake and in its own terms. We can admire and appreciate the unique adaptations and capacities of other species no matter how remotely related to ourselves they may be. We can also discover in nature *nonresource instrumental values,* that is, sources of value to humans that are entirely different from what is yielded when we transform nature into a commodity. We all recognize that nature has profound aesthetic, symbolic, historical, and spiritual importance to us, including the potential for psychological renewal.[35] In short, we value nature as a whole as well as specific parts of nature both as means to our own ends—physical, mental, and spiritual health—and as things to celebrate and cherish for a wide variety of other reasons.

We are now in a position to consider the role animal agriculture plays in undermining species diversity. U.S. Vice President Al Gore has written that "at the current rate of deforestation, virtually all of the tropical rain forests will be gone partway through the next century."[36] It is difficult to establish a precise correlation between animal agriculture and rain forest decimation,[37] since the forests are cleared by humans seeking firewood, settlement space, farm plots, monoculture plantation holdings, oil, minerals, and pastureland for cattle. Hydroelectric projects, roads, and other development schemes also take their toll. Although these pressures are numerous and diverse, grazing may be identified as a major contributor to the process of destruction.

The conversion of tropical forests to pastureland for cattle has proceeded at a remarkable pace in Central America since mid-century.[38] The inherent nature of rain forests is such that when cleared, only poor quality, unsustainable pastureland remains, and this contributes to the expanding destruction as new grazing areas are sought to replace older, exhausted areas.[39] Norman Myers contends that from Mexico to Brazil, "the number one factor in elimination of Latin America's tropical forests is cattlegrazing."[40] Most of the beef produced in this region is exported to the U.S. market, although an increasing portion goes to Western Europe and Japan.[41] The United States contains only 5 percent of the world's population, yet it produces, imports, and consumes more beef than any other country.[42] The beef imported from Latin America ends up as fast-food burgers, processed meats, and pet foods. Myers notes that "convenience foods . . . constitute the fastest-growing part of the entire food industry in the United States"; 50 percent of all meals are now consumed in either fast-food or institutional settings.[43] According to Arnold Newman, for each North American fast-food hamburger, "the environmental cost is half a ton of rainforest. . . . Expressed as forest area, the cost is 67 square feet—more than 6.25 square meters of forest—for every hamburger sold."[44] This pattern demonstrates forcefully the connection between meat-eating and rain forest destruction— what Myers calls "the 'hamburgerization' of the forests"[45]— and offers yet another moral indictment of the omnivorous diet. We cannot save the forests just by excluding fast-food hamburgers from our diets, but we can help turn things around if enough of us make this and other, related dietary decisions, and thus set an example for the rest of the world.

The case of rain forest decimation by cattle grazing may be read as a typical ecological horror story. But the situation in fact is much more complicated, for it is merely one of the many examples of our species's tendency to treat nature and natural biological systems purely as instruments to achieve human, and often very narrow, objectives.

According to the manipulative mind-set, nature and parts of nature (such as members of nonhuman species) are merely a collection of resources for our disposition, use, and disposal. The slash-and-burn practice that seals the fate of rain forests that are viewed as obstacles in the way of profit to be gleaned from low-cost meat provides but one example. While the rain forests are treated as dispensable, the animals now bred on this land are themselves no more than commodities destined for some distant stockyard, just further contents of the organic cash till that is nature. The attitude that permits such ruthless domination and exploitation of cattle from rain forest regions is in fact no different from that which approves the widespread practice of animal confinement on factory farms. It is not enough that animals give their lives (and deaths) to the food industry and to the consumers of food, however. Now the silent laws of demand, supply, economic growth, and profit make it necessary for them to be genetically "improved" to be even more efficient food generators. Over a decade ago a report prepared for the U.S. Congress predicted (perhaps a bit overzealously) that "before the turn of the century cattle ranches in Texas may be able to raise cattle as big as elephants. California dairy farmers may be able to . . . increase milk production by more than ten percent without increasing food intake."[46] Pigs twelve feet long and five feet high are not beyond scientific speculation.[47] Such laboratory triumphs, which have been aptly called "monstrosities of utility,"[48] may never come to be, but clones (genetically identical copies) of superproductive animals are already on the way.[49]

These developments should not surprise us, as purpose-bred life-forms are now being patented,[50] and animals are being genetically engineered to grow improved body parts that can be harvested for human transplant surgery.[51] Some have even mooted the possibility of breeding animals without pain receptors, which would turn these creatures into the insensate machines Descartes fantasized all animals to be.[52] Pigs with modified physiologies that experience little or no stress are the subjects of active research.[53] If these experiments succeed, then (the thinking presumably goes) it will be all right to treat these animals as mere things, and major ethical objections to factory farming, animal research, and similar types of exploitation will simply melt away. (This is not the case, however, as I show in Chapter 8, Section 9.)

What does all this mean? The meat industry, itself feeding off human demand for certain types of food, is ushering in a form of animal rearing and use that is totally lacking in compassion and a sense of connection with nature. Genetic engineering arguably aggravates the animal suffering inherent in factory farming, as it manipulates breeding stocks to produce new animal types.[54] One author observes that "the disastrous effects of industrialised agricultural methods are being repeated with new biotechnology."[55] We seem to be learning slowly to connect on one level—with ecological issues—while badly disconnecting on another. Most people wouldn't visit a slaughterhouse for any reason,[56] and from what they know of modern livestock production processes, wouldn't dream of allowing their pets or any animals they cared about to be treated as food animals routinely are. But at the same time the consumer selection of meat and meat products as foods goes on and simply isn't analyzed. In this manner we are conditioned to accept the manipulation of nature that as sensitive, caring people we ought to be aware of and reject. We thus find ourselves caught in a trap of our own making. We can, however, seek a way out by reflection and choice of a lifestyle that does not rest on the subjugation of nature and the suffering of nonhuman forms of life. This is the vegetarian option.

3. World Hunger and Injustice

World hunger, like the human manipulation of nature, is likewise an enormously complicated problem. It too has many causes and aggravating factors both domestically and in developing nations, which prevent bountiful produce from being equitably distributed. Some of these factors are shifting and often feudal patterns of land ownership, profiteering in the agriculture industry, unemployment, political corruption, war, overpopulation, economic mismanagement, inadequate educational resources, disease, weather, natural disasters, dependence on petrochemicals and fossil fuels, and the replacement of traditional farming by Western monoculture. We must therefore be on guard against seeking one-dimensional explanations of this problem as well, although it is still possible to identify how meat production contributes directly to world hunger.

Over twenty years ago, in an early edition of her now famous classic *Diet for a Small Planet,* Frances Moore Lappé described the wasteful feedlot process of rearing cattle for beef as "a protein factory in reverse" (16 units of protein input for each 1 of output;[57] other estimates place the ratio as high as 20 to 1, and the ratio of caloric input to output for human consumption at 10 to 1).[58] She also reported her "discovery that in 1968 the amount of humanly edible protein fed to American livestock and not returned for human consumption approached the whole world's protein deficit!"[59] And this is not just an issue for Americans. The world's food animals are a very hungry lot: The cattle, buffalo, sheep, goats, pigs, and poultry have a combined biomass greater than that of the world's total human population.[60] Lappé pointed out that ruminants can graze on marginal rather than prime agricultural land because they produce protein efficiently from cellulose. She observed that the poorer countries of the world are often net exporters of food to the more affluent countries, and that the North American food production system basically feeds animals, not people.

These findings are confirmed by recent studies. Developing countries in Latin America, the Caribbean, and Asia are still exporting more agricultural products (by U.S. dollar value) than they import, while African nations export almost as much as they import, and these trends are projected to continue into the new millennium.[61] Alan Durning, senior researcher at the Worldwatch Institute, contends that nearly 40 percent of the world's grain and 70 percent of American grain are fed to livestock.[62] Meanwhile Oxfam estimates that 14.6 million hectares (36.1 million acres) of often choice land in developing nations is dedicated to producing animal feeds for European livestock.[63] Michael Redclift gives an even higher estimate of 21.6 million hectares (53.4 million acres).[64] According to another report, "worldwide over one-third of all grain is grown to feed livestock, whilst at least 500 million people are malnourished."[65] These are scarcely rational uses of abundant but ever more precious planetary resources.

Simply put, large-scale meat production absorbs vast quantities of raw materials and energy of all types in order to produce relatively meager returns to humans. Ecologically, nutritionally, and calorically, it is a losing proposition. Nor does it make sense from the standpoint of collective human welfare and the quest for global equality and social justice. The "right to adequate food" or to freedom from hunger has been affirmed numerous times by international organizations, and is part of the Universal Declaration of Human Rights of 1948.[66] If there exists a basic human right to the minimum nutrition needed to survive and be healthy, then the meat-based economy of agriculture is simply immoral, for it systematically prevents this right from being acknowledged respectfully and realized in practice.

Everyone knows that not only in North America but around the world the gap between rich and poor is widening. The "protein factory in reverse" is evidently an aggravating factor in this overall process. Perhaps we can understand this truth more fully if we examine some actual and possible food distribution and consumption patterns.

The fundamental social and economic inequalities that form the underpinning of poverty and create serious deficiencies in the basic needs of life are the same everywhere. As Andy Crump indicates, hunger and malnutrition are "found predominantly among those people who lack the cash income to buy—or the land and inputs to grow—the required amounts of food for them and their families. This is true even in the richest of countries."[67] Patricia L. Kutzner remarks, more succinctly, that the world's rural poor simply lack "access to productive land and water."[68] In the Latin American rain forests, a major factor shaping this state of affairs is the concentration of land in fewer hands and the dispossession of the poor and indigenous peoples, who are driven therefrom to settle in new wilderness areas or in already swollen urban centers.[69]

We have been confining our attention to the developing nations in which food shortage is most obvious and severe. And here the statistics are indeed appalling. For example, 14 million children die each year from hunger and hunger-related causes.[70] The number of people unable to meet their basic subsistence needs has reached 1.1 billion, according to the World Bank.[71] In Brazil, where the rain forests are ravaged daily for cattle grazing and other uses, the average person annually consumes less beef than does a domestic cat in the United States.[72] Meanwhile, large food stocks (principally grain and dairy products) continue to pile up in the United States, Canada, and the European Economic Union due to government subsidies, and such "surplus" stocks, while not on the market, have the effect of lowering world prices for these commodities.[73]

The average North American is overfed and overproteinized; this is too well known to be debated any longer. According to Pimentel, per capita daily consumption of protein in the United States is 102 grams (3.57 ounces), 70 grams (2.45 ounces) of which are of animal origin, while the United Nations Food and Agricultural Organization's recommended level is 41 grams (1.44 ounces).[74] As Robbins points out, people in the developing world "are copying us. They associate meat eating with the economic status of the developed nations and strive to emulate it. The tiny minority who can afford meat in those countries eats it, even while many of their people go to bed hungry at night, and mothers watch their children starve."[75] He estimates that "a given acreage can feed twenty times as many people eating a pure vegetarian (or vegan) diet-style as it could people eating the standard American diet-style." The same acreage would feed between six and seven lacto-ovo vegetarians.[76] Meanwhile, based on figures provided by the Overseas Development Council, Robbins projects that a mere 10 percent reduction in American meat-eating could free up enough grain to feed all of the millions of human beings who starve to death annually.[77] He concludes that "hunger is a social disease caused by the unjust, inefficient and wasteful control of food."[78] Exploitation is clearly a principal feature of this "disease," as the poorest countries of the world increasingly find their traditional agricultural practices and diets undermined, their peoples undernourished, their lands deforested for grazing, their position in international markets deteriorating, and other negative effects visited upon them by the multinational corporations that control the international agricultural and meat economy.[79]

Production and distribution of food and control of world, regional, and local markets are complex, dynamic elements that reinforce and perpetuate these forms of exploitation. Their scope goes beyond what we have space to consider here.[80] In addition to these factors, there are others—some transient, some more durable—that also affect food supplies. An example of the former is what is euphemistically called "structural adjustment in debt-burdened countries," which results in a "sharp reduction of government health and nutritional programs"; an instance of the latter is the disproportionate access to and consumption of world resources by developed in contrast to developing nations.[81]

But despite the enormity and complexity of the issues we need to understand in order to develop an agenda for action and change, everyone *does* have a choice between abetting the conditions that enable the "social disease" of world hunger to flourish and confronting them by means of her or his own dietary commitments. In her careful analysis of the problem, Kutzner concludes that in the future, "diets will need to obtain most of their calories and protein from grain directly instead of by feeding the grain first to animals where grain is converted into nutrients much less efficiently."[82] Our individual food purchases of course cannot by themselves change the world. We can, however, change ourselves, which indeed is the starting point for all change. We can exercise an influence on those who look to us for examples or for leadership. Small, incremental, grassroots changes should not be undervalued, for they often lead to much larger ones at the societal or even the international level. We may not realize the contribution our microchanges make to macrochanges until, after the fact, there is the time and the method for sifting and interpreting the evidence. In any event, it is important, one might say, to do the right thing when it stares us in the face.

4.   Interconnected Forms of Oppression

A principal aim of this book is to encourage the reader to make the significant ethical connections that lead to the choice of a vegetarian diet. In recent times, a number of philosophical outlooks have grown up around the theme of exploring connections among different forms of domination, oppression, and exploitation. These efforts are directed toward enhancing our understanding of the dynamics of subjugation and enabling us to see how apparently unconnected phenomena are related symptoms of a common cause. I refer to this cluster of views as *antidomination theories,* and among them may be listed Marxist ecology, social ecology, Greenism, ecofeminism, and the environmental justice movement.[83] This is a wide field of activity, but what is common to all these schools of thought is the affirmation of a connection between the domination of humans and of nature by humans. For our purposes, ecofeminism has the most to offer, since it is the only one that addresses issues concerning the treatment of animals and (at least occasionally) endorses vegetarianism on ethical grounds.

The character of ecofeminist thinking is revealed in the following statement by Taiwanese educator Huey-li Li: "Ecofeminists' ethical concerns regarding environmental issues are extended to any indication of brokenness and disharmony in the web of life. War, class exploitation, poverty, and animal experimentation are not regarded as peripheral to other urgent ecological issues, such as air and water pollution, oil spills, and the extinction of wilderness and wildlife."[84] Here Li expresses a dedication to preserving the integrity and health of the biosphere and of the human community, as well as to seeing things holistically rather than piecemeal. The theme of relatedness is evident not only in the way in which various concerns are linked, but also in the implication that the harmonious connection between life-forms is a desirable state that can provide a source of values for living. Li's comments seem to resonate with an ancient wisdom in which a caring and responsible attitude toward nature and other human beings is paramount, rather than expressing proprietorship, instrumentalism, and domination.

One should not assume that all ecofeminists speak with one voice, however. Some ecofeminists (and other feminists) either do not see the connection between women's liberation and animal liberation or else do not affirm it strongly in their work and lives.[85] However, Jane Meyerding explains very clearly why they *should:* "It is a contradiction for feminists to eat animals with whom they have no physical or spiritual relationship except that of exploiter to exploited. . . . I think concern for the lives of all beings is a vital, empowering part of feminist analysis; I don't think we can strengthen our feminist struggle against one aspect of patriarchy by ignoring or accepting other aspects."[86] The point here is not just that people ought to be ·

consistent in thought and action, but rather that one's failure to address parallel forms of domination, oppression, and exploitation in fact reinforces them and unknowingly undermines one's own efforts in other areas. Meyerding's claim is strengthened, I believe, by accounts of women who have undergone a process of experiential identification with animals as commodified or objectified bodies, and as beings whose acts or natural functions are under the control of another person or agency. Some women have an awareness of themselves as being manipulated and defined within patriarchy in the same way as animals are.[87] Others come to this realization in a particularly forceful way by being exposed to certain kinds of advertising or pornography, or by being victims of male violence.[88]

In view of the foregoing considerations, use of the term *ecofeminism* hereafter will refer to that version that acknowledges and takes seriously the connection between the domination of women and that of animals. Ecofeminism, then, is the attempt to diagnose what has gone wrong in disharmonious relationships between humans, and between humans and nonhumans, in order to take remedial action. Because disharmonious relationships have to do with power imbalances, ecofeminism is inevitably a political theory. This will become clearer if we define some terms.

Domination refers to power that is exercised over someone or something, and that in a vital way diminishes or circumscribes the domain of that being's activity. Domination by one party creates in another an inferior or subordinate status. Power may be wielded over others either de jure or de facto. In the de jure sense, power is held to be justifiably exercised, and the justification is often sought by appealing to *natural law,* some moral argument or the rules of a duly constituted political process. In the de facto sense, power is simply recognized as being exercised, whether justifiably or not, and there are those who claim that power over others is never exercised justifiably, if this is taken to mean "by right." Famous thinkers, such as

Niccolò Machiavelli (1469–1527) and Thomas Hobbes (1588–1679), have attempted to justify the use of power in human affairs, while others, like the anarchists William Godwin (1756–1836) and Peter Kropotkin (1842–1921), have vigorously denied that it can ever be justified. The most important source of the justification for the domination of nature by humans, known as *dominion,* is of course the Book of Genesis in the Old Testament. While there is considerable controversy over the meaning of God's granting of dominion over nature to humans because Genesis itself offers conflicting accounts,[89] a despotic self-image of our species vis-à-vis nature has been unquestionably formative in the development of Western culture. (For more on biblical dominionism, see Chapter 7, Section 5.)

Oppression is the unwarranted and/or arbitrary denial of freedom to some being that has a claim to it. This denial is usually understood to be injurious to the being in question because it is contrary to its will or thwarts the pursuit of its significant interests (such as liberty, physical and psychological inviolability, or the realization of basic needs).[90] An oppressor creates a being that is subjugated and subservient—an oppressed being. Peter Singer generated a heated discussion by arguing that the oppression of animals is as morally objectionable as sexism and racism.[91] Most animal liberationists and animal rights supporters agree, while others find this view outrageous and unacceptable.[92] It is not necessary here to determine whether animals are oppressed in precisely the same ways and to the same degree as are humans, however. It is plainly true that in factory farming and many other areas, animals are dominated by humans, and that this results in the suppression of their species-typical behaviors and a great deal of manifest suffering. Since animals have a significant moral status, including an interest in their own welfare and a desire to live, this process bears the marks of oppression.

Exploitation, finally, refers to the treatment of some being in a purely instrumental fashion, that is, as a means to ends other than its own and with no serious concern for its welfare. In exploitation, a dominator callously and calculatingly takes advantage of another in order to gain something. Allen W. Wood takes this point somewhat further by stating that "proper respect for others is violated when we treat their vulnerabilities as opportunities to advance our own interests or projects. It is degrading to have your weaknesses taken advantage of, and dishonorable to use the weaknesses of others for your ends."[93] While this comment helps crystallize the analysis of exploitation, Wood makes no mention of animals as members of the class of beings who may be exploited. It is as if concepts like respect, degradation, and dishonor simply do not apply to interactions between humans and other animals, no matter how similar to us they might be; it is as if the entire contemporary debate concerning the moral status of animals does not exist. Interestingly (and disappointingly) the readings with which Wood's essay appears in book form contain no mention of animals, notwithstanding the publisher's claim that they "take us to the very cutting edge of current discussions of exploitation."[94] (Nature, according to some contributors to the volume, can be exploited, but animals, apparently, cannot be.) I believe this omission is a serious shortcoming that reveals the anthropocentrism still clinging to ethics and social philosophy even when some people assert that the scholarship represents the "cutting edge." Surely the body of high-quality philosophical work that has been done to clarify and defend the moral considerability of nonhumans deserves to be recognized positively rather than ignored in discussions such as this. In contrast, the definition of exploitation I offer above is deliberately inclusive, and makes it possible to affirm that wherever forms of cruelty and manipulation are practiced, we have examples of *animal exploitation*.

Before we proceed we must deal with an objection. In a recent article Beth A. Dixon takes issue with the way of speaking I am advocating. She maintains that "animals do not share with women the cognitive capacities and the social and cultural context that would allow them to benefit from equal treatment."[95] Furthermore, comparing women and animals with respect to oppression, she argues, "is not compelling once we detail the ways in which animals and women are dissimilar."[96] On the first of these points, Dixon simply begs the question concerning the cognitive capacities of animals, assuming without argument that they occupy a completely different psychological realm. But considerable recent investigative literature testifies to the contrary.[97] In addition, animals of course are in some crucial senses excluded from our human "social and cultural context." But in other ways they are not: Zoos, circuses, museums, schools, farms, home life, art, literature, science, and the media are all areas of social and cultural activity in which the presence of nonhumans is keenly felt. Dixon is correct to observe that equality is absent in our dealings with members of other species, and that we as yet have no clear idea how animals would or might benefit from such equality if they were to win it from us. However, we should bear in mind that, as Singer has carefully articulated, the notion of equality does not entail identity of capacities or of treatment, and is more meaningfully understood as standing for equal consideration of interests, so far as comparisons between them can be made.[98] Thus, for example, when animals show signs of being in pain, being traumatized, or being bored in situations similar to those in which humans have such experiences, we are obliged to take their welfare into account and to avoid doing things that cause them gratuitous harm. Dixon's second point misses the mark if the general characterization of oppression I have given above is accepted, and also if we once again acknowledge the growing body of evidence about animals' awareness, needs, and sophisticated capacities.

Feminists (pretty much by definition) have been in the vanguard of cultural criticism for as long as they have been around. Margaret Cavendish, duchess of Newcastle (1623–1673), for example, was a self-taught thinker who confronted Descartes both in person and in correspondence over his views on animals as machines. She was also among the first to frame a concept of animal rights.[99] Josephine Donovan notes that "there is a long list of first-wave feminists who advocated either vegetarianism or animal welfare reform," including Margaret Fuller Ossoli (1810–1850) and Charlotte Perkins Gilman (1860–1935), each of whom proposed a utopian vision of a nonviolent, vegetarian society.[100] The pro-animal strand of ecofeminism should be appreciated as the successor to this tradition. But beyond this ecofeminism elaborates a theoretical basis for deconstructing Western cultural tendencies that inferiorize women, nature, and animals. This in turn clears a conceptual space within which new, empowering relationships between human beings, humans and nature, and humans and animals can develop. It gives voice to concerns previously silenced by the modes of thought and discourse that have shaped our culture, as well as to neglected values within our ethical tradition.

Ecofeminism identifies Western culture as thoroughly patriarchal. This means that society is structured in such a way as to ensure and enhance male supremacy. Bonnie Kreps suggests that more is involved, defining patriarchy as "the institutionalized system of male dominance in which (1) all women are subordinated *and* (2) a small elite of men further subordinate other men and appropriate for themselves a vastly disproportionate share of power and wealth."[101] It would be difficult to deny that there is a very close fit between this description and our own society, even if we make allowances for the fact that society and its institutions are constantly evolving and that some elements of progress toward greater egalitarianism are discernible. Within a patriarchal framework women, nature, and animals (and, one should add, children) are positioned ontologically, evaluatively, and politically in relation to men, whose attributes are taken to be the norms against which we measure other things. Men are considered (by men, of course, since they control the dominant discourse) to be more real, perfect (or at least perfectible), valuable, and deserving of power than women are or any nonhumans ever could be.

The elements of the ecofeminist approach can best be understood in relation to the Western philosophical, religious, and political tradition. Ecofeminists argue, first, that domination, oppression, and exploitation arise from two factors: dualistic thinking and hierarchical valuation. Dualistic thinking is manifested most plainly in the body/soul (or body/mind) dichotomy characteristic of Plato, and is rooted in Christianity and its prominent philosophical architects such as Saint Augustine (354–430), Saint Thomas Aquinas, and Descartes. The body is the material and perishable component of our being, which is the source of physical needs and dependencies, illness, desire, emotion, perceptual and other kinds of error, and finally (with Christianity) sin. The soul (or mind) is the seat of reason and of the essential, immaterial, immortal self that each of us allegedly is. Our humanity, perfectibility, and capacity for salvation all derive from this part of our being. For dualistic thinkers, animals typically lack souls (or at most have souls of an inferior grade), and consequently possess neither the higher potentialities nor the immortality of humans. Body is identified with nature, and hence a second dualism between nature and humans comes into play (insofar as humans are *essentially* soul or mind and not body).

Such dualism is also reflected in the opposition between men and women, male and female, and masculinity and femininity, and here the contrast between humans and nature exercises an important influence. Because they experience menstruation, pregnancy, and childbirth; nurture the young; and have allegedly greater emotionality, women are identified more closely with the body, animals, and nature, and therefore too with the physical principle that limits ideal human self-betterment. Genevieve Lloyd points out that "from the beginnings of philosophical thought, femaleness was symbolically associated with what Reason [as the creative energy of the universe] supposedly left behind—the dark powers of the earth goddesses, immersion in unknown forces associated with mysterious female powers. The early Greeks saw women's capacity to conceive as connecting them with the fertility of Nature. As Plato later expressed the thought, women 'imitate the earth.'"[102] This symbolic identification of women with nature—frequently forged through physical and psychological linkages with animals—is juxtaposed to men's identification with reason and intellectual and spiritual perfectibility. Christianity later absorbed these Greek ideas and embedded them firmly in our culture.

Through the habitual practice of dualistic thinking, difference, opposition, and otherness became taken as aspects of reality and fixed as ontologically and epistemically primary. That is, from the standpoint of how things are and how they are to be known, the fundamental dichotomies under review were ingrained in our collective view of the universe, our paradigm for understanding.

An almost inseparable phase of this process is the relative evaluation of differences. Here hierarchical rankings enter into our thinking and order entities in arrangements of positive/ negative, better/worse, superior/inferior, above/below, and so on. Men are superior to women and humans to nature and animals, and it is better to be the former of each pair than the latter. While this may seem a fairly simplistic and mechanical caricature, it is difficult to deny that we have a very strong tendency to organize our judgments about the world in such terms. Elizabeth Dodson Gray, one of the earliest ecofeminists, notes that "almost in the same instant that we perceive difference, we are looking to ascertain rankings of power, moral or economic value, and aesthetic preference. We do this whether it is a different animal, a different culture, or a skin pigmentation that is different."[103] In all the struggles against inequality and injustice (for example, against racism, "ethnic cleansing," homophobia, and ageism), this attribution of relative values to what are merely differences can be found, and fair-minded people continually need to monitor their own perceptions in order to guard against it. Lloyd also substantiates the claim that hierarchical thinking is endemic to our species by tracing it back even farther than we have thus far—to a "table of opposites" framed by the Pythagoreans in the sixth century BCE in which male/female and other differences are enshrined as unchanging formative principles of the cosmic order.[104] Meanwhile, more recent work by ecofeminists such as Val Plumwood and Ariel Salleh[105] and by body theorists such as Elizabeth Grosz[106] goes still farther, collapsing or transcending male/female and masculine/feminine dualities and working toward a challenging new definition of human nature.

The second major emphasis of ecofeminism is on power relationships. Hierarchical rankings become incorporated into an ideological worldview that comprehensively explains how things are and ought to be thought about and related one to another, and that by the same token legitimates the power some beings wield over others. Just as men are "naturally" superior to women, so they are "destined" to rule over them, and the same reasoning "justifies" humans' domination over nature and exploitation of all other species. Nature and nonhuman entities are alien or other; humans are apart from nature even while being part of it. It isn't clear whether patriarchal political and social systems generate hierarchical thinking, or vice versa. Very likely there is a complex reciprocal causation between the two, such that power relationships stimulate the search for a justifying ideology, and the justifying ideology in turn shores up the evolving power relationships. At any rate within patriarchy it is men who control the discourse and hence are able to fashion philosophical, religious, and other outlooks to suit the needs of their political agenda.

The third level of ecofeminist theory contends that the domination, oppression, and exploitation of women and nature, or women and animals, form "interlocking systems."[107]

This means that we must not only understand each in terms of the other, but also attack both together at their common root. When dualism and hierarchical valuation are deconstructed (or taken apart through analytical thought), their veneer of legitimacy is stripped away. What remains is an awareness that what seemed to be a truthful perspective on reality is merely an ideology of domination. It is revealed that patriarchy operates on the underlying principle that "might makes right"—a doctrine that in its undisguised form our ethical sensibility would never tolerate. What appeared to be a de jure exercise of power now shines forth as having only a de facto status. This insight can then lead the way to change, or to the egalitarian *re*construction of relationships between men and women, and humans and nonhumans. Ecofeminist theory and, more generally, the study of cultural attitudes toward women and animals teach us that these attitudes are socially constructed. In other words, they are embedded in a network of meanings, symbols, values, and images that are themselves historically situated. We are part of this process of social construction, whether or not we are explicitly aware of it, and whether or not we choose to be involved in it. But critical awareness introduces a fundamental change of direction, as the way in which women and animals (as well as men and human beings as such) are defined can be altered through a process of conscious, deliberate reimaging and revaluation. This is an ongoing development that many of us are now witnessing and participating in. For those who see themselves as part of this process, vegetarianism represents a commitment to redefining the human-animal relationship on a more harmonious footing, where violence and exploitation no longer hold sway. Feminist thinking is in many respects leading the way, providing, as it does, new directions in ethical theorizing that build upon connection and relatedness, reciprocity and community, experiential data, bodily self-awareness, acknowledgment of moral emotions (such as love and compassion), caring, celebration of life, nonviolence, and respectful acceptance and affirmation of difference.[108]

5. Common Threads

Embedded in ecofeminist thinking is the larger project of healing a fragmented picture of human nature itself. From both practical and philosophical standpoints, vegetarianism represents a significant step in this process. I shall develop this theme in the remaining chapters. For the moment, however, it is useful to reflect that all the issues and arguments reviewed thus far tend toward the same conclusion: our health, our treatment of animals, our relationship to the environment and to the biosphere as a whole, our management and distribution of the earth's bounty, and our relationships with one another in a global community and economy are all directly connected with our fundamental attitudes about ourselves and how we fit within the natural world. Indeed, it is not too much to say that our vision of our place in the universe is also implicated— whether we see our species (or some privileged part of it) as specially gifted and central to creation, or else adopt a more humble, open-minded approach to what is other than ourselves.

Vegetarianism is a commitment to taking greater responsibility for these attitudes and for understanding their impact on a larger circle of human activities. It is a way of redrawing the mental geography with which we negotiate around our world so that it includes an expanded sense of what has value in and of itself. Above all it is a path leading to less harm to the planet and more peaceful coexistence with other sentient life-forms. This should recommend the vegetarian choice to persons who believe that our species should move in the direction just described. It is often observed that human beings cannot nourish themselves without killing *something*. Some people use this fact to support an argument for meat-eating, as if there were no differences of degree or kind between killing plants and killing animals, and as if the ecological consequences of both were the same. However, there is no reason to believe that plants are capable of experiencing pain and suffering, while many animals plainly can. In killing animals for food we also destroy life-forms that exhibit consciousness and other sorts of mental capacities and psychological characteristics that we greatly value in ourselves. Furthermore, the environmental impact of large-scale food animal production is extremely negative. Therefore, a vegetarian diet is, both ethically and ecologically, a more sound and sane alternative.

Meat-eaters place themselves at the top of the so-called food pyramid, which is a graphic way of depicting the relationship among food sources and eaters. The broad base of the pyramid comprises vegetative matter, next comes a smaller level of exclusive herbivores, and finally there are still smaller levels of carnivores and omnivores that feed off the levels below. It is a curious fact that humans, who are omnivores, for the most part do not eat strict carnivores (except for fish and occasional exotic reptiles and amphibians), but rather poultry and ruminant herbivores, probably because of their relative ease of domestication. But we usually visualize ourselves as occupying the top of the food pyramid nonetheless. What we need to realize is that as omnivores we not only consume the herbivores we serve up as meat but also all the vegetative matter they have consumed, whereas if we ate at the lowest level of the pyramid we would only ingest what we need to survive, which is less than is required by the herbivores we kill for food. The food pyramid, then, represents a concentration of environmental consumption and exploitation as we move upward (just as the so-called food chain represents an increasing concentration of toxic substances as we move from agricultural crops to meat). We do ourselves and the planet a favor, then, by eating a vegetarian diet. And we earn the additional reward of being able to cultivate in ourselves a more harmonious outlook on the world of which we are a part.

CHAPTER

Arguments for Vegetarianism: III

1. Wisdom Traditions and Modern Parallels

Every traditional worldview, whether Western or non-Western, touches upon the relations between humans and nature and either implicitly or explicitly contains principles governing the use and treatment of animals. These may be very general, such as injunctions to show kindness or to consider all animals as existing to serve human needs, or they may be very specific, such as prescribed dietary practices, slaughter methods, or provisions for working animals. We may collectively refer to the teachings from which such principles are derived as "wisdom traditions." Many of them (but by no means all) are associated with or derived from religious and spiritual outlooks. We shall examine both sacred and secular views and observe that each sort has recognizable counterparts in the other.

Unlike most of the mainstream religions, the systems of

113

belief of native peoples throughout the world are characterized by mythic elements that connect humans intimately with
animals and other natural objects. Through creation stories,
instructive fables, and rituals, these myths foster a sense that
vital, ongoing interactions between humans and nonhumans
are taking place. Mainstream religions, on the other hand,
seldom, if ever, have this feature. Martin Palmer has noted
that "many . . . 'indigenous' belief systems . . . have never
seen themselves, nor sought to be seen, as universal, or as
having universal significance."[1] Among the principal world
religions, some have proclaimed their universality and have
had a corresponding history of proselytizing. Others, however, have no such self-image or self-aggrandizing ambition.
I believe that the same division can be found among secular
philosophies, not withstanding the declaration of Friedrich
Nietzsche (1844–1900) that every metaphysician secretly
wishes to be the " 'unriddler of the world.'"[2] That is, some
philosophers are bent on creating a universal standpoint,
while others (like Nietzsche himself) have more humble, per-
spectival objectives. For these reasons, it is wrongheaded to
expect that every view to be considered will yield a full-
fledged argument for vegetarianism. But as Jim Nollman observes, "spiritual truth is both universal and immanent, no
matter what name it chooses to register under."[3] That is, if
we listen carefully, we may find elements in any outlook that
can serve us well in a practical sense as we journey through
life. My suggestion, then, is that we look upon each spiritual
or religious orientation as providing a possible route to a vegetarian way of life and that we be prepared to learn and borrow from it as we see fit. And if we are already committed to
a particular spiritual or religious viewpoint, we may be able to
consider its vegetarian potential as we may not have done before. Consequently, we shall explore not so much *arguments*
as *directions* in which our thinking about animals and dietary
choices might be guided.

2. Interspecies Kinship and Compassion

The idea that all life-forms comprise a natural order in which each has its special place and function is a very ancient one. Most expressions of this idea, however, feature a hierarchical arrangement, with humans or deities occupying the highest rank or manifesting the greatest level of perfection or degree of actuality. Concealed within this mode of thought is not only the desire to explain why things are (or appear to be) a particular way, but also to rationalize or justify certain norms of conduct. If a god is "above" us, then it is proper to adopt an attitude of subservience toward him or her. Toward nonhuman animals that are "below" us, however, we may act as dominant. We are their "lords and masters," as the gods are ours. But there is also a minority or dissident viewpoint in human history that conceptualizes the relationship between humans and nonhumans as one of kinship or more or less equality.

The idea of interspecies kinship has both religious and secular roots. Some belief systems affirm the fundamental goodness of all creation and the duty to honor and esteem its many manifestations. Others see in natural objects and animals divine or spiritual embodiments. Still others postulate that some deities have or assume animal forms. Beyond these interesting notions, which we shall revisit later, there are also nonreligious perspectives of the same general type. We have considered (especially in Chapters 1 and 5) conceptions of animals as beings that are closely similar to us in important, morally relevant respects, such as the ability to experience pleasure and pain and the desire to maintain a state of well-being. These awarenesses have given rise to a sense of the need for an expanded moral community that includes humans and (at least some) nonhumans. Association with companion and farm animals has created in many generations of humans a bond of friendship with and love for animals. Astute observation has furnished scientists, animal handlers, naturalists, and laypersons alike with insights into the connections between living things. And there are philosophers who, on purely secular grounds, have posited what Tom Regan calls a "kinship ethic." As Regan explains, "these thinkers share the belief that only *conscious* beings can have moral standing. I refer to theories that embody this belief as *kinship* theories because they grow out of the idea that beings resembling humans in the quite fundamental way of being conscious, and thus to this extent kin to us, have moral standing."[4]

Some of these sources of kinship thinking are anthropocentric in that they draw conclusions concerning interspecies unity from evidence that animals meet human requirements for moral consideration. This is laid out in an especially clear fashion in the passage I have cited from Regan. Here we see that it is not how humans resemble animals that counts but the reverse; and not just any resemblance will do, for it must be along the lines of something that is highly prized by us. Yet the sense of kinship is cultivated in other ways that do not rely on how humanlike animals are or might be under certain unusual circumstances (e.g., when saving humans' lives), or within artificially constructed environments (e.g., laboratory experiments designed to test problem-solving abilities). Stephen R. Kellert has recently examined in detail the complex phenomenon known as "biophilia." This term (proposed earlier and independently by Erich Fromm and Edward O. Wilson) "emphasizes our physical, emotional, and intellectual inclinations for nature and life."[5] Now as in the distant past, Kellert observes, "people continue to need rich and textured relationships with natural diversity in order to achieve lives replete with meaning and value."[6] This need, rather than being anything particularly strange or far-fetched, is thought to be biologically based, since it confers adaptive advantages on humans. Typical examples of biophilia include the well-known role that companion animals play in preserving human health, changing deviant behavior, and relieving loneliness; the aesthetic appreciation of wild animals; insights gained from the observation of animals; and the more pragmatic utilization of animals in the service of human ends. While not all bonds, connections, or affinities between humans and other animals stem from a feeling of kinship, many do, and its expositors therefore regard kinship as an important ingredient of biophilia.

Another time-honored way in which kinship with animals reveals itself to us is through empathy. While a few have discovered within themselves a resonance with the lives and psychological states of animals, this kind of attunement is relatively rare. Enough of us do catch glimpses of it in our dealings with animals, however, that we are able to understand what others mean when they describe the experience of knowing intuitively what an animal is thinking or feeling. We may not have the special gifts and opportunities of a Jane Goodall or a Dian Fossey, but we can share their observations vicariously. More common is the response to perceived suffering in animals, which is the origin of our aversion to cruelty toward nonhuman creatures. Empathy in the face of suffering is also the catalyst for compassion, a moral emotion that is found at the heart of such important ethical systems as Buddhism and the theories of David Hume and Arthur Schopenhauer, an admirer of Hume who was perhaps the first Western philosopher to borrow ideas self-consciously from Buddhism.

Schopenhauer considers compassion to be an "everyday phenomenon" and defines it as "the immediate *participation*, independent of all ulterior considerations, in the *suffering* of another, and thus in the prevention or elimination of it." To his way of thinking it is "the great mystery of ethics."[7] The capacity for compassion is simply something we are born with, an endowment that we cannot ultimately fathom. He maintains that "boundless compassion for all living beings is the firmest and surest guarantee of pure moral conduct, and needs no casuistry."[8] By this he means that the ability to empathize with the suffering of other humans and nonhumans, if it is cultivated in ourselves by repeated practice and uncorrupted by other influences, will suffice to ground our ethical outlook on the world. No beliefs concerning extramundane realities or deities and no eschatological doctrines (about repentance, redemption, final judgment, heaven, and hell) are required to sustain the compassion that flows from us naturally or to bestow on it enduring moral significance. And when we experience compassion we are simultaneously inclined toward doing what we can to prevent or relieve the suffering with which we empathize. This comes very close to saying that compassion is the whole of morality. Indeed Schopenhauer, having declared that "virtue is as little taught as is genius," puts us on notice that in his works "no precepts, no doctrine of duty are to be expected; still less will there be set forth a universal moral principle, a universal recipe, so to speak, for producing all virtues."[9] Thus the avoidance of causing harm, the prevention of harm, and the alleviation of suffering seem to be what ethics has to teach; but each of us has the capacity to be kind and caring that our parents and teachers, but in the final analysis we ourselves, must nurture for the good of all.

It is easy to locate problems in this view, such as the idea that suffering is always a bad thing, that the experience of compassion automatically inclines us to want to help other beings, or that ethics can be devoid of principles. But these are not at issue or in need of being resolved here. The point of this discussion is rather to illustrate that empathy and compassion are strongly tied to the feeling of kinship with other sentient beings, and that such a sense of unity with them can provide ethical direction to our lives. Where would this direction lead? One obvious application of feeling kinship and hence empathy and compassion toward animals would be that we ought not to eat them, particularly if in doing so we cause them suffering, as we inevitably do. One might also say that such an ethical position would prohibit the instrumental treatment and exploitation of other creatures. As someone near and dear said to me,

"If you *care* for animals, why would you want to *eat* them?"[10] Oddly enough, this application was not obvious to Schopenhauer in spite of his strong animal advocacy. While he condemned the maltreatment of animals and recognized animal rights, he argued that meat-eating was justified on the most flimsy consequentialist grounds that the suffering of animals is outweighed by the gustatory pleasures of humans. It is remarkable how historically durable this blind spot and gross inconsistency has proved to be.

Kinship with and compassion toward animals express themselves, somewhat differently, in views that prominently feature concepts such as "reverence for life," "respect for life," and "respect for nature." The reverence-for-life theory of Albert Schweitzer is an unlikely amalgam of Christian ethics and Schopenhauer's atheistic metaphysics of the will. Within this worldview, all living things are regarded as being sacred because of their common creation, as embodying the same will to live, and hence as having equal footing with respect to their daily struggles to survive. All sentient beings thus are cosufferers with us in the world as it is constituted, and it is therefore appropriate and obligatory, in the spirit of universalizability on which morality is founded, to adopt an ethics of compassion in our dealings with them. As Schweitzer writes, "ethical is nothing but the reverence felt by my will-to-live for every other will-to-live."[11] Reverence signifies the impulse to care for, nurture, identify with, and develop an acute sensitivity toward other life-forms and their common or comparable needs and interests. Schweitzer's basic ethical principle is that "it is good to maintain and to promote life; it is bad to destroy life or to obstruct it."[12] The lifestyle prescribed by this principle is one to which, it would seem, only an obsessive-compulsive personality could consistently conform. For such an individual "tears no leaf from a tree, plucks no flower, and takes care to crush no insect. If in summer he is working by lamplight, he prefers to keep the window shut and breathe a stuffy atmosphere rather than see one insect after another fall with singed wings upon his table."[13]

But one should avoid too hasty a dismissal of Schweitzer's outlook. It is true that his life's project involved clearing jungle vegetation to establish medical treatment centers and eradicate disease organisms. He also carried a gun at all times to dispatch threatening predators. All of these actions are "tragically necessary," he reflects, and occasions for guilt. Schweitzer despairs that "reverence for life is an inexorable creditor!"[14] It might be inferred that this means we may continue to exploit animals as long as we feel guilty while doing so (or immediately afterward at the very least). Schweitzer has something else in mind, however. He acknowledges that human interests and the interests of nonhuman animals sometimes come into conflict. In addition he perceives an unavoidable clash between the principle of reverence for life and one's actions when one is getting on with the business of living. What all of this shows is not that his ethics amounts to an unrealizably stringent absolutism, but instead that the reverence-for-life principle states a prima facie obligation that can only be overridden in very special, carefully circumscribed situations. Therefore, we must always begin with the assumption that injuring or taking life is wrong, and then work our way to a justification of doing so that will succeed only under exceptional circumstances.[15] When contemplating action against an organism a reverential individual should not ask questions about how valuable or deserving of existence it is, whether it has instrumental value from a human perspective, or whether some minor disutility it causes oneself or our species should be tolerated. Rather, this individual should allow the organism to exist in its own unique way as much as possible, avoiding interference or damaging behavior if at all possible, even if doing so poses minor to moderate levels of inconvenience and hardship to him- or herself.

Whether all conflicts between human and other forms of life can be resolved ethically is far from clear. Schweitzer grappled with the problem and did not find a satisfactory solution, but at least he recognized that there is a problem to be addressed, and we should not lose sight of his unique contribution. His theory represents an attempt to transcend human arrogance and anthropocentrism and to respond effectively to an awareness of the interdependence of life-forms. If the ethics of reverence for life were to prove unviable, it would nevertheless still offer a central concept regarding an important moral emotion: reverence. Even though we cannot *always and consistently* act out of reverence for life, this does not mean that we *never* can. One of the easiest and most effective means by which we can do so is by deciding not to raise and/or kill animals for food ourselves, or ask others to raise and/or kill them for food on our behalf. Disappointingly, Schweitzer himself was not a vegetarian, although arguably he lived up to the potential of his own theory in other ways. Here again we have a perspective whose implications surpassed its author's capacity or willingness to realize them fully.

A more contemporary, purely secular life-centered moral theory is Paul Taylor's "ethics of respect for nature." Taylor holds that all living things—whether sentient or nonsentient—possess equal worth, and that each such being, having a characteristic well-being, welfare, or good of its kind that it strives to realize or maintain, is "deserving of moral concern and consideration."[16] It follows, he believes, that "all moral agents have a prima facie duty to promote or preserve the entity's good as an end in itself and for the sake of the entity whose good it is."[17] There are two ideas of outstanding interest for our purposes in Taylor's approach. The first is that he grounds his theory in a worldview that he calls "the biocentric outlook on nature." Taylor elaborates as follows: "from the perspective of the biocentric outlook, one sees one's membership in the earth's Community of Life as providing a common bond with all the different species of animals and plants that have evolved over the ages. . . . When one looks at this domain of life in its totality, one sees it to be a complex and unified web of inter-dependent parts."[18] Common membership in the biotic community is but another name for kinship, seen this time through the lenses of evolution and ecology. We come to appreciate the unity of life, Taylor suggests, by perceiving teleologically—by discerning the shared, built-in drive toward realization of a species-specific optimal state (see Chapter 5, Section 2). The second relevant idea in Taylor's theory is that of basic and non-basic interests.[19] A basic interest of an organism is one that guards its welfare or life. Having a supply of food and water, not being harmed or caused to suffer, and not being killed are interests of this kind; all the rest are nonbasic interests. Taylor holds (as do many other animal rights advocates) that basic interests cannot normally be outweighed (or "trumped") by nonbasic ones, regardless of which species are in conflict. We need not explore all the intricacies of this theory, however. It will suffice to conclude from the grounds Taylor has provided that causing animals to suffer and killing them to be able to eat meat (a nonbasic interest for most of us) cannot override the basic interests of the animals concerned. And this conclusion is reached by reflecting on and reasoning from our natural connections to nonhumans within the web of life.

Western philosophies of kinship and compassion have been influenced by Buddhism, as we have seen. Buddhism is indelibly marked by compassion for all living things that can suffer—so much so that Siddhartha Gautama, the Buddha (c. 563-c. 483 BCE), is often referred to simply as "the compassionate Buddha." To understand compassion properly, it is necessary to comprehend that, from the Buddhist perspective, all things are connected. Thich Nhat Hanh, a contemporary Vietnamese Buddhist monk and peace activist, writes that "wealth is made of non-wealth elements, and poverty is made by non-poverty elements. It is exactly the same as with the sheet of paper [that is made of non-paper elements]. So we must be careful not to imprison ourselves in concepts. The truth is that everything contains everything else. We cannot just be, we can only inter-be. We are responsible for everything that happens around us."[20] Hanh is saying that there is a subtle ecology linking all things that exist, a mutual dependency that often goes unnoticed and seldom receives conscious acknowledgment. Things and events are determined and configured by their opposites, which, as inseparable from them and yet distinct, both are and are not the same. Compassion comes alive when the illusion of complete separateness is broken. Hanh writes that "real efforts for reconciliation arise when we see with the eyes of compassion, and that ability comes when we see clearly the nature of interbeing and interpenetration of all beings."[21] As indicated, such occasions of insight and caring concern are rare and likely to be fleeting. But while we have them, they are powerful and instructive. Stephen Batchelor, who was extensively trained in both Tibetan and Zen Buddhist traditions, observes that "for as long as these fragile moments last, I inhabit a world where all living things are united by their yearning to survive and be unharmed. I recognize the anguish of others not as theirs but as ours. It is as though the whole of life has been revealed as a single organism."[22] To a large extent, Buddhism involves the process of transforming compassion, thus understood, from a transitory into a more durable expression of the psyche. One does this through meditation and practice of the Buddhist *dharma,* or time-honored teachings.

At the heart of Buddhist teachings are the "Four Noble Truths."[23] These specify, first, that suffering is an inescapable part of life for nonhumans as well as humans. (Suffering is not held to be continuous but rather unavoidable.) Second, suffering arises from desire or craving. Third, in the absence of desire or craving, there is no suffering. Fourth, an "Eightfold Path" toward personal betterment and reduction of desiring, and hence also of suffering, is prescribed. In addition Buddhists accept a very different picture of reality from that which is prevalent in Western religions. This can be summarized in its conception of the wisdom of life: "Wise people, realizing the impermanence of all things including themselves, should not become emotionally attached to things. Wise people are detached from both material goods and images of themselves."[24]

While Buddhism offers the possibility of supreme enlightenment and attainment of nirvana (especially for monks), it functions for most persons on a much more practical, everyday level. Here, it is to be noted that the first of the five fundamental moral precepts of Buddhism is to refrain from the killing of living beings. This translates into adherence to the principle of nonviolence (or *ahimsa*) that we shall investigate in the next section, but not necessarily into a vegetarian imperative. According to a recent scholarly account, "most Buddhist laity do eat meat and do kill insects and small animals as necessary to make life bearable, but there remains in Buddhism to this day the ideal of minimizing the harm one brings to other creatures, no matter how small."[25] Reporting on the Buddhist culture of Ladakh in northern India, Helena Norberg-Hodge comments that meat is usually eaten during the winter, when food is more scarce in the high altitudes of the Tibetan plateau: "Fish is never eaten, as it is thought that if you are going to take a life, it is better for it to be the life of a large animal that can supply food for many people; if you ate fish, you would have to take many more lives. The killing of animals is not taken lightly and is never done without asking for forgiveness and with much prayer."[26] However, important Buddhist sects have been and still are committed to vegetarianism, as are many of the Buddhist clergy. The reader may also recall Aśoka (Chapter 1, Section 2), the Buddhist emperor of India in the third century BCE who established a vegetarian regime.

3.   Universal Nonviolence (*Ahimsa*)

To live according to a strict code of nonviolence is an idea that may be foreign to most of us. Yet it remains true that for the vast majority of us, for the greater part of the time, nonviolence characterizes our personal conduct, at least in relation to other humans. But what about in relation to animals? Here, as I have indicated, the story is rather different, with most of us literally buying into the system of animal torment and killing from which we obtain our daily meat. Before we address this problem again, however, let us consider what it means to live nonviolently and where this idea originates.

The roots of the philosophy of nonviolence extend far down into the soil of both Eastern and Western thought. In the East sources of this approach to life can be found in Hinduism, Jainism, Taoism, and Buddhism. In the West there are strains of nonviolent thinking associated with Judaism, Christianity, and Islam.[27] I shall focus on Jain religious theory and practice, and the widely influential nonviolent way of life developed by Mohandas Karamchand Gandhi, a figure whose intellectual formation owes much to both East and West.

Jainism is unique among the world's religious and spiritual outlooks for its absolutely fundamental concern with nonviolence (or *ahimsa*) and its systematic commitment to practices intended to avoid the causing of harm to any lifeform. Originating in India, probably in the sixth century BCE (although argued by some to be much older), Jainism promulgates doctrines of *karma* (the lingering effects of one's actions), cycles of rebirth or reincarnation, and liberation of the soul by means of right conduct and ritual. Souls exist in various gradations throughout reality, and the lowest of these are situated in animals and plants. For this reason all actions must be monitored and regulated carefully so that one refrains from engaging in harmful conduct that leads to bad *karma* and hence the encumbrance of one's own soul in its journey toward purification.

Within a complex code of right conduct that prescribes principles for guiding individual Jains to liberation, nonviolence is the most important and is even considered to be part of the ground and meaning of other principles, such as that of truth-telling (intentional falsehoods, for example, are often injurious to others). To avoid causing any harm, one is to eat as little as is minimally necessary and forgo honey, root vegetables (which host abundant microorganisms), and any fruits that may likely contain insects. The images of Jains wearing face masks to avoid breathing in tiny life-forms and sweeping the area where they plan to walk are fairly well known. Jains are also forbidden by tradition from entering occupations that may cause animal suffering, even indirectly.

An important Jain text states that "a wise man should not act sinfully towards the earth, nor cause others to act so, nor allow others to act so."[28] Within the context of Jainism, this seems to entail, among other things, that one should not kill animals oneself for food, nor expect others to slaughter for them, and should do what one can (peacefully) to prevent such killing. Such practices are described as "motivated by altruistic concern for other beings,"[29] but a different understanding would portray them as self-centered or egoistic, since detachment from earthly things is pursued for its essential contribution to the process of liberating one's soul. This alternate, less generous interpretation is mistaken, however, for ultimate emancipation occupies a realm that lies altogether beyond the confines of the individual ego. Because of this, one cannot engage in liberatory practices for selfish gain but only in order to surpass personhood or any other kind of bondage to embodiment.

Gandhi's teachings on nonviolence sprang from his reflection on sources as diverse as Hinduism, Jainism, the Christian pacifism of the great Russian novelist Leo Tolstoy (1828–1910), and the writings of Henry David Thoreau (1817–1862) on civil disobedience as a defining duty of good citizenship. Always an activist as well as a thinker, Gandhi evolved his eclectic approach from various "experiments with truth,"[30] or the ongoing process of trial, error, and revision that characterized his many involvements with social and political issues of the day, most notably the liberation of India from British colonial rule.

Essential to an understanding of Gandhi's position are the concepts of *ahimsa* and *satyagraha* (soul-force or truth-force). "*Ahimsa,*" he tells us, "means not to hurt any living creature by thought, word or deed, even for the supposed benefit of that creature."[31] The basic meaning of nonviolence unfolds itself in knowledge of the truth plus the determination always to seek the truth and to live peacefully in light of it. Gandhi believed absolutely in the power of truth and in its invincibility in the face of wrongdoing. He took a very broad view of violence, as we shall see. Because of this, his vision of living peacefully includes not only avoiding obvious forms of violence (that is, the use of hurtful or coercive force) but also refraining from harming others by actions and words. Later, Gandhi applied *ahimsa* to political activities by focusing on *satyagraha,* the channeling of spiritual resolve into defiant but peaceful acts of resistance to injustice. But *satyagraha* also means not acting out of anger or a retaliatory frame of mind; it entails returning love for hate and has a resolute purpose: "it brings good both to the *satyagrahi* and his adversary."[32] This good, Gandhi states, is "truth, which is the very substance of the soul."[33] Ignorance, lying, deceit, and violence are therefore corruptions of the soul and of the human essence. Lying and violence are intimately connected in Gandhi's thinking (as in Jainism), and are harmful ways of treating others as well as oneself. Treachery, the use of physical force, and domination are ultimately self-defeating because they do not promote truth, fail to respect the moral personality of the opponent, do not generally resolve conflicts of interest, infect the end toward which one struggles, and have the unhealthy consequence of leading to further acts of the same kind. In addition violent behaviors cannot help us attain the end of life, which is to "realize God who dwells within our hearts."[34] Only by following the path of truth can we achieve this, and if others deviate from it we must help them find their way back. Gandhi firmly believed that "a truthful man cannot long remain violent. He will perceive in the course of his search that he has no need to be violent and he will further discover that so long as there is the slightest trace of violence in him, he will fail to find the truth he is searching."[35] *Satyagraha*, as a form of non-violent resistance to violence, aims "to open up the opponent's mind and heart so that rational discussion could take place in a climate of goodwill and critical self-reflection."[36] In this process the practitioner of Gandhi's method shows respect for the humanity of his or her opponent as well as faith in the possibility of meeting, eventually, in a dispassionate spirit of negotiation and on a level of equality.

The quest for truth, in Gandhi's view, does not culminate in political freedom, nor does it cease when this is secured. Indeed, it is a lifelong process. But truth, peacefulness, and nonviolence must also govern our relations with nature as a whole: "God-realization means seeing Him in all beings. Or, in other words, we should learn to become one with every creature. This can happen only when we voluntarily give up the use of physical force and when we develop the nonviolence which lies dormant in our hearts."[37] Needless to say, this implies that animals should be treated with kindness and that vegetarianism is obligatory. Gandhi even went so far as to affirm that "the greatness of a nation and its moral progress can be measured by the way in which its animals are treated."[38] Since animals are by long tradition the lowest-placed occupants of the moral ladder, or perhaps negligently not even placed on the first rung, their status can be used to gauge the ethical and spiritual health of a society as a whole.

Psychological strength and consistency of thought and action are required of those dedicated to nonviolence. First, nonviolence must be identified with active engagement and self-empowerment, not with weakness and passivity. While nonviolence is always morally preferable to violence and is almost always the right course of action, there may be exceptional circumstances (such as saving a victim of life-threatening violence) in which, as Schweitzer also believed, violence may be used, although it does not cease to be an evil. In such a situation, Gandhi asserted, "using physical force with courage is far superior to cowardice."[39] Second, since life itself is a process, not a result, nonviolence must always be the goal that we strive to realize, even though we will sometimes fall short of our ideal. Gandhi recognized clearly that moral perfection is beyond the reach of human beings. As he acknowledged, "to observe this principle [ahimsa] fully is impossible for men."[40] In practical terms, then, living nonviolently is equivalent to causing the least amount of harm possible, or as Gandhi put it, "the least possible destruction, such as is caused by [the] taking of vegetable life."[41]

4. Earthdwelling: Native Peoples' Spirituality

Most of the world's indigenous peoples have depended, to some extent at least, on meat-eating. Some (such as the Haida of the Pacific Northwest) have relied on hunting and fishing for a major part of their food supply. Others (such as the Australian Aborigines and the Iroquois of eastern North America) have obtained most of their food from foraging (including, of course, for insects).[42] Isn't it therefore paradoxical to look to them for sources of inspiration that may direct us toward vegetarianism? In one sense it is, but certainly no more so than to sift through the past history of Christianity or Judaism with the same purpose, as many have done (and as we shall do in the next section). Yet in another sense it is not contradictory, for these are cultural groups whose ways of life embody what Nollman calls "spiritual ecology," or a mix of belief and practice that exhibits a sense of complete interconnectedness with nature.[43] Sean Kane suggests that "early humanity negotiated a dialogue with nature that has gone on variously for the better part of 100,000 years. It is still going on today." He identifies the general feature of this "dialogue" as "earth-relatedness." Of Paleolithic and Mesolithic (that is, preagricultural) civilizations,

Kane asserts that "these were people who greeted all forms of life on earth as intelligent kin and, as far as we can tell, saw themselves as just another species sharing a habitat."[44] The Australian Aborigines' concept of the "dreaming" (or "dreamtime") illustrates what is at work here. Anthropologist Diane Bell describes this intricate system of thought that knits the mythical past to the present as "a living and accessible force in the lives of people today, just as it was in the past." The dreaming embraces an epistemology, sources of meaning, and a moral code that are expressed in "an all-encompassing Law which binds people, flora, fauna and natural phenomena into one enormous interfunctioning world."[45] Thus human life is intimately bound with the landscape and its other inhabitants, the history of creation, and nature in all its many moods.

There has been much discussion of the relationship between indigenous peoples and nature, and it has proved difficult for many scholars as well as laypersons to avoid romanticizing this issue, thus obscuring not only the harsh conditions of existence faced by some native peoples, but also the fact that they sometimes have transformed the land by such methods as systematically burning off cover and cultivating crops. In addition, their treatment of animals has not always been kind. Inuit sled dogs are often subject to rough handling, Australian Aborigines would use boomerangs to maim kangaroos prior to killing them, and the ritual slaughter of animals in tribal India and Indonesia has been a cruel and appalling business.[46] Nevertheless, to speak of the ecological way of life of indigenous peoples—part spiritual, part intuitive, part experiential—is not a misnomer but a vital reality that we in the West can only capture poorly with expressions like "living with respect for nature." These societies were not perfect; human societies never are. But if we can see beyond their defects, there is much to be learned. As Alice Walker writes, "That the Indians were often sexist, prone to war, humanly flawed, I do not dispute. It is their light step upon the Earth that I admire and would have us emulate."[47]

Characteristically, indigenous worldviews are transmitted via traditions of oral storytelling, and this process has the effect of energizing the stories, keeping them fresh ("within living memory," as we say), and creating an intimate bond between generations as well as between humans and their surroundings. (In North American Indian society it is not uncommon to encounter the notion that today's choices must be understood as having consequences for seven generations into the future.)

Kane observes that in ancient myths plants and animals are depicted as "the spirit-children of supernatural progenitors." He adds that "the first myths were about the powers and intelligences of animals. What the animals knew was considered sacred."[48] Well, what *did* the animals know? For one thing, they knew about ecological balance and the need to cherish and conserve resources. Their lives and wisdom were intertwined with and inseparable from the culture of the myth-tellers, governing both ritual and daily activities as well as rationalizing penalties for transgression against nature, meted out in the first instance by nature itself. Ecological myths of this type combine elements of spirituality, morality, social structure, group and personal self-identification, metaphysics, causal explanation, and practical knowledge, all of which act together to nourish a rich sense of oneness with and caring responsibility for the environment. Nature is the Great Provider, and the place of animals within indigenous worldviews must be understood within this context. Outlooks of this sort are therefore anthropocentric, but of a character that expresses stewardship and cooperation rather than domination.

We can gain insight into this special relationship through the folklore of indigenous peoples. *Tyendinaga Tales*,[49] a group of traditional oral stories from the Mohawks of eastern Ontario, Canada, offers a representative sample of such narratives. Many of these stories center on animals and are concerned with origins—of the earth and its features; of the natural order; of the solar system and the constellations; of animals' physical features, capacities, and behaviors. In them animals have personhood, language, emotions, reasoning, and humanlike motivations. They are figures of strength who possess special powers and sometimes act as agents of the Great Spirit or Creator. Their bodies or body parts transform into and hence explain other features of the landscape (such as trees and plants, or the color of autumn leaves). Humans and animals communicate and sometimes struggle with one another, sometimes experience mutual friendship. Humans are saved or otherwise helped by animals, and they work together as allies. The solution to a human problem may come by way of dream about an encounter with an animal. Although it is clear that Mohawk males prided themselves on their hunting skills and bravery, animals are depicted in one story as being thankful to a great hunter who showed them kindness and as bringing him back to life after he was killed in battle.

The question of how vegetarians can draw upon native sources such as this has been raised above, but it is perhaps just as puzzling to ask why indigenous peoples have seen nothing wrong with meat-eating. I think both questions must be answered together. The following reflection by an Onondaga Indian provides a key to our understanding: "Being born as human to this earth is a very sacred trust. We have a sacred responsibility because of the special gift we have, which is beyond the fine gifts of the plant life, the fish, the woodlands, the birds, and all the other living things on earth. We are able to take care of them."[50] According to this view, even though humans have been given the gifts of nature—both flora and fauna—for their use and nourishment, everything in nature is to be venerated as holy both in itself and in its connections with all else. Natural and spiritual harmony are interdependent and can be preserved only if humans respectfully look after the earth and the forms of life that dwell upon it. Taking animals for food with gratitude, being mindful of their numbers, their role in the ecosystem, and their own sacred endowments, does not transgress against creation.

The world desperately needs this sense of harmony in living. Yet it might be argued that, knowing what we now do about animal pain and suffering, and having multiplied as a species far beyond a level our indigenous ancestors could possibly have imagined, greater harmony (and hence a greater positive moral good) can be sought today by refraining from killing animals for food. There is much evidence (such as we have reviewed in Chapter 6) that points in this direction. If native spirituality normalizes and valorizes meat-eating, then the practice must be viewed from within the perspective of the original peoples for whom this spirituality is a vital force. Outsiders have no right to criticize this way of life. As products of modern, industrialized, consumption-driven Western culture, we can neither simply transport the life context of indigenous peoples into our own nor casually appropriate their sensibilities and modes of conduct. What we *can* build upon, however, is their commitment to respecting and valuing other animals, which, placed as we are, we can best carry out by promoting their welfare. This translates into taking a vegetarian stance. Meat is not essential to our well-being and we have no excuse for failing to seek harmony with nature by adopting a vegetarian diet.

5. Major Religions and Minority Voices

In addition to Buddhism and Jainism, other major religious traditions are sometimes associated with vegetarianism, including Hinduism, Judaism, Christianity, and Islam. Of these, Hinduism has the most profound connection with a vegetarian way of life and the strongest claim to fostering and supporting it. Judaism, Christianity, and Islam present pathways to vegetarianism that reach their full potential only in minority sects.

Hinduism, the most ancient of all the world religions, derives from many and diverse scriptural sources, a number of which have injunctions against meat-eating. Some texts oppose violence against other life-forms, which are held to be equally sacred; others link caring for animals with one's journey toward spiritual purity and self-betterment; another group admonishes that the karmic consequences of meat-eating are drastic (one will experience a miserable life when reincarnated or be eaten by the same kinds of animals one has killed in the present life). Steven Rosen observes that while Hindu scriptures, like the Jewish Old Testament, sanctioned the eating of sacrificial animals, these texts carefully circumscribed what was permissible and "never endorsed the wholesale slaughter of animals so prevalent today."[51]

The Vedas, considered to be of nonhuman (although not necessarily divine) origin, are the most venerable scriptures of Hinduism and yield its core of belief, hymns, incantations, and prescriptive way of life. Vasudha Narayanan comments that although there are many contrasting opinions within Hindu texts, "the theoretical, ritual, and epistemological significance of the *Vedas* has been unquestioned."[52] According to the Vedic tradition, all creatures manifest the same life force, and hence merit equal care and compassion. The soul that is present in animal form is of no lesser significance than that which is embodied in human form. Because benevolence toward animals is the root of benevolence toward fellow humans, it is to be cultivated with diligence. Other monumental Hindu epics, recognized as being of human authorship—the Ramayana and the Mahabharata (which includes the popular Bhagavad Gita)—also advocate a vegetarian diet on religious grounds. The Bhagavad Gita specifies that vegetarian foods (fruits, vegetables, grains, nuts, and dairy products) be presented as devotional offerings, and that those who consume such items, having first offered them to God, are especially blessed.

Hinduism, then, is demonstrably positive toward vegetarianism. Furthermore, it has contributed immeasurably to the evolution of ideas about compassion toward and equal treatment of animals, the connection between kindness toward animals and toward humans, and hence nonviolence as the ideal way of life, all of which we find resurfacing in other contexts and belief systems, some very far removed, geographically and temporally, from their Eastern birthplace (e.g., in the International Society for Krishna Consciousness, better known as the Hare Krishna movement). This having been said, however, it remains unclear whether India's vast majority Hindu population is primarily vegetarian. Rosen strongly asserts that it is, while Narayanan just as adamantly declares that it is not.[53]

Judaism and Christianity have a common scriptural source, which provides the same challenge to their vegetarian adherents. It is widely acknowledged that in the Old Testament the story of creation is told in two versions. The first contains a "dominionist" account of humans' relationship to nature wherein God tells our species: " 'Be fruitful, multiply, fill the earth and subdue it. Be masters of the fish of the sea, the birds of heaven and all the living creatures that move on earth'" (Gen. 1:28).[54] The second story, which also begins the Garden of Eden parable, is often described as "stewardly." It states that "from the soil, Yahweh God caused to grow every kind of tree, enticing to look at and good to eat, with the tree of life in the middle of the garden, and the tree of the knowledge of good and evil. A river flowed from Eden to water the garden, and from there it divided to make four streams" (Gen. 2:9–10). After describing the four subsidiary bodies of water the narrative continues, and we learn that God "took the man and settled him in the garden of Eden to cultivate and take care of it" (Gen. 2:15). God then cautioned: " 'You are free to eat of all the trees in the garden. But of the tree of the knowledge of good and evil you are not to eat'" (Gen. 2:16–17). In this idyllic setting humans appear to be vegetarians, and no mention is made of their mastery over animals. But even in the first, so-called dominionist creation story that precedes this tale of Paradise, it is not so clear that God has given humans license to exploit and dine on animals. The text is ambiguous, for immediately after the instruction to "conquer and subdue" comes the following: "God also said, 'Look, to you I give all the seed-bearing plants everywhere on the surface of the earth, and all the trees with seed-bearing fruit; this will be your food'" (Gen. 1:29). Whether "this will be your food" refers to plants and trees or animals as well remains problematic. Therefore it appears possible that even within the dominionist creation story, a vegetarian diet is prescribed.

However this may be, by the time of the great flood (Gen. 6–8) humans had certainly fallen away from vegetarianism, just as they had from obedience to the commands of God in general. After the flood, a promising new beginning for humankind occurs, which at the same time constitutes a grim outlook for animals, as God tells Noah and his sons: "'Breed, multiply and fill the earth. Be the terror and the dread of all the animals on land and all the birds of heaven, of everything that moves on land and all the fish of the sea; they are placed in your hands. Every living thing that moves will be yours to eat, no less than the foliage of the plants'" (Gen. 9:1–3). Rosen and other scholars regard this as "an expedient in a crisis. As all vegetation was destroyed, God indeed gave Noah a *concession*—not a commandment—to eat meat."[55] Unfortunately, this interpretation seems most implausible for a number of reasons. The most weighty of these is that the permission to eat meat is never revoked and is indeed reinforced many times over in both Old and New Testaments, although it is often accompanied by baffling, almost unintelligible dietary prescriptions. Furthermore, the communication to Noah and his sons cited above was made as a prelude to God's announcement of a new covenant between himself and humankind. However, because humans are firmly fixed as meat-eaters within the context of the Fall of Man, we are invited to see it as a condition from which we need redemption. This holds out the hope that with a return to grace, when harmony reigns among animals (Isa.

11:6–7, 65:25) and between humans and animals (Isa. 8–9; Hos. 2:18), not only will all animals be herbivorous, but humans will also return to their prelapsarian vegetarianism. Indeed one biblical scholar has this to say of the repeated references to the state of Paradise regained: "We may note above all that the ideas of indescribable fruitfulness, of unbroken peace among men and animals, and of eternal life have entered into the Old Testament expectation of salvation."[56]

This is not the place to detail the mental gymnastics through which both Jewish and Christian interpreters have attempted to extract a vegetarian message from the Bible. These efforts have been of three principal types: understanding dietary laws and various other divine pronouncements concerning food as symbolic and instructional rather than literal; retelling or "revisioning" biblical scenarios to give them new meaning; and focusing on the many examples in both the Old and New Testaments of kindness toward animals and merciful treatment of both humans and nonhumans. Of these three tactics, the last is perhaps the most common, although it is often found in conjunction with the other two. There is certainly no shortage of biblical stories upon which to dwell if one seeks paradigmatic compassionate acts done in the interest of animals' welfare, and many are the role models one could choose in order to ground benvolent conduct toward other creatures. Most intriguing of all, reflection on the commandment against killing (Deut. 5:17), especially when combined with a concept of stewardship of the earth, may lead to a life of nonviolence with respect not only to humans but also to nature as a whole.

Aside from these more or less direct appeals, there are many significant figures in the postbiblical history of both Judaism and Christianity who have instantiated more positive and caring attitudes and behaviors with regard to animals, some well known and some not (see Chapter 1). These are the minority voices who have tried to work out compassionate, sometimes vegetarian ways of life that are anchored in religious sources and who serve as inspirations and provide opportunities for others.

Like Judaism and Christianity, Islam is not a religion most would identify with vegetarianism, even though some scholars and adherents contend that its founding prophet, Muhammad (c. 570–632), conveyed a vegetarian message both by word and deed. Many of his sayings and actions are concerned with the need to show love, kindness, compassion, and mercy to animals.[57] The Qur'an (or Koran), the book of revelation of which Muhammed is the messenger, also contains suggestive hints of the following kind: "All the beasts that roam the earth and all the birds that soar on high are but communities like your own. We have left out nothing in the Book. Before the Lord they shall be gathered all" (Surah 6:38).[58] "He laid the earth for His creatures, with all its fruits and blossom-bearing palm, chaff-covered grain and scented herbs" (Surah 55: 9–11). In Islam our species is not granted absolute dominion over the earth, since the earth does not belong to us; humans are but nature's caretakers, the vice-regents of Allah, for whose glory all acts are performed.[59] This, taken together with the prescription always to act out of justice, kindness, and charity (Surah 16:90), seems to call for a caring, protective stance toward animals.

According to Rosen, there is evidence from independent accounts of his life that Muhammad himself preferred a vegetarian diet, but was unable to require it of his earliest followers because he was mindful that such strictures would likely alienate them. He thus favored the "techniques of gradualism,"[60] meaning that he aimed, via coaxing and personal example rather than prescription, to move people in the right direction. Rosen also notes that there is a robust and compassionate vegetarian standpoint emanating from the Sufi (or Islamic mystical) tradition, and that (as in Judaism) the strictest dietary laws are solely concerned with the slaughter of animals and forbidden and permissible forms of meat-eating.[61] There is, then, an opportunity for vegetarianism to take hold within Islam too.

6. Vegetarian Building Blocks

In this chapter we have surveyed a large range of worldviews and disparate belief systems, whose richness and complexity can only be hinted at here. Nevertheless, we can see that there are many more avenues to vegetarianism than most of us have ever imagined. Michelangelo (1475–1564) is said to have remarked that when he looked at a block of stone he saw a finished piece of art waiting to be liberated by the actions of his chisel. A vegetarian can apprehend a particular spiritual outlook or body of religious doctrine in a similar fashion—as a solid, seemingly impenetrable object that resists appropriation but can be made to work for one if sufficient skill and the right tools are brought to the task. Such activity can unlock the hidden potential of the human spirit, allowing it to take shape.

I hope that the reader will reflect on the material presented in this chapter not as an interesting and engaging kaleidoscope of images and thoughts, but instead as a stimulus and challenge to further inquiry and personal growth. Vegetarianism is an orientation to life, and should be integrated with the other elements that constitute the point of view from which one sees and acts in the world. And for most of us spiritual or religious dimensions help to define that personal viewpoint.

CHAPTER

Arguments Against Vegetarianism

1. The Consequences of Vegetarianism

Vegetarianism was born and has evolved in a swirl of controversy. It is no surprise, then, that many sorts of arguments are used *against* vegetarianism, and these must be addressed and dealt with. Possibly the most obvious objection to vegetarianism concerns its impact, especially if universally adopted.[1] While this approach, which is commonly called "consequentialism," might take numerous avenues I shall concentrate on its most developed expression.

In *Rights, Killing, and Suffering: Moral Vegetarianism and Applied Ethics,* R. G. Frey lists some fourteen severe effects that a shift to universal (worldwide) vegetarianism would allegedly entail.[2] These include the collapse of the animal food, leather, and pet food industries (and thus a significant part of the economy); social disruption; and the loss of *haute cuisine*. Frey is correct in judging that the impact of this change would be monumental and indeed revolutionary. Many livelihoods that depend on meat would be undermined, as would countless others in diverse occupational areas that depend substantially or completely on it, such as the advertising, shipping, packing, and publishing trades. Lifestyle alterations would be significant too, since as we have seen (Chapter 2), many forms of social interaction and ritual center upon the sharing of meat. However, several subsidiary claims he makes to support these conclusions seem just plain silly. For instance, Frey voices skepticism over the possibility that all the restaurants of the world could adapt to vegetarian meals and find enough menu variety to stay in business, and he laments the end of barbecue cooking and its associated social life. But it is evident that anyone who entertains these worries seriously has never considered with care what makes restaurants flourish rather than fail (the availability of meat being only one among many factors), or sampled outstanding vegetarian cuisine, or examined top-notch vegetarian recipe books, or visited parts of the world where vegetarian restaurants predominate, or explored the opportunities for vegetarian backyard cooking.

Even if some of his arguments may be defective in regard to details, however, the issue Frey forces us to confront is a real one: instituting a vegetarian economy would have widespread ramifications that should not be ignored by those who argue that it is more desirable than the present meat economy. In general, unless philosophical theories that have ethical content or implications are tested in some measure by reference to the consequences of their adoption, they remain free-floating abstractions. Frey and others like him are not concerned with consequences as such but with greater and lesser utilities. That is to say, they strive to evaluate which of a choice of scenarios produces the optimum proportion of benefit to harm for all concerned. Frey claims that leaving things alone (that is, preserving the meat economy) is preferable in this sense, because the number of good relative to bad consequences in the existing meat economy is greater than what would be the case in the alternative vegetarian economy. This is of course quite an assertion, and its force is difficult to assess, since it is based on hypothetical projections. For this reason Frey is careful to document his case by envisioning a plentiful number of likely or possible impacts. However, in evaluating questions of utility, particularly this one, another problem intrudes, namely, *which utilities are to be considered in the overall calculation*. Frey has considered only human utilities, having decided that animal utilities (pleasures, pains, sufferings, senses of well-being) count for little or nothing by comparison, and hence may conveniently be ignored in any final reckoning.

I challenge this assumption on two grounds. First, the moral status of animals is coming to be seen as more significant than Frey allows (see Chapter 4, Section 4). In fairness to him, much of the scientific and anecdotal evidence on which this new and evolving perspective is based has come to light since he published his book in 1983. Be that as it may, it is now becoming clearer that animals should be counted among those whose lives bear the brunt of decisions we humans make concerning our dietary choices. Second, even if animals' experiences are characterized by very low levels of utility compared to our own, the vast scale on which animal lives are sacrificed to human gustatory preferences, together with the incredible amounts of pain and suffering we inflict on them in the course of satisfying these preferences, may very well outweigh all other considerations. When billions upon billions of food animals are slaughtered annually worldwide, including billions in North America alone, and between several hundred and a few thousand during our individual lives for our own personal consumption, this speculation can scarcely be written off as exaggerated or inapplicable. Moral philosophers and laypersons alike commonly assume that only considerations of human utility (positive benefit and negative harm) are significant in these discussions, or at any rate that human pleasures in eating meat and preserving the present meat economy are the only things that matter. In short, the assumption is that humans benefit more than animals suffer. But utility as a whole (taking animals into account) tells a different story from this myopic and now arguably outmoded view, and is more likely to be maximized by the vegetarian alternative, which avoids the infliction of suffering and death on incalculable numbers of sentient beings.

Frey's consequentialist, antivegetarian argument also assumes a disaster scenario. That is, he depicts, as do many similar critics, a massive, overnight conversion to vegetarianism, for it is only on this imaginary hypothesis that the shift may be seen to generate cataclysmic results. But this is quite unrealistic. Macrochanges in society do not generally occur in this fashion, but instead take decades or even centuries to unfold. (There are naturally exceptions; we are now, for example, living through a period in which the so-called information technology revolution and right-wing economic and political agendas have created radical change and social disruption in just a few short years.) There is no reason to think that a change to universal vegetarianism, if it ever occurred, would take place abruptly, especially since it would not be driven by technology alone. Rather, it is much more likely to happen gradually and as much as a result of changes in consciousness as of environmental and resource crises. A slower rate of change is clearly less likely to rend either economic or social fabrics. Time to adjust to new ways of doing things has always been demanded by important changes such as the introduction of universal education, machinery, railroads, and automobiles. It would be foolish to deny that such developments have caused much conflict and upheaval and exacted a heavy toll on many sectors of society. But the point is that they *have* occurred, that society has absorbed them (for better or worse), and that life goes on, even if in strikingly different directions than before. Farmers and others whose livelihoods depend on the meat economy would find other ways to make a living, and government and industry would have the responsibility to retrain people to this end and to ease the transition in other ways (for example, by relocating workers). People would still have to eat, and the opportunities for food production, distribution, processing, packaging, shipping, and sales, as well as commodity trading and new secondary industries, would certainly not evaporate. These openings would be as many and varied as human ingenuity could make them. One can use as a comparison the many visions of a sustainable society that ecologically minded futurists have promulgated, committed as they are to moving beyond present forms of natural resource exploitation.[3]

Perhaps a better and more pertinent example of socioeconomic change is that of slavery. In one form or another slavery was once practiced in many parts of the world. Now it scarcely exists at all, at least in any publicly avowed and legal sense. There was a time not too long ago, however, when many people not only thought slavery was justifiable, even sanctioned by God, and were sure that they—and society—couldn't survive without it. What this meant was that their lifestyle, economic well-being, and position of power and privilege couldn't survive without it, which is quite a different matter. In the United States, in the period after the emancipation of black slaves, there was enormous social disruption, unrest, and repositioning, and the economy of the South had to be rebuilt. Historians observe that the effects are ongoing today. But no one argues that the overall social utility was greater during the times of slavery. This is not because it is "politically incorrect" to do so but because, when all relevant benefits and harms are taken into account, it is manifest that slavery was a vicious and irredeemably cruel institution. That black slaves were treated like animals is no secret to most, and the wrongness of such treatment is self-evident today. But only recently have some even dared to suggest that *animals* are routinely treated as slaves had been and that there is a comparable degree of wrongness involved in this. Marjorie Spiegel observes that "there are distinct social, political, and economic factors which create and support the subjugation of animals, as well as differences between the possible manners in which blacks and animals could respond to their respective enslavements. But, as divergent as the cruelties and the supporting systems of oppression may be, there are commonalities between them. They share the same basic essence, they are built around the same basic relationship—that between oppressor and oppressed."[4] And Gary Francione shows that under a legal regime (such as ours) that treats animals as property, "nonhumans are, for all intents and purposes, the *slaves* of humans," for "virtually every aspect of our lives is involved in some way or another with the institutionalized exploitation of some animal or another."[5] Spiegel reminds us that "any oppression helps to support other forms of domination,"[6] an idea we examined earlier (Chapter 6, Section 4). Along this pathway too, the negative utility of the meat economy can be charted.

The slavery analogy brings us to a further but deeper issue concerning the consequentialist approach: its exclusive focus on results. Many would contend that what's wrong with slavery first and foremost is that it represents an egregious violation of human rights. Even if (contrary to fact) slavery produced a system of positive social utility (such as the greatest happiness of the greatest number), it would still have been fundamentally evil and wrong, because slaves were persons deserving of respect, dignity, justice, and protection from harm. Are animals (or at any rate *some* animals) also deserving of the same? I believe that they are (see Chapter 4, Section 4), and that, this being the case, their systematic oppression in the course of providing flesh for human consumption is likewise fundamentally evil and wrong. So even if (again, I think, contrary to fact) the meat economy yielded a system of positive utility, it would be unsustainable from a moral standpoint. Therefore harsh though the consequences of introducing universal vegetarianism may be, if an institution that is deeply embedded in society is immoral through and through, then it must be rooted out, even if a high price has to be paid in the short term for doing so. To bring about justice is often costly, given that centuries, if not millennia, have passed during which the profits of injustice have been systematically reaped by some.

There may be an appearance of glibness to the above remarks. But this can be dispelled if we look at the larger consequences of a shift to vegetarianism. In other words, a purely consequentialist approach not only considers practical impacts alone but also too narrowly construes the relevant consequences. Large-scale consequences of radical social changes *are* quite important, but when we ponder these, we ought to cast as wide a net as possible. For example, we should weigh the benefits of a society whose food output does *not* rest on the massive, mechanized carnage of sentient creatures and environmental damage against the costs of one that *does* so depend. We could also include in our calculation the health costs to society of a meat diet as opposed to a vegetarian one, and many other factors. Once this were done, it would be clear that, even on consequentialist grounds, a vegetarian society would emerge as manifestly preferable to the flawed society in which we live at present.

Another aspect of the consequentialist viewpoint we must examine deals with the fate of the newly "liberated" animals themselves after the shift to a completely vegetarian economy. What would happen to the many millions of animals that had been waiting to be killed and eaten? Would they simply be allowed to roam the streets, pasturelands, parks, barrens, and wildernesses of the world? Would we be bound to treat them like so many sacred cows? How could we responsibly address the issue of their uncontrolled reproduction? *If* we were to face the disaster scenario painted by Frey, then clearly we would confront a daunting problem in the postmeat era, an ecological puzzle of impressive magnitude, to say the least. But as I have indicated, there is no reason to suppose that the worst case imaginable is the one we would actually face. Instead meat-eating would gradually decline as vegetarianism gained adherents, with the net effect that as demand for meat declined, so too would the supply. Fewer and fewer animals would then be reared for slaughter, and the problem of unwanted surplus animals would diminish correspondingly. A certain number of animals would presumably continue to be bred and maintained under more enlightened conditions than those prevailing on today's factory farms, and what they produced would continue to be utilized by humans. Thus, for example, sheep could still provide wool, cattle milk, and poultry eggs. There seems to be little moral objection in principle to animal husbandry of this sort.

Many practical problems would, of course, remain to be worked out. For instance, cattle must be impregnated periodically in order to maintain lactation. Since the veal, leather, and other industries have customarily absorbed excess male calves (i.e., those not needed for breeding), new, relatively noninvasive methods would have to be discovered for controlling reproduction and selecting the sex of offspring. In like manner the proportion of male chicks would have to be managed in the poultry industry. The dwindling numbers of other animals (pigs, for example) would have to be maintained until their natural death at taxpayer expense or else as pets. These solutions, awkward and interventionist as they may sound, are nevertheless preferable to the cruelty of releasing stock into the wild, where they would be at the mercy of predators and would inevitably spill over into the harsh world of humans, who surely would not tolerate their presence. Finally, new secondary industries would need to be developed to secure the replacements for leather, pet food, and other products now derived from animals.

2. Humans as Natural Carnivores

But isn't it *natural* for humans to eat animals? Don't we even have a *right* to do so? It would help, in answering questions such as these, if we knew what "natural"—always a troublesome word—is supposed to mean in this context. Some have argued that humans are hunters by instinct and evolution. We have already looked at the myth of "man as hunter" (Chapter 2,

Section 2), so this need not detain us further here. There is also the argument that humans are physically adapted to the role of carnivores. This is highly controversial, for there is much anatomical and behavioral evidence to the contrary.[7] But the more interesting assertion is that humans, as part of nature, are somehow *justified* in eating meat.

No less a personage than Benjamin Franklin (1706–1790) found this appeal persuasive. Franklin, who had been a vegetarian since age sixteen, discovered on a sea voyage that fish, when cut open, contained lesser fish, swallowed whole. He therefore concluded that since it was nature's way for one animal to eat another, so too it must be natural for humans to eat animals, and henceforth he abandoned his vegetarianism in naive self-satisfaction.[8] The argument seems to be this: Humans have a natural place in the food chain, and, being animals like all the rest, may eat other species just as they eat one another. Elizabeth Telfer points out that there is a crucial ambiguity here, however. Either an *entitlement* claim (i.e., that humans are justified in eating animals or have the right to do so) or a *desert* claim (i.e., animals deserve to be eaten by us because they eat each other) is being asserted. But in either case, she remarks, the claim fails the test of logic. With respect to the first, "we do not think that we are entitled to do to people everything that they do to others, so why should we be entitled to do it to animals?" In relation to the second, the argument at most "justifies us in eating carnivores," and since such animals are generally thought to be "incapable of morality," they "cannot either deserve or not deserve anything."[9]

The argument persists, however, in the form that animals have been placed on earth for the pleasure and use of humans—a view with a lengthy tradition and biblical sanction. Very little of what is said in this book will make any impression on one who believes this. But many scholars have argued that our species should assume a stewardship or caretaking role in relation to others, and have grounded this alternative position in biblical sources as well. We have examined some of these views earlier (Chapter 7, Section 5). Let us look, then, at the secular argument that humans are superior to animals and thus entitled to eat them. Aside from the fact that this alleged "natural superiority" is far less obvious to many people than it once was, we may note some major problems with this stand. First, even if humans are simply deemed superior to other animals (in, say, language, reasoning ability, tool use, and complexity of social relationships), this does not (following Telfer) justify our eating them anymore than it does our eating human infants or severely mentally defective members of our own species who are also "inferior" in the same respects. Second, if humans are considered to be superior in certain respects but inferior in others (e.g., evolutionary longevity, or ability to fly, see in the dark, or control aggression), but are claimed to be superior to other animals nonetheless, then we are merely witnessing the dogmatic assertion of a speciesist principle ("humans are always and forever superior just because they are members of the species *Homo sapiens*"). And both positions open up the unpalatable possibility that an extraterrestrial species, more highly advanced in intelligence and technology but of a different moral persuasion, might use these same arguments to turn the tables on us. Finally, humans have the capacity to think and feel ethically. From this perspective, we are not animals who cannot act otherwise than as nature dictates; we are beings who can deliberate and make choices. To appeal to our "natural" place in the food chain or to the "naturalness" of our eating animals, given that they routinely eat each other, is precisely to abdicate this responsibility to reason and take charge of our actions. It is to deny one of the capacities that is supposed to mark us as different from and superior to other animals. Since humans *do* have the choice as to what they may and will eat, and since this choice has an enormous range of consequences, then they ought to exercise it cautiously and thoughtfully.

As a postscript, it is worth remarking that the concept of "naturalness" is itself notoriously slippery. Many things are justified merely on the grounds of being "natural" (greed, war, heterosexuality), and many are condemned on the equally flimsy pretext of being "unnatural" (altruism, pacifism, homosexuality). Meat-eating is thus considered natural (or "normal") and vegetarianism unnatural (or "abnormal"). But does this mean anything more than that meat-eating is commonplace and vegetarianism comparatively rare? Meat-eating may be the (statistical) norm within our present society, but it in no way follows that it is any more "correct," "good" or "valuable" a practice than vegetarianism. In fact, *nothing at all follows* with respect to value judgments. No normative conclusions can legitimately be drawn from the statistical distribution of types of behavior or personal traits. Average musical, artistic, or scientific ability is far more common than talent or genius, yet we wouldn't say that the former is better or more worthy of cultivation. So the naturalness argument settles nothing; the debate (on whatever issue is at stake in a given case) must be settled elsewhere.

3.   Animals as Replaceable

"If you have seen one redwood, you have seen them all." This brazen remark, often attributed to Ronald Reagan, outraged both environmentalists and ordinary citizens in the 1960s. Whether Reagan really said this remains moot,[10] but the thought behind this type of rhetoric is not unfamiliar in debates about nature and natural kinds. Many people seem to think, for example, that "if you've seen one animal (of a particular species), you've seen them all." Stated this bluntly, we may find the claim absurd, even offensive to our sensibilities. But as judged by the the meat-eating majority's behavior and general lack of concern with issues that pertain to the raising and killing of animals for food, it must be supposed that they regard domesticated "farm" animals as fully replaceable. What does "replaceability" mean here? It doesn't mean that animals are in every respect indistinguishable from one another. Rather it represents the belief that, for all intents and purposes, they are the same, and more specifically, that the lives of animals of the same sort are fully interchangeable and lack what we may call "moral residue." In other words, it is assumed that the place of each animal killed for food will be filled, without loss, by another that is more or less identical. All we need to do, at most, is make sure they are treated humanely along the way.

We may begin to see how callous and narrow-minded this approach is if we consider that those who have companion animals (or pets) already know in their heart of hearts that the above view is false. People don't think that their special animal friends are fully replaceable without moral residue; in fact they don't believe they're replaceable at all. That is why they treat them specially, grow so attached to them, grieve over their loss, and often memorialize them after death. The suggestion that a favorite pet who has just died is fully replaceable would be treated by a great many as both flippant and hurtful. Of course we are speaking of dogs, cats, birds, rabbits, rodents, and a few other kinds of animals, and perhaps we cannot extend the point any further. But while it might be tempting to draw such a limit, let us reflect that small-scale farmers and their families get to know their livestock animals well, easily identify them, know their individual traits, give them names, and sometimes bond with them. In order to slaughter them or send them to slaughter elsewhere, they may have to practice the kind of distancing and compartmentalization described in Chapter 3. Such experiences with members of other species should not be dismissed lightly, for they reveal that people do frequently understand and appreciate intuitively that animals are individuals and thus, in a certain sense, irreplaceable. Those who have had the special gift of having lived in the midst of or in close association with chimpanzees, gorillas, elephants, wolves, dolphins, and other wild animals, whether in domesticated or natural settings, commonly report the same discovery.

Notwithstanding all of this, there are philosophers who have framed a replaceability argument such that it would be morally permissible or even right to rear and kill sentient animals for food, provided that the following conditions are met:

1. the nonhuman in question would not otherwise have existed;
2. the nonhuman has had a pleasurable life;
3. the death of the nonhuman causes it no pain, fear or other disutility;
4. those close to the nonhuman (e.g., mothers, mates) are not allowed to suffer as a result of its use and killing; and
5. the nonhuman is replaced at death by another nonhuman for whom conditions 1–4 hold.[11]

It is clear that this argument, which might work for those who adhere to a classical pleasure/pain version of utilitarianism, is little more than a bad joke within the context of modern factory farming, where the only condition that can plausibly be said to be met is the first. Perhaps, then, it might apply to animals reared in free-range environments and slaughtered in accordance with conditions 3 and 4. But even the staunchest defender of utilitarianism and founder of the animal liberation movement, Peter Singer, expresses doubts, admitting that "the proposition that the creation of one being should somehow compensate for the death of another does have an air of peculiarity."[12] The reason is that Singer recognizes that sentient animals, like humans, have preferences, including one to continue living. Furthermore, they have accumulated experiences, relationships to the world around them and to each other, anticipations, and possibly other dimensions of consciousness that cannot merely be swept aside or nullified by those of a different creature that succeeds them in time. Additionally troubling is the point, made by Evelyn Pluhar, that "the replaceability argument applies to any individual with a welfare, including human beings."[13] The idea is not that humans as such are replaceable, but rather that certain purpose-bred humans might be, provided they were reared and killed in conformity with the five conditions laid out above. And this is, to most people, a profoundly disturbing implication. Finally, there is the problem of trying to figure out what to make of the first condition. The difficulty here is not whether we can meaningfully deliberate about the possible quality of life of future beings who have not yet been conceived, as well as of ones that have already been conceived, for we do this all the time in planning ahead as a society and as individuals. The problem instead resides in bringing about lives that we knowingly intend to terminate, which may have some value independent of human interest, and which could be fuller, richer, and even more diverse (for all we are aware) if allowed to continue.

All of these conundrums could, of course, be eliminated by a rejection of the utilitarian approach, or at least by the acknowledgment that, as we have seen, it will not suffice as a theoretical approach to issues of animal use and treatment because it does not do justice to aspects of these issues we must not overlook. If, for example, animals have some basic rights, it will not do to manipulate their lives in the casual, purely instrumental way that the replaceability outlook seems to mandate. But further, if (as appears to be increasingly evident) animals' conscious life is far more complex than we have hitherto thought, its psychological, ethical, and aesthetic character surpasses the criteria of assessment on which the replaceability argument rests.

4. An Ecological Objection

J. Baird Callicott, whose views we have examined (Chapter 3, Section 4), contends that "a vegetarian human population is . . . *probably* ecologically catastrophic" and that "meat eating . . . may be more *ecologically* responsible than a wholly vegetable diet."[14] His reasoning is as follows. Vegetarian humans would require more plants than exist at present. But a greater supply of plant food would cause the human population to increase and place a corresponding drain on environmental resources of all sorts. In turn, nonhumans that depend on plant life would decline in numbers. All of these outcomes are unsustainable. In addition, according to Callicott, vegetarianism represents "a paradoxical moral gesture toward those animals whose very existence is dependent upon human carnivorousness."[15]

In Chapter 6 we took a careful look at the ecologically unsound practices upon which the worldwide meat economy is built. Considering this, there is no force to the argument that increased plant agriculture would exact a still greater toll, especially since this would, in many areas of North America at least, represent a move toward restoring some of the land to vegetative cover (prairie grasslands and forests, for example) that existed prior to white settlement. While this statement may be controversial, it is clear that growing crops for human food is a significantly more efficient and environmentally sound use of land than growing grain for livestock food. In addition, some rangelands now used for grazing could be converted to food production, and the remainder, plus acreage of marginal quality, could be returned to the wild. But we should also note that Callicott's argument focuses on secondary or indirect effects of enhanced plant production within a vegetarian economy, namely, those resulting from a projected increase in the human population. The possibility that humans might someday learn to limit their numbers is not considered by him, nor is any credit accorded to the prospect that agriculture in general might become more sustainable. A worst-case scenario is the conclusion reached, not unexpectedly, in this facile manner. Like some other antivegetarian arguments, this one is based entirely on speculation and a dim view of human nature, adaptability, imagination, and inventiveness.

Callicott implies that phasing out herds of domesticated food animals would be wrong, since their existence is a function of our meat-eating. This is suspiciously reminiscent of the replaceability argument considered above. Perhaps it is enough to add that those animals that we bring into existence for the primary purpose of serving as our food, would scarcely lavish moral praise and gratitude on us if they knew what fate awaited them and were able to articulate their preferences in the matter. We must agree that after having brought food animals into being and perpetuated their kinds through millennia of special breeding, we have an important moral obligation toward them. But to suggest that we better fulfill this by continuing to slaughter and eat them than by releasing them once and for all from exploitation, servitude, and inevitable abuse betrays an anthropocentrism that we can and should move beyond.

5.   The Necessity of Killing

"Humans have to kill in order to survive," some say. Just like many other organisms, we are killing machines by nature; life feeds off death. If causing death to living things should concern us, then, the argument goes, the difference between meat-eating and vegetarianism is no longer clear, for vegetarianism would require us to kill many more living things than we do at present. This reasoning is confused. First, there are vegetarians (fruitarians; see Chapter 4, Section 1) who do not kill things in order to nourish themselves. Second, it is overdramatized and inaccurate to assume that life must feed off death. Many forms of herbivorous harvesting, such as picking fruit and corn; collecting nuts, rice, and other grains; and gathering fruits and vegetables that grow on vines, do not necessarily involve killing plants. Other forms, such as potato digging, lettuce picking, and carrot pulling, do, of course. But in all cases, seeds or cuttings may be saved for regeneration of the plants, and plants that are not harvested generally spread their seeds, thereby reproducing themselves. (In principle, of course, these things might be said of animals too. We can take "cuttings" from live animals and create new ones through cloning; we can breed new animals as we kill older ones; and animals left to their own devices will self-replicate. But what we *cannot* say is that there are any animals we can eat without killing them.) Third, there is little substance to the claim that in a vegetarian economy many more living things would be killed than at present. Humans would eat more vegetative matter than they do now, to be sure. But so long as we remain at the "top" of the food chain, in effect we ingest (and are thus "responsible for") all the plants that the animals we eat have themselves eaten. Therefore it seems highly unlikely that in eating the amount of vegetative matter we need in order to survive, we will consume more of it than we do as meat-eaters. Fourth, animals suffer, and plants do not, so even if our choice were between killing things that suffer and killing things that do not, it is apparent that the latter is preferable.

6.   A Feminist Critique of Vegetarianism

While many feminists have not yet drawn a connection between the oppression of women and animals, many others have, and one's expectation is that feminists who do address the moral issues that surround the eating of meat will argue for vegetarianism (see the discussion of ecofeminism in Chapter 6, Section 4). In several controversial recent articles, however, Kathryn Paxton George has argued that a universalizable ethical commitment to vegetarianism cannot be grounded in traditional moral theories (in particular utilitarian and rights theories), because they assume the normalizing standpoint of a privileged, white, male subject.[16] In addition she adduces empirical support for the claim that the impact and risk factors of a strict vegetarian (or vegan) diet are much less likely to be borne by this class of individuals than by many women, infants, children, adolescents, the elderly, some nonwhites, and vast numbers of persons in developing countries. This large group—always nutritionally shortchanged in patriarchal societies—stands to lose even more by being deprived of meat, however scarce the supply at present. These differential effects are masked by treating the implied male subject of ethical discourse as a representative of all of humanity, and construing his health requirements as correspondingly universal. In brief, what George labels "the vegetarian ideal," or "ethical veganism," rests upon arguments that "presuppose a 'male physiological norm' that gives a privileged position to adult, middle-class males living in industrialized countries."[17]

George's position has spawned a heated exchange, and some challenges to both her interpretation of the nutritional literature and the soundness of that literature itself.[18] These issues are not likely to be settled by *philosophers* shouting at one another in print or in person. The fundamental question George raises—an important one—is whether anyone in today's fragmented world may arrogate to him- or herself the right to speak on behalf of everyone on matters such as this. Ethics, many would assert, must be capable of reflecting diverse standpoints as never before, or, in short, of being framed and applied contextually.

George poses a serious challenge to the view that people will improve their overall health and well-being by choosing a vegetarian diet. In general her view is that although we may grant that animals have rights, "we have no duty to make ourselves substantially worse off for the sake of other rights-holders" (i.e., sentient nonhuman animals).[19] Whether any given human being should be a vegetarian, therefore, "would depend solely on whether [his or her] own particular biological nature is suited to maintaining good health and vigour on a [strict] vegetarian diet."[20] What George tries to show is that it is actually a notably small minority of the global human population that morally ought to be strict vegetarians. We should not regard those who are entitled to eat meat as comprising a class of people who are merely exempt from an overriding duty to be vegetarian, for, she holds, there is no such general or universal obligation. Rather, humans may consume *some* meat and other animal products unless and until it is shown that, in their specific life circumstances, vegetarianism can plausibly be said to be obligatory for them as individuals.

Is vegetarianism then only "a provisional duty [that] depends upon biological and situational facts,"[21] as George contends? It may be that *veganism* is, and this would hinge on the outcome of unbiased nutritional studies. But even if we were to grant this point for the sake of argument, nothing at all would follow with respect to other forms of vegetarianism (see Chapter 4, Section 1). We have canvased a wide variety of arguments for vegetarianism and noted that they have a cumulative impact, which is up for consideration and evaluation in its totality. Perhaps it may be conceded that a complete ethical defense of vegetarianism, which is sensitive to the full range of issues raised by environmentalists, development experts, agricultural experts, feminist thinkers, and others, awaits refinement and the proverbial "finishing touches." Yet George herself "continue[s] to affirm that we have moral obligations to animals and that killing or harming any animal is an evil and is often wrong."[22] She also "assume[s] that any feminist ethic will in some way incorporate a recognizable version of the equal worth of differently situated individuals, whether human or animal."[23] It seems clear that these ethical commitments will have to play an integral role in any more comprehensive theory concerning the way humans ought and ought not to use and treat animals, and that their implications will therefore have to be worked out somehow within the dietary choices each of us makes, however different our standpoints and situations may be. And, as George would no doubt agree, we cannot simply pass on to animals the costs of whatever difficulties our singular life situations pose. This has been the path of least resistance and compromise that humans have followed for far too long by granting little or no moral status to nonhumans. Doubtless we must make sacrifices to implement the equal-worth-of-lives criterion cited earlier. Exactly which sacrifices are needed and how these will come into play remain to be determined from a particular standpoint and cannot be settled entirely by a detached, global theory of obligation.

Having said all this, however, it should not go unmentioned that George's own position, even if persuasive to a degree, does not range very far. She does not, for instance, take up the issue of meat diets and social injustice, which surely ought to be weighed against the injustices she contends vegetarianism would create for those likely to suffer from inadequate nutrition because of it. We must not overlook the fact that many people in developing nations, as well as in our own, are nutritionally deprived *precisely because of* capitalist control of meat production, world agriculture, and food distribution. Bearing this in mind, we may focus on real risks to life and health that stem from the tie between food shortage and the world meat economy, which a shift to increased vegetarianism might alleviate. Introducing vegetarianism, let alone veganism, on a world scale without changing anything else about the way things are done undoubtedly would be unwise and would aggravate some nutritional trends that already have a negative impact. But to concentrate on the imaginary bogey of universal veganism, taken out of context, seems to misdiagnose the problem.

7.   Indigenous Peoples, Cultural Imperialism, and Meat-Eating

Among the many objections to vegetarianism, the most difficult to address may be that concerning its relationship to indigenous peoples. Some might say that the answer is simple: There is no relationship because the first peoples of the world have, for the most part, always hunted and relied on meat as an essential, even crucial component of their diet. Hence we must not question their right to do so now and in the future, since any claim to the contrary engages in cultural imperialism and is unacceptable. I believe this response contains a good deal of the truth, but not all of it. We have seen (Chapter 2, Section 2) that the time-honored anthropological portrait of "man as hunter" is open to question. The self-sufficiency and flourishing of human groups have often depended mainly on herbivorous gathering as much as or more than on the irregular yields of the hunt. But there have been and are still peoples, frequently nomadic, who depend entirely on wild animal meat for sustenance, and on a ready supply of animal hides, bones, and other body parts for clothing and artifacts for daily use. The Inuit of Canada's far north provide one example, and Russia's Arctic nomads, the Nenets, another. The Nenets have followed reindeer migratory patterns for many centuries, traveling 900 kilometers (559 miles) twice a year. As one leader observes, "'for us in the tundra, the reindeer are life itself. There is nothing we can do without reindeer. It's our food, our clothing, our transportation and every other necessity. You can't survive without reindeer. A person without reindeer is a nobody.'"[24]

One cannot imagine a clearer statement of the total dependency of a people on animals. Cases such as this, where the very survival of a traditional culture is at stake, require that an exception be made. This may be justified by the principle that while humans may have no greater right to live than members of any other species, they also have no lesser right to live. And where the issue comes down to the stark choice between the need to kill animals and self-extinction, meat-eating may be sanctioned. However, the culture in question must be a genuinely traditional one, with a long history of dependency upon wild animal food. Typically such indigenous peoples kill within a context of reverential spirituality, endowing hunted animals with value and unique powers (see Chapter 7, Section 4). They thus affirm a relationship to the animals that is both personal and laden with significance within the scheme of creation—a dimension that is quite unknown to a Western outlook. They also kill only what is needed for their use and avoid wastage, thereby promoting sustainability of the resource.

With these qualifications in mind, we may conclude that the natural condition of indigenous peoples presents us not with a counterargument so much as a limitation on universal vegetarianism that takes account of very special and unavoidable circumstances. It should be added that if similar "very special and unavoidable circumstances" were to exist in the life of *any* individual or group, meat-eating might likewise be justified. As an example, consider someone who, for some medical reason, can only digest meat or can extract only from meat certain vital nutrients that others can derive perfectly well from a herbivorous diet. I think we would have to concede that such an individual has the right to eat meat, although again he or she would have to confront the choice between obtaining meat from factory farms or from free-range animals. Another example is provided by people cut off from the outside world by an act of nature or accident. Many would be prepared to argue that in such cases not only meat-eating but also cannibalism can be morally justified.

Having acknowledged the right of traditional peoples living off the land to eat meat, it must be noted that appearance is not always the same as reality in deciding what is truly a "traditional" or "subsistence" lifestyle. Consider the following examples: Caribou are now herded to slaughter with the aid of all-terrain vehicles, snowmobiles, and electronic navigation tools;[25] satellite tracking systems, sonar, and speedboats are employed in native whaling expeditions;[26] and whales hunted under a "subsistence" quota granted by the International Whaling Commission are butchered and fed to captive polar foxes, themselves soon to be slaughtered for the Russian fur trade.[27] We may question whether meat-eating is still justified in such indigenous societies in which the subsistence harvesting of animals has been replaced by commercial hunting and the purchase of factory-farmed meat at local supermarkets, and in which the use of native implements has been supplanted by technology and practices imported from the dominant white culture.

On a different note, Jane Meyerding has pointed out that people of color within the dominant North American culture frequently grow up within a meat-eating subculture that has its own strong traditions. Thus at events (such as feminist conferences) where most participants are white and a vegetarian menu prevails, these individuals are prohibited from connecting with their traditions, and hence experience vegetarianism as a reiteration of the institutional racism that victimizes them in everyday life.[28] Against this background, Meyerding asks whether it is morally acceptable to enter into a critical dialogue with cultural traditions in relation to meat-eating and concludes, with qualifications, that it is. The objective of such a dialogue is to encourage people of color to reconsider their commitment to meat-eating. But this process must avoid self-righteousness and encourage self-examination. It must take place within the framework of a commonly shared political analysis of society and a set of values that oppose oppression and exploitation—of humans and nonhumans. Cultural traditions can and do change, but ultimately they must be stimulated to do so from within.

I believe Meyerding's bold approach to this sensitive topic is on the mark. While we may abhor historical examples of, and present tendencies toward, cultural imperialism, we should not shrink away from cross-cultural criticism just because it is easier to hide behind the façade of an ethical relativism that tolerates everything. This is no less true in regard to issues like female circumcision and the persecution of religious minorities than it is to meat-eating. But there is bound to be a need for a delicate balance that allows the voice of legitimate moral protest to be heard without being drowned out by the perception of old-fashioned, condescending modes of domination.[29]

8.   Preventing Carnivorous Behavior in Nature

If humans have a moral obligation to prevent the suffering and death that meat-eating causes, should they also try to prevent nonhumans from eating one another? Probably only a philosopher would ask this question, but it deserves a hearing nonetheless, for it raises an important point, not unlike the one discussed in the preceding section: How far does our vegetarian obligation extend? Many of us experience an empathetic reaction when we see a vulnerable creature being attacked or about to be attacked by another, fiercer animal that covets it as a food source. We might even intervene and chase the predator away if we can do so without risking too much danger to ourselves or other humans. Does it follow that we should always do this? That we should crusade through nature seeking far and wide for such opportunities? I don't think so. For one thing, predatory animals (we assume) are not moral agents, and so they cannot be held accountable or blameworthy for their actions, however unpleasant to witness. While what they do might be or would be considered wrong if humans committed such acts, animal behavior has to be perceived from a different (nonmoral) viewpoint if it is carried out by beings that are not moral agents. Indeed, this is precisely the distinction philosophers often insist upon when contrasting behavior with action. *Behavior* is bodily movement that is instinctually driven, reflexive, conditioned, or accidental, while *action* is bodily movement or some other kind of doing that has an evaluative dimension. Accordingly, we are responsible for our actions but not for our mere behaviors. Now if animals never *act*, then they never can be responsible agents, and it is an error to suppose otherwise.

But it still remains true that animals do a great deal of damage to one another, and that some of this (how much is unclear) could be prevented by humans. Now some people choose to feed their companion animals a vegetarian diet and in this way reduce the total amount of carnivorous behavior in the world. But to attempt this kind of intervention universally would require a dedication to controlling other species on a scale so vast and expensive that it defies the imagination. Such a policy would also in all likelihood be ecologically disastrous and would require the same sorts of suppression of instinctual ways for which we condemn factory farming. It hardly seems correct to perpetuate and expand these negative consequences in order to prevent others from occurring. Furthermore, as John Benson points out, "the proper fulfilment that we desire for one creature sometimes involves the pain and death of another."[30] To play favorites among nondomesticated species is irrational enough; to extend the practice throughout nature would not only compound this irrationality but also eventually lead to conduct on our part that would defeat our own preferences. This would occur if certain species (e.g., jungle cats) were to become endangered by our act of removing their primary food sources from them. The alternative—placing all carnivores in zoos or carefully controlled wildlife refuges—is not only unmanageable but also manifestly undesirable. In sum, if humans were to police all the eating that goes on in nature, we would merely replicate and consolidate our arrogant role as "lords and masters" over all that lives.[31]

9. Eating Shmoos and Other Consenting or Indifferent Animals

Suppose certain animals positively *want* to be eaten and can even communicate this fact to us. Imagine some animals that don't care whether they are eaten because they lack consciousness, or that have limbs that shed themselves and regenerate. These fanciful scenarios are assembled as part of a comprehensive challenge to vegetarianism by Michael Martin.[32] The first example is provided by the *shmoo,* a fictitious being invented by American cartoonist Al Capp.[33] The shmoo delights in being eaten by humans, and indeed it desires nothing more. We might, Martin suggests, imagine real animals that, were they able to communicate with us, would express the same desire.[34] Genetic engineering may even create such animals in the future. His second example raises the possibility that genetic engineering might someday yield animals that can neither suffer nor be aware in general of what is happening to their bodies. Martin's third case also leans on genetic engineering as the source of animals that provide body parts for human consumption but do not have to be killed in the process. He contends that in each of these situations there is no moral objection to eating meat thus supplied.

All of these examples have, of course, been imagined for a specific purpose, but such thought experiments have an important place in testing philosophical viewpoints and theories. It is thus worth taking a moment to look at them seriously. We have inquired into the manipulation of nature, including non-human animals (Chapter 6, Section 2), and saw that all sorts of "monstrosities of utility" are being contemplated by those who possess the ingenuity to splice genes. In doing so, they also boast the capacity to perfect the ideal animal-machine—an organism that has absolutely no reason for existing, no quality of life, no physical or mental properties other than those selected by humans for their own beneficial exploitation and collective self-aggrandizement. This totally sedentary kind of animal, passive in the extreme, a mere blob of inert and insensate flesh awaiting consumption, is scarcely an animal at all. It might as well be a plant, since it exhibits so completely that "vegetative torpor" the French evolutionary philosopher Henri Bergson (1859–1941) believed to be characteristic of primitive life-forms.[35] It appears that one either finds this trend disturbing and highly objectionable, or does not. I believe it presents a great deal to concern thoughtful people. Making animals into sheer machines represents a throwback to the Cartesianism of the past, another technological triumph over nature, a denial and cancellation of animals' independent congenital characters, and a grave form of our own alienation from the biosphere. These tendencies will contribute (and arguably are now contributing) to our own species's self-destruction as well as to the devastation of the environment. And even if we somehow escape or postpone this fate, they may help usher in a "brave new world" so repugnant in its artificiality none of us would wish to inhabit it.

Martin's scenarios are additionally objectionable because of the exploitation they entail. He suggests that if a shmoo (or shmoo-like real animal) wants to be eaten, we may happily and with a free conscience oblige it. To see what is wrong here, compare the situation of a human slave who rejoices in being enslaved or an ordinary human who wishes to sell him- or herself into slavery. Should we object, and if so, why? This issue has a lengthy history, and it touches upon other matters, including the moral status of sadomasochistic relationships, suicide, abortion, and euthanasia, far removed from the subject of meat-eating. John Stuart Mill insisted that "over himself, over his own body and mind, the individual is sovereign."[36] If we accept this influential principle, we seem to be committed to the view that anything related to the disposition of one's own self is permissible. But obviously many do not accept so broad an interpretation of the position, as controversies over the above examples indicate. To etch this in greater relief, note that very few would agree that if a person wants to be murdered or to have him- or herself subjected to mind control, then it is acceptable to have this desire fulfilled by someone else. What makes the problem vexing is that most of us do believe that sovereignty over ourselves is supremely important— at least up to a point—and that in certain instances (e.g., abortion, euthanasia), if this right exists, one may need to depend on another person to insure that it is respected and implemented. This is not the place to attempt to resolve such complex issues. But when the sovereignty-over-self principle is invoked, we generally presuppose that a mature being, capable of responsible deliberation, is the subject of concern, not an animal that is deficient in this regard or a fleshly robot that has been constructed to give a preprogrammed response. We also often draw the line when others are called upon to guarantee an agent's exercise of sovereignty, since this requires that they perform actions that they would not willingly or ethically contemplate in normal circumstances. Just because someone wants to die or be tortured, for instance, it does not follow (without further consideration) that another person should be the agent of this wish. Similarly, it does not follow that if an animal wants to be eaten, we may eat it.

Martin maintains that even if it would be wrong to create animals that want to be eaten, it would be cruel *not* to eat them, once they have been created, if that is their strongest desire. This is so, he adds, even if we must cause them suffering in order to eat them. We are now in rather bizarre territory, to be sure, but while this reasoning may in some sense be true (just as it would be "cruel" not to kill, enslave, maim, or torture a human whose strongest desire this were), we are obligated *not* to do so all the same, unless there are overwhelmingly powerful arguments to persuade us differently. And certainly none are supplied by Martin.

Of the three cases invented by Martin, plainly that of the animal that sheds its limbs is the least questionable from an ethical standpoint, for this animal does not care what happens to its cast-off body parts. (Similarly, one of my students argued that we may eat "roadkills" and animals that have died of natural causes without moral concern.) But it still remains that this animal, like all the other "miracles" of genetic engineering, is an artifact of exploitation, built to satisfy a human want (the desire for meat) that masquerades as a *need* (sustenance).

10.   Why Not Eat Free-Range Animals?

I frequently hear the objection that arguing for vegetarianism is in reality only arguing against factory farming. That being the case, why should we not simply refrain from eating meat that comes from this source, perhaps even campaign for laws that will prohibit factory farming, but feel free to eat meat (like other animal products) obtained from free-range animals? The objection is held to be particularly weighty if it is made on behalf of those who do their own slaughtering.

This argument has some appeal for two main reasons. First, less grain—perhaps none at all—would be required by free-range ruminants. These animals can convert cellulose into protein and can graze on marginal lands as well as grasslands. Their subsistence need not be as taxing on natural resources as it is at present, and the scandalous calorie intake-to-output ratio of livestock could be reduced. This would clearly be a positive gain. Second, the wrongfulness that attaches to killing animals for food is arguably less in the free-range situation. Where meat-eating is not part of a mechanized system of carnage, and others are not asked to do the dirty work for us, it is a less culpable activity.

There are some problems with this viewpoint, however. First, whether the grasslands and marginal lands of the world are sufficient to maintain the many millions of cattle, sheep, goats, and other ruminants needed to supply meat to everyone who wants it is extremely doubtful. It is evident at least that sustainable agriculture is incompatible with anything like today's level of meat gluttony on the part of the affluent. Second, to reduce wrongfulness is not to eliminate it. "Free-range" does not always mean what we would like to believe. Many aspects of an animal's life may be controlled and manipulated outside of a factory farm, and to presume otherwise may be to be beguiled by childhood portrayals of the happy innocence of farm life. It should not be assumed that animals on traditional farms, whether pastured or raised in feedlots, are spared suffering. Branding, castration, dehorning, tail docking, separation of mothers from young, diseases, parasitic infestations, and predation are a few examples of the fate of farm animals in the past as well as the present. Then there is the final act of slaughtering, which for many kinds of animals entails extreme suffering and by definition also death. These evils can be abolished by a turn to vegetarianism. Rather than rationalize them as "necessary" or as "more humane" than those perpetrated by factory farming, then, our obligation is to try, both individually and collectively, to put an end to the conditions that produce such harms. Therefore we only mislead ourselves when we think that eating meat from free-range animals is morally acceptable.

11. The Requirement of Moral Sainthood

Vegetarians who use leather articles such as shoes or belts (even if acquired before they became vegetarians), commonly encounter hostile critics who hastily seize upon these items as evidence of their duplicity and hypocrisy. If you are a herbivore who speaks on behalf of your beliefs (perhaps only when pressed to do so), you are expected to be morally unblemished, for only the morally unblemished can serve as examples to others. If you aren't 100 percent morally consistent, it is assumed, your message can be (and deserves to be) aggressively discredited.

This complaint against the vegetarian is not only unjust but also displays an unrealistic view of the world. No one is morally perfect, nor should perfection be the standard by which we judge people's character and behavior. I suggest that the above criticism emanates from a guilty conscience and is the special currency of those who have a particular grievance against vegetarians. Jean-Paul Sartre (1905–1980) succinctly pointed out that we all have "dirty hands" in our moral and political lives.[37] Sartre's claim seems especially true today, when our consumer goods come from parts of the world where sweatshops and child labor are the rule; where there are few or no environmental regulations; where human and animal rights are flagrantly and systematically abused; where multinationals exploit and impoverish many; and where, in our own society, many serve our needs by working for low wages in dangerous and demeaning occupations. Perhaps it would be better if vegetarians, especially those who are committed to converting others, spoke, dressed, and acted in a way that gives a uniform and seamless message: "I don't engage in or support *any* activities that exploit or destroy animals." But then it would be a far better world if *everyone* could say this, and could in fact extend the statement to include the impact of their behavior and choices on other humans and the environment as a whole. This having been said, it must be admitted that vegetarians, like everyone else, can and sometimes do practice compartmentalization in their ethical life, and to this extent also manifest dissonant moral thinking (see Chapter 3, Sections 1–3).

Four additional points must be made, however. First, anyone who regards it as part of his or her moral responsibilities to help others (whether these "others" be humans or nonhumans) will devote a certain amount of time and energy to such projects. But, no matter how much time and energy are spent in attempting to improve the lot of others, still more singular dedication is possible. The logical outcome of this line of reasoning is, of course, that in order for a conscientious person to avoid doing less than he or she *might* conceivably do, unremittingly self-sacrificing service to others is required. Instead of enjoying recreation, family time, and other pursuits, or even accommodating natural functions such as eating and sleeping, full-time altruism and self-denial, even self-neglect, are thus the price of moral consistency. This obviously absurd outcome has been aptly labeled "caring burnout" by Rita Manning.[38] It is easy—especially if one is unsympathetic to vegetarianism for whatever reason—to overlook the effort required to maintain a caring attitude at all times. As one individual interviewed by Susan Sperling reflects:

> I try to be a vegan, which means not using any animal products at all. It's impossible. I've got a piano and it's got felt. This is rubber, and vulcanization includes some kind of animal products. A lovely desk that has some kind of polish uses oil from an animal. I use rennetless cottage cheese for my animals. Rennet is an enzyme from the stomach of a calf which is used to cure cheese. So this is rennetless, but it's from cow's milk. It's hard, and you argue with yourself. You could be a total vegan, but it takes up so much of your time, and you should be spending your time doing other things, right?[39]

The point is not that the vegetarian should be exonerated from all responsibility to do more in the cause of animals, but that each of us has to decide for him- or herself how far an obligation to help must be extended in terms of not only the opportunities that present themselves but also the time, energy, and resources available. While there is always room to argue with others and oneself over where the line is to be drawn, hypocrisy and inconsistency are not so readily apparent in a generally dedicated life as some allege. In any event, vegetarianism is a process that grows and evolves, an ongoing lifestyle choice that does not and need not follow a fixed pattern.

Second, as Carol J. Adams has indicated, "meat eating is the most oppressive and extensive institutionalized violence against animals."[40] If this is true—and certainly in quantitative terms the amount of death, pain, and suffering caused to animals in the food industry far outweighs that caused by any other animal industry—then vegetarians do more good by reducing harm to animals through their dietary choices than they could possibly do in any other single way. According to the U.S. Department of Agriculture, in 1994 Americans' per capita consumption was 114.8 pounds (52.8 kilograms) of red meats, 15.1 pounds (6.8 kilograms) of fish, and 63.7 pounds (28.9 kilograms of poultry, for a total of 193.6 pounds (87.8 kilograms).[41] While it is difficult to translate these statistics into numbers of animals killed, it is clear, especially in the case of poultry, that the per capita cause of animal death is significant. Vegetarians also lighten their impact on the planet in the several respects discussed in Chapters 5 and 6. And the stricter the form of vegetarianism, the greater the benefits.

Third, meat-eaters who criticize vegetarians for being inconsistent are themselves not willing to alleviate animal pain, suffering, and death in a manner that is both effective and demands no sacrifice of their own basic needs, given that a vegetarian, even vegan, diet is capable of providing complete nutrition. The sole forfeitures in switching to vegetarianism are those of dietary preferences and a certain amount of pleasure, which are nonbasic needs at best and mere wants at worst, and can arguably be fully satisfied in alternative ways once one makes the transition. So it seems that those who are doing little or nothing to help animals are, morally speaking, on very shaky ground when they criticize those who are already doing much for not doing more. And what kind of example does *this* set?

Fourth, as Telfer points out, "since most people fail to live up to their principles some of the time, it is not clear how an accusation of inconsistency counts against any doctrine in general, or vegetarianism in particular."[42] Arthur Schopenhauer wrote that "it is . . . just as little necessary for the saint to be a philosopher as for the philosopher to be a saint; just as it is not necessary for a perfectly beautiful person to be a great sculptor, or for a great sculptor to be himself a beautiful person. In general, it is a strange demand on a moralist that he should commend no other virtue than that which he himself possesses."[43] The critic of inconsistency need not concede this much, however. Conceiving of oneself as an activist moral reformer, or at any rate someone who has taken a moral stand that goes against the grain of prevailing social norms, surely requires that one attain credibility in the eyes of others, or at least of oneself. And this involves a determined attempt at creating harmony between one's words and deeds—an attempt that will probably fall somewhat short of its objective. While Schopenhauer may have overstated the case, perhaps for unconscious reasons of his own, it is difficult to gainsay Telfer's position. If we take a circumspect attitude toward belief systems, we ought to state that many Christians, Jews, Hindus, and Muslims (for example) do not practice their faiths consistently; but even if this were true of the majority, it should not be taken as discrediting what these religions have to teach. Similarly, the basic message of vegetarianism, if compelling, is not undermined by incomplete adherence of the sort we have been investigating.

12.   Some Observations

There are doubtless many more arguments against vegetarianism that could occupy our attention (others have, in fact, been addressed throughout this book), but those discussed here are the most significant ones currently encountered. I have tried to show that none presents an insurmountable obstacle to the change in diet and lifestyle I am endorsing. Certain critical perspectives we have reviewed possess relevance with respect to one or another argument *for* vegetarianism, but we must remember that the vegetarian position is not one-dimensional. What counts, when all is said and done, is the combined force of all the arguments for vegetarianism. But then can't the same be said of the arguments *against* vegetarianism? Don't they have a cumulative weight and effect too? Clearly they would, if they were to go unanswered, and we would either have a stalemate or witness the collapse of the vegetarian viewpoint. However the counterarguments have been confronted and defused, and while we may appreciate and to a degree sympathize with some of the worries that give rise to them, they need not detain us any longer.

Part of what gives life to these counterarguments is fear of the unknown. The future is always in this domain, notwithstanding how often one hears (and uses) hackneyed phrases like "the fore-seeable future." One cannot deny that vegetarianism posits a very different kind of future for the world than the one toward which it is headed at present. In the minds of most meat-eaters and many others besides, this is an unsettling thought, and thus a natural response is either to ridicule or endeavor to undermine such a perceived threat. Thinking about future possibilities isn't our strongest suit as a species. We do not necessarily embrace creative new directions for the future with open minds. As Elise Boulding has written, "if one tries to work toward the future from the present, the known realities cling like tendrils to every new idea, smothering it with awareness of what won't work because of the way things are."[44] To verify this observation, you need only compare the number of people who will eagerly show you how something *can't* be done with those who will help you find a way to do it. So we may look upon the effort to state the case for vegetarianism in the face of many, often strong objections as part of a process of removing barriers to envisioning alternatives that may help heal ourselves, our planet, and our relationship to it. We will explore this suggestion further in the final chapter.

CHAPTER

Conscience and Change

1. The Vegetarian Conscience

In the preceding chapters I have tried to demonstrate ways in which vegetarianism arises from the ability and willingness to see connections between what we believe and do, and how vegetarianism enhances our perception of these crucial relationships. Vegetarian thinking draws on numerous resources as it consolidates its position, and we have reviewed and revisited many of these as our discussion unfolded. Converging lines of argument and visions of the world bring us to vegetarian conclusions and a commitment to changing our dietary habits not only for reasons of health but also for the sake of animals, fellow humans, and the planet. We may say, therefore, that there is such a thing as a *vegetarian conscience,* and that this expression designates an ethical perspective from which decisions governing one's place in the community of nature may be made.[1]

The vegetarian conscience takes humans to be *a part of* nature, not *apart from* nature. It therefore predicates human activity on an understanding of interconnections between the human and nonhuman spheres. It is egalitarian with respect to other humans, regardless of their differences, and acknowledges the intrinsic value of diverse nonhuman life-forms and forms of consciousness. It recognizes the importance of ecologically sustainable human activity and affirms the requirement that we seek to minimize our impact on the planet and the amount of harm we do in the course of looking after our own essential needs. Clear thinking and mindfulness of both the short- and long-term consequences of individual choice and collective human behavior are hallmarks of the vegetarian conscience. The vegetarian's goal is not moral perfection but rather compassionate cohabitation with other species and respect for the earth, to the greatest extent that these precepts can be followed daily, both in one's own personal activities and in social policies and planning.

Lester R. Brown of the Worldwatch Institute has remarked that "an era of food scarcity is looming" for the human population of the earth, adding that "there will eventually come a point in each country, with each grain, when farmers will not be able to sustain the rise in yields."[2] Crop yields can be increased by only two methods—"either by expanding cultivated area or by raising land productivity"[3]—and both clearly have their limitations. This is a matter for all citizens of the world, particularly those in affluent countries, to consider with the utmost seriousness. When we know that most of our grain goes to feeding livestock, that water and arable land are in short supply, and that meat production is not only harmful to animals but also wasteful of resources and damaging to the environment, we ought to do what we can to address the looming food scarcity problem in a constructive way that takes account of these factors and their contribution to creating the mess in which we find ourselves. But in doing so, we must be aware that what it is appropriate for us, in the affluent part of the world, to do may not be universalizable. Kathryn Paxton George confronts us with this realization when she writes that "in some places in the world, there is not a broad selection of food, and people must eat what is available at the time regardless of their economic class. The health and lives of these people are threatened by protein, vitamin, and mineral deficiencies all of their lives. A moral rule of vegetarianism cannot apply to these people."[4] This point has already been conceded in the discussion of living off the land (Chapter 7, Section 4 and Chapter 8, Section 7). Given these exceptions, those of us who can do more to address the world food crisis, which our nations and industries have done much to create, surely ought to do so.

Vegetarianism may not be the only means of bringing about such change, but might it be the most effective? There are many indications that it is, if we view all the problems posed by meat-eating holistically, that is, as aspects of a general set of attitudes toward and interactions with the natural world. Global threats never have simple and immediate remedies because they are complex, have taken a long time to develop, and are perpetuated by institutional inertia, selfishness, and political divisiveness. The most we can say is that inasmuch as nearly everyone is part of the problem, nearly everyone has a part to play in devising a solution. Organic farming, vegetarianism, and other allied movements are processes that hold out the promise of being able to exercise an increasingly powerful, positive impact as more people subscribe to them. In order to make the transition to sustainable societies and sensible lifestyles, we need not embrace extreme altruism and self-denial, just good sense and a sense of proportion. If we can assure our health and quality of life and look after the environment at least as well by practices that do not depend on the suffering and death of great numbers of sentient beings, then should we not prefer this alternative to the status quo?[5] There can be but one answer to this question, whether or not one identifies with the vegetarian conscience.

2.   Vegetarianism or Veganism?

Numerous forms of practice fit under the heading of vegetarianism, as Chapter 4 revealed. Throughout this book, I have purposely refrained from prescribing any particular kind of vegetarian commitment, because I regarded my main task as that of convincing readers to accept the vegetarian viewpoint in general. The time has arrived, however, to consider whether veganism, sometimes called "strict" or "pure" vegetarianism, is the path we ought to follow.

For the vegan, no animal products are allowed either in the diet or for other personal uses. Now the issue that always lurks in the background in discussions of vegetarianism is this: How far should vegetarianism extend? Is veganism the only morally acceptable outcome of the reflections that led to one's initial vegetarian commitment? Are we in an all-or-nothing predicament? It is not easy to give a short and definitive answer. If it were true, as George contends, that "*most* people would be at substantial risk of being made worse off in a strict vegetarian world,"[6] then clearly there would be serious cause for concern about promoting veganism. If diets were changed globally without altering the social, economic, and political causes of inequity, George would probably be right. But if we envisioned a more general transformation, so that everyone had access to the necessities of life, there seems to be no reason to suppose that a healthy, vigorous human species that is vegan could not emerge worldwide.

Nevertheless, at the present time veganism is a challenge many well-meaning vegetarians are not ready to meet. And the difficulty of maintaining a vegan commitment should not be underestimated, particularly if one does not have the time to shop and cook properly, or travels and eats out a great deal. In

many places, it is hard enough to find adequate and varied supplies for a vegetarian diet, let alone restaurants offering suitable
choices. Such problems are harder still for vegans. These are
not the only issues confronting would-be vegans. Recall the
remarks of the individual who pointed out that animal by-
products are used in the processing of a limitless array of commercial goods, many of which one can scarcely avoid using
(Chapter 8, Section 11). They are nearly invisible supports of
our quality of life, as things stand. Faced with these dilemmas,
there seem to be two choices: one can either be a vegan when
circumstances permit (for example, when one is at home); or
be a nonvegan vegetarian who tries to cause the least amount
of harm possible (buying organic and free-range foods, striving to avoid products that contain animal-derived ingredients,
etc.). In a practical sense, this may be as far as most of us are
able or willing to go if we wish to avoid the "caring burnout"
described in Chapter 8, Section 11.

Veganism nevertheless remains an ideal toward which we
should aim. Without too great a level of sacrifice, people can
ease their diets off dependency upon animal foods, if they deem
this vital. Others may decide that taking eggs from free-range
hens and milk from cows that are kept on traditional farms, not
in any way tied into the meat or leather industries, and allowed
to live out their normal life spans, is acceptable. Honey is fairly
easy to do without. On the other hand, leather is *not* so easy to
do without, at least for shoes, given the available alternatives—
canvas or rubber shoes and shoes made of uncomfortable, un-
breathing synthetics that may themselves be manufactured using environmentally unsound processes—which are not
suitable for all persons or for all occasions. But as with food,
new demand will no doubt stimulate entrepreneurial inventiveness. Furthermore, one can consult such helpful guides as *Personal Care for People Who Care,* published in the United States
by the National Anti-Vivisection Society,[7] which lists a wide
range of cruelty-free personal and household products, and

provides information on which companies do animal testing, which charities fund animal research, and related topics. By reference to such aids, one can fashion and implement a compassionate consumer profile of one's own.

3. New Directions and Creative Thinking

The establishment of an alternative vegetarian economy and society will require foresight, imagination, and ingenuity on a broad front of human activities. We shall need to think and dream differently to get through a difficult transitional period to a world of cruelty-free food choices. One area ripe for development is nut cultivation. British vegan author Kath Clements cites a United Kingdom Ministry of Agriculture leaflet to the effect that "the yield per acre of well-managed hazel trees may reach at least two tons." She then makes a remarkable observation that incorporates the research of nutritionist and health reformer John Harvey Kellogg (1852– 1943): "In fact, a larger amount of food per acre can be produced by tree-growing than by any other means. Walnuts, for instance, have an astonishingly high food value and supply many essential nutrients. 'An acre of walnuts will supply more than 1,000 lbs [453.6 kg] of shelled nuts. . . . This is 20 times the amount that the same acre would yield in beef. The protein quality of the nuts would be as great as in beef and of superior quality.' "[8]

Equally instructive is the case of the lowly peanut (actually a legume or seed), which is easy to cultivate and plentiful in the southern United States. George Washington Carver (1864–1943), the great African American scientist and inventor, did extensive, lifelong research on the practically limitless number of products that can be derived from this crop. Peanuts yield high-quality protein, are relatively low in saturated fat, and contain a good amount of omega-6 (linoleic) fatty acids, which are essential human nutrients.[9] Some might despair at the thought of sitting around all day munching on nuts. But this is not at all what might be in store for future generations. Consider the following: In 1916 Carver compiled and published 105 recipes for dishes made from peanuts, and his students at Tuskegee Institute in Alabama once treated ten guests to a five-course luncheon—"soup, mock chicken, creamed as a vegetable, salad, bread, candy, cookies, ice cream, coffee—all from peanuts; and as varied and tasty as one could ask."[10] Carver produced and displayed at agricultural fairs many more of his incredible but edible peanut inventions over the years: "a dozen beverages, mixed pickles, sauces (Worcestershire and chili), meal," not to mention "mock oysters, curds which could hardly be distinguished from meat," and most impressive of all, a cream that could be used to produce "an inexpensive, palatable, and long-lasting cheese . . . ; where a hundred pounds of cows' milk made ten pounds of cheese, the same amount of peanut milk made thirty-five pounds."[11]

These facts should incline us toward a view of the post-meat era as one of refreshing and vital new opportunities in eating, just as our awareness of Asian, East Indian, and other vegetarian cuisines does now.

4.   A Way of Life

Enough has been said, perhaps, to persuade most readers, whether they are pro- or antivegetarian, that vegetarianism is a way of life. That is, it involves a view of the world, a moral vision, and an integrated set of beliefs and practices. For those who take the vegetarian option seriously and adopt it as their own, it may well connect with their spiritual or religious orientation, even their sense of meaning and purpose in life. Some might see these as grandiose claims, but the point is that vegetarianism sheds light upon, and is in turn reflected by, our philosophical outlook on ourselves, our world, and our place in it.

Richard Manning has recently argued that vegetarianism is a "city-bred" phenomenon, "a product of distance" or of lack

of contact with animals and the land.[12] He concedes that vegetarians "assert—correctly and importantly—a vital message of
postindustrial design: that it is necessary that our energy needs
be met by current solar radiation. . . . Eating grain and vegetables in general is simply a way of conserving existing solar
energy."[13] But in spite of this, Manning goes on to propose a
nostalgic alternative scenario for our time of the solitary hunter
killing his or her own animals and living off grassland yields.
This, he asserts, is a more energy-efficient way of life than (generally) supermarket-dependent vegetarianism.[14]

Let us consider these comments for a moment. That vegetarianism is an urban-generated movement should come as no
surprise. An increasing proportion of the world's population is
located in cities, and it would be natural to expect ever-greater
moral direction to emerge from this context. In addition, past
moral and social reform movements have sprung most often
from urban settings, where improved education and greater
awareness of issues are present. That city-dwellers are less in contact with animals and the land is no doubt true, for the most part,
but this kind of proximity seems less important as a factor in
moral progress than a desire to be well informed, an inclination
to be reflective about the consequences of individual and collective human behavior, and a strong sense of responsibility. Ur-
banites are no less likely to be *caring* toward animals and ecologically sensitized than rural-dwellers are to be *uncaring* toward
animals and alienated from nature. Finally, ethical issues other
than mere energy efficiency are involved in the assessment of
hunting; nor is it at all plausible that an entire population of millions could sustain itself by returning to a lonely and outmoded
hunter-gatherer form of existence. In addition, many vegetarians
are now enjoying the options of shifting their business from supermarkets to farmers' markets, cooperative farms, and market
gardens, or else cultivating their own small plots of land.

We see here that the vegetarian way of life actually offers
many the chance to reestablish contact with the land and with

nature, the loss of which Manning and many others rightly lament. We may hope that this process will continue and broaden in the future, as more and more people come to realize that vegetarianism, rather than being confining, is liberating as it frees us *from* the exploitation of animals, the domination of nature, and the oppression of one another, and frees us *to* discover ourselves in more positive, life-affirming ways.

Finally, a word on what it means to be an agent of change. It is easy to feel that one's personal efforts are insignificant—a mere drop in the bucket—in the face of large-scale injustices or social ills that cry out for a remedy. But to begin, if any practice—such as meat-eating—is wrong, then it is right for each of us not to engage in it, even if this does not by itself change the world. We are better in ourselves for making this decision. We must also remember that every revolutionary social movement begins with a dedicated few who push it forward and act as the surrogate conscience of others, helping them gain a greater awareness and acquire the courage of new convictions.

The global human population is growing by 250,000 daily, which presents us with a set of problems that urgently need to be addressed. Even a vegetarian approach to feeding everyone will place additional stress on planetary resources, biodiversity, and ecosystem carrying capacities, and there is no easy solution in sight. Nevertheless, one estimate suggests that there are already some 4 billion vegetarians in the world today—about 2.3 billion in China and India alone.[15] Taking all factors into consideration, it appears evident that if there is to be a hope of feeding everyone in the future, an even greater shift toward herbivorous diets will be essential.

Such thoughts as these I hope will guide the reader when coming to her or his own conclusions about the issues raised in this book.

Notes

Chapter 1: A Historical-Philosophical Overview

1.   William James, "Pragmatism's Conception of Truth," in *Essays in Pragmatism,* ed. Alburey Castell (New York: Hafner Publishing, 1968), p. 159. This lecture was first published in 1907. My thanks to Andrew Sneddon for locating the source of this quotation.

2.   Daniel A. Dombrowski, *The Philosophy of Vegetarianism* (Amherst: University of Massachusetts Press, 1984), p. 1.

3.   Ibid., p. 2.

4.   Søren Kierkegaard, *Concluding Unscientific Postscript to "Philosophical Fragments,"* trans. Howard V. Hong and Edna H. Hong (Princeton, Princeton University Press, 1992), pp. 120, 121.

5.   George Santayana, *The Life of Reason, or the Phases of Human Progress,* vol. 1, *Reason in Common Sense* (New York: Scribner's, 1905–6), p. 284.

6.   G.W.F. Hegel, *Reason in History,* trans. R. Hartman (Indianapolis: Bobbs-Merrill, 1959), p. 50.

7.   Henry Ford, interview, *Chicago Tribune,* 25 May 1916.

8.   E. Lyttelton, "Vegetarianism," in *Encyclopedia of Religion and Ethics,* ed. James Hastings (Edinburgh: T. & T. Clark, 1934), vol. 12, p. 618.

9.   See the works by Carol J. Adams *(Sexual Politics of Meat),* Janet Barkas, Ryan Berry, Jon Gregerson, and Colin Spencer.

10.   See, for example, Neal D. Barnard, *The Power of Your Plate: A Plan for Better Living* (Summertown, TN: Book Publishing, 1990), chap. 8; Carol J. Adams, *The Sexual Politics of Meat: A Feminist-Vegetarian Critical Theory* (New York: Continuum, 1991), pp. 147–48; and Peter Cox, *The New Why You Don't Need Meat* (London: Bloomsbury Publishing, 1992), chap. 1. The argument that humans are naturally—physiologically and anatomically—suited to be vegetarians rather than meat-eaters goes back at least as far as the thinking of Jean-Jacques Rousseau (see Adams, *The Sexual Politics of Meat,* pp. 116–17).

11.   Paul R. Amato and Sonia A. Partridge, *The New Vegetarians: Promoting Health and Protecting Life* (New York and London: Plenum Press, 1989), p. 2.

12.   As Richard D. Ryder remarks, "Hinduism and Buddhism quite early in their development abandoned animal sacrifice, and the feeling against

185

unnecessary destruction of life led to widespread vegetarianism in both Hindu and Buddhist societies from the third century BC onwards" (*Animal Revolution: Changing Attitudes Toward Speciesism* [Oxford: Blackwell, 1989], p. 25).

13.   Jon Gregerson, *Vegetarianism: A History* (Fremont, CA: Jain Publishing, 1994), pp. 19–20; Colin Spencer, *The Heretic's Feast: A History of Vegetarianism* (Hanover, NH: University Press of New England, 1995), pp. 85–86. I am grateful to Hugh Campbell for introducing me to Spencer's work.

14.   Cited by Spencer, *Heretic's Feast*, p. 47n.

15.   Plutarch, "Whether Land or Sea Animals Are Cleverer," in *Moralia*, trans. Harold Cherniss and William C. Helmbold (Cambridge: Harvard University Press; London: Heinemann, 1957), vol. 12, pp. 323–24 (959D–60A).

16.   Aristotle, *Nichomachean Ethics*, bk. 2, chap. 1.

17.   Amato and Partridge, *The New Vegetarians*, p. 2; Daniel A. Dombrowski, "Was Plato a Vegetarian?" *Apeiron*, 18 (1984): 1–9. See also Plato, *Republic* 373.

18.   Gregerson, *Vegetarianism*, chap. 6.

19.   Vegetarians in the West are always out of step with their times. As I shall argue, they are also ahead of their times. High-profile vegetarians are especially so, and many have been sharp social critics and activists. This has frequently brought them into conflict with established authority and settled public opinion, and they have paid the price. Today vegetarians still are subject to social ostracism and ridicule, and they are regularly challenged to justify their dietary choice, while meat-eaters are seldom called upon to defend theirs. (See, for example, the story of k. d. lang in Chapter 2, Section 2.)

20.   Porphyry, *On Abstinence from Animal Food*, trans. Thomas Taylor and ed. Esme Wynne-Tyson (London: Centaur; New York: Barnes & Noble, 1965; reprint, Watchung, NJ: Albert Saifer, 1989). As Wynne-Tyson records (p. 5), Porphyry was born in Phoenicia, and his original name was "Malchus, the root of which in Semitic languages signifies 'a King.' Later, he preferred to be known by the Greek equivalent, Basileus, and finally was persuaded by Longinus, his tutor at Athens, to change it to Porphyrius, meaning the purple used for royal garments."

21.   Ibid., pp. 54–55, 60.

22.   Ibid., pp. 60–61.

23.   Ibid., pp. 63, 105.

24.   Ibid., pp. 64, 78.

25.   Porphyry's view is that "to the Gods, indeed, the most excellent offering is a pure intellect and an impassive soul, and also a moderate oblation of our own property and of other things, and this not negligently, but with the greatest alacrity" (ibid., p. 107).

26. This argument has recently been revived and christened as "new" by Jordan Curnutt in "A New Argument for Vegetarianism," *Journal of Social Philosophy*, 28:3 (Winter 1997): 153–72.

27. Porphyry, *Abstinence*, pp. 70–71.

28. Ibid., p. 109.

29. Ibid., pp. 131–34, 138.

30. Ibid., p. 111.

31. Ibid., p. 114.

32. Ibid., p. 124. The argument that animals should not be regarded as inferior or "failed" humans has been rediscovered by John Rodman in "The Liberation of Nature?" *Inquiry*, 20 (1977): 93–94. At least two present-day philosophers have learned that the sort of point made by Porphyry is a sword that cuts two ways. In *Beyond Prejudice: The Moral Significance of Human and Nonhuman Animals* (Durham and London: Duke University Press, 1995), Evelyn Pluhar observes that such an argument invites us to contemplate "a very ominous disjunction: 'Either *both* marginal humans and any nonhumans who are similar to them in all important morally relevant respects are maximally morally significant, or *neither* are'" (p. 66 [emphasis in original]). Pluhar's book contains a very extensive treatment of all aspects of "the argument from marginal cases." Peter Singer goes even further in *Animal Liberation* (new rev. ed. [New York: Avon, 1990]), venturing to suggest that "normally . . . if we have to choose between the life of a human being and the life of another animal we should choose to save the life of the human; but there may be special cases in which the reverse holds true, because the human being in question does not have the capacities of a normal human being" (p. 21).

33. Porphyry, *Abstinence*, pp. 112, 115.

34. Ibid., p. 113.

35. Ibid., pp. 115, 123–24.

36. Ibid., pp. 116–17, 119.

37. Ibid., p. 119. The same point is made by Plutarch, "Whether Land or Sea Animals Are Cleverer," pp. 339–43 (962D–63A); and by Cicero *De Natura Deorum*, 2.13.34.

38. Porphyry, *Abstinence*, p. 122.

39. Ibid.

40. Ibid.

41. Ibid., p. 123.

42. See, for example, John Rawls, *A Theory of Justice* (Cambridge: Harvard University Press, 1971); Carl Cohen, "The Case for the Use of Animals in Biomedical Research," *New England Journal of Medicine*, 315:14 (2 October 1986): 865–70; Jan Narveson, "On a Case for Animal Rights," *The Monist*, 70 (1987): 31–49; and Peter Carruthers, *The Animals Issue: Moral*

Theory in Practice (Cambridge: Cambridge University Press, 1992). I once argued this way myself; see Michael Allen Fox, *The Case for Animal Experimentation: An Evolutionary and Ethical Perspective* (Berkeley and Los Angeles: University of California Press, 1986), chap. 3.

43.   This observation, at least, needs to be modified in animals' favor. See Frans de Waal's important study *Chimpanzee Politics: Power and Sex Among Apes* (London: Counterpoint, 1982).

44.   Porphyry, *Abstinence,* pp. 124–25.

45.   Ibid., p. 123. This principle was "discovered" recently by Paul W. Taylor. For a discussion of "the rule of fidelity," see his *Respect for Nature: A Theory of Environmental Ethics* (Princeton: Princeton University Press, 1986), pp. 179–86, and 193–98.

46.   Porphyry, *Abstinence,* p. 127.

47.   Ibid., pp. 127–28.

48.   Ibid., p. 130.

49.   Ibid., p. 140.

50.   E. O. Wilson, *Biophilia* (Cambridge: Harvard University Press, 1984).

51.   The underlying assumption, obviously shared by Porphyry and in fact quite commonly assumed in these discussions throughout the ages, is that inhumane behavior, practiced by us or by someone who serves as a model for us, threatens to radiate through the human character and to undermine our disposition to carry out our direct duties to fellow humans. See Immanuel Kant, "Of Duties to Animals and Spirits," in *Lectures on Ethics,* ed. Peter Heath and J. B. Schneewind, and trans. Peter Heath (Cambridge: Cambridge University Press, 1997), pp. 212–13. This piece was compiled from his students' notes taken in 1762–94 and published posthumously.

52.   Dombrowski, *The Philosphy of Vegetarianism,* p. 2.

53.   Saint Thomas Aquinas, *Summa Contra Gentiles,* 3.113.

54.   Ryder, *Animal Revolution,* p. 35.

55.   Spencer, *Heretic's Feast,* p. 163.

56.   Ibid., pp. 128, 161, 166, 185–86,

57.   Ryder, *Animal Revolution,* pp. 34, 36, 37.

58.   Ibid., p. 39.

59.   On this point see Bernard Rollin, *Animal Rights and Human Morality,* rev. ed. (Buffalo: Prometheus, 1992), pp. 30–32.

60.   Ryder, *Animal Revolution,* p. 43.

61.   For a detailed discussion of Descartes's views, see Daisie Radner and Michael Radner, *Animal Consciousness* (Buffalo: Prometheus, 1989), pt. 1; for an opinion that dissents from the common interpretation of Descartes,

see John Cottingham, "'A Brute to the Brutes?': Descartes' Treatment of Animals," *Philosophy*, 53 (1978): 551–59.

62. Michel Eyquem de Montaigne, "Apology of Raymond Sebond," cited in Ryder, *Animal Revolution*, pp. 50–51. This work is part of the body of essays Montaigne published in several revised and expanded editions after 1580, to which he added further marginalia in his own copies. References to the capacities of animals are scattered throughout Montaigne's essays.

63. Spencer, *Heretic's Feast*, p. 198.

64. Ryder, *Animal Revolution*, pp. 46, 47, 53.

65. Ibid., p. 52. It seems likely that Ryder is referring to one of the following works by Tryon: *Health's Grand Preservative, or the Women's Best Doctor* (London, 1682); or *The Country-Man's Companion* (London, 1694).

66. Ryder, *Animal Revolution*, p. 53.

67. Spencer, *Heretic's Feast*, p. 230. For the books by Paine see *Common Sense* (Baltimore: Phoenix Publishing, 1776); and *The Rights of Man*, 4th American ed. (Boston: I. Thomas, 1791).

68. James Turner, *Reckoning with the Beast: Animals, Pain, and Humanity in the Victorian Mind* (Baltimore: Johns Hopkins University Press, 1980), p. 18. Oswald's work is *The Cry of Nature; or, An Appeal to Mercy and to Justice, on Behalf of the Persecuted Animals* (London: J. Johnson, 1791).

69. George Nicholson, *On the Conduct of Man to Inferior Animals* (Manchester, 1797).

70. Joseph Ritson is the author of *An Essay on Abstinence from Animal Food as a Moral Duty* (London: Phillips, 1802).

71. Ryder, *Animal Revolution*, p. 62. Paley thus rediscovered Plato's argument.

72. Ibid. Ryder observes here that "by the end of the eighteenth century the inconsistency in eating animals while advocating their rights began to worry some humanitarians."

73. Jeremy Bentham, *An Introduction to the Principles of Morals and Legislation* (London: T. Payne, 1789), chap. 19, sec. 1.

74. Arthur Schopenhauer, *On the Basis of Morality*, trans. E.F.J. Payne, Library of Liberal Arts ed. (New York: Bobbs-Merrill, 1965), sec. 19, point 7. First published in 1841.

75. Ryder, *Animal Revolution*, p. 96.

76. Amato and Partridge, *The New Vegetarians*, p. 4.

77. Spencer, *Heretic's Feast*, pp. 259–61.

78. Jon Wynne-Tyson, *Food for a Future: The Complete Case for Vegetarianism* (London: Centaur Press; New York: Universe Books, 1979), Appendix.

79. Spencer, *Heretic's Feast*, p. 285.

80.   Ryder, *Animal Revolution,* pp. 95–96.

81.   Percy Bysshe Shelley wrote two essays on vegetarian themes: *A Vindication of Natural Diet* (London: J. Callow, 1813; new ed., London: F. Pitman, and Manchester: J. Heywood and the Vegetarian Society, 1884); and *On the Vegetable System of Diet* (Bungay, Suffolk: Richard Clay and Sons, 1929), which was only published posthumously. His long poem *Queen Mab; A Philosophical Poem* (London: P. B. Shelley, 1813) sketches out Shelley's vision of a vegetarian utopia.

82.   Mary Wollstonecraft Godwin Shelley, *Frankenstein; or, The Modern Prometheus* (London: Lackington, Hughes, Hardy, Mavor, & Jones, 1818; rev. ed., London: Coulburn and Bentley, 1831). First published anonymously.

83.   For a recent and illuminating discussion see Adams, *The Sexual Politics of Meat,* chap. 6.

84.   Ryder, *Animal Revolution,* p. 92.

85.   Charles R. Magel, *Keyguide to Information Sources in Animal Rights* (London: Mansell; Jefferson, NC: McFarland, 1989), p. 9. Salt's piece is: "The Rights of Animals," *Ethics,* 10 (1899): 206–22.

86.   Magel, *Keyguide,* p. 9. Salt's book is entitled *Animals' Rights Considered in Relation to Social Progress* (London and New York: G. Bell, 1892; rev. ed., London: G. Bell, 1922; reprint, Clarks Summit, PA: Society for Animal Rights, 1980).

87.   Mohandas Karamchand Gandhi, *An Autobiography: The Story of My Experiments with Truth,* trans. Mahadev Desai (Boston: Beacon Press, 1957), p. 48. First published, in two volumes, in 1927 and 1929.

88.   Leonard Nelson, *System of Ethics,* trans. Norbert Guterman (New Haven: Yale University Press, 1956), pp. 136–44. This work is a translation of Part 1 of Nelson's *System der philosophischen Ethic und Paedagogik* (Goettingen: Verlag "Öffentliches Leben," 1932).

89.   Magel, *Keyguide,* p. 10.

90.   Nelson, "Duties to Animals," in *System of Ethics,* p. 142.

91.   Ibid.

92.   Ibid., p. 144.

93.   See n. 32 above. First published as *Animal Liberation: A New Ethics for Our Treatment of Animals* (New York: New York Review/Random House, 1975).

94.   Singer, *Animal Liberation,* pp. xiv–xv.

95.   Stanley Godlovitch, Roslind Godlovitch, and John Harris, eds., *Animals, Men and Morals: An Enquiry into the Maltreatment of Non-Humans* (London: Gollancz; New York: Taplinger, 1971).

96.   Peter Singer, "Animal Liberation," *New York Review of Books,* 20/5 (5 April 1973), pp. 17–21.

97.   Tom Regan, *The Case for Animal Rights* (Berkeley and Los Angeles: University of California Press, 1983).

98.   See n. 10 above.

Chapter 2: You Are What You Eat (Almost)

1.   *"Der Mensch ist, was er isst"*; in Jacob Moleschott, *Lehre der Nahrungsmittel: Für das Volk*, *"Advertisement"* (Erlangen: Enke, 1850). Earlier, French jurist and gourmet Jean Anthèlme Brillat-Savarin wrote, "Tell me what you eat and I will tell you what you are" (*"dis-moi ce que tu manges, je te dirai ce que tu es"*). This is the fourth of the *aphorismes pour servir de prolégomènes* in his *Physiologie du Goût* (Paris: A. Sautelet, 1826). A much earlier version of this insight can be found in Sir Thomas Browne, *Religio medici* (London: Andrew Crooke, 1642), pt. 1, sec. 37: "*All flesh is grasse*, is not only metaphorically, but literally true. . . . Nay further, we are what we all abhorre, *Anthropophagi* and Cannibals, devourers not only of men, but of our selves; and that not in an allegory, but a positive truth" (in *Selected Writings*, ed. Sir Geoffrey Keynes [Chicago: University of Chicago Press; London: Faber and Faber, 1968], p. 44 [emphasis in original]).

2.   Karl Marx, "Alienated Labor," *Economic and Philosophical Manuscripts* (1844), trans. Loyd D. Easton and Kurt H. Guddat, in *Writings of the Young Marx on Philosophy and Society*, ed. Loyd D. Easton and Kurt H. Guddat (Garden City, NY: Anchor, 1967), p. 293 (emphasis in original).

3.   I would like to thank my colleague Henry Laycock for clarification on this point.

4.   Ed McGaa (Eagle Man), *Mother Earth Spirituality* (San Francisco: Harper Collins: 1990), p. 203.

5.   For a classic statement of this view, see José Ortega y Gasset, *Meditations on Hunting*, trans. Howard B. Wescott (New York; Scribner's, 1972). See also Patrick F. Scanlon, "Humans as Hunting Animals, in *Ethics and Animals*, ed. Harlan B. Miller and William H. Williams (Clifton, NJ: Humana Press, 1983), pp. 199–205; and Ann S. Causey, "On the Morality of Hunting," *Environmental Ethics*, 11 (1989): 324–43.

6.   See, for example, Fred R. Myers, *Pintupi Country, Pintupi Self: Sentiment, Place, and Politics Among Western Desert Aborigines* (Washington, DC: Smithsonian Institution Press; Canberra: Australian Institute of Aboriginal Studies, 1986), pp. 74–76; Diane Bell, *Daughters of the Dreaming*, 2nd ed. (Minneapolis: University of Minnesota Press, 1993), pp. 54–55.

7.   Some works of interest by this "new school" are Nancy Makepeace Tanner, *On Becoming Human* (Cambridge: Cambridge University Press, 1981); Marija Gimbutas, *Goddesses and Gods of Old Europe, 7000–3500*

B.C. (Berkeley and Los Angeles: University of California Press, 1982); and Riane Eisler, *The Chalice and the Blade: Our History, Our Future* (San Francisco: HarperCollins, 1988).

8. Nick Fiddes, *Meat: A Natural Symbol* (London and New York: Routledge, 1991), p. 173.

9. Ibid., p. 65.

10. J. Twigg, "Vegetarianism and the Meanings of Meat," in *The Sociology of Food and Eating: Essays on the Sociological Significance of Food,* ed. A. Murcott (Aldershot, Hampshire: Gower, 1983), p. 21.

11. Noëlie Vialles, *Animal to Edible,* trans. J. A. Underwood (Cambridge: Cambridge University Press; Paris: Editions de la maison des sciences de l'homme, 1994), p. 4. My thanks to Linda Whiteside for bringing this book to my attention.

12. Mary Midgley, *Animals and Why They Matter: A Journey Around the Species Barrier* (Harmondsworth, Middlesex: Penguin, 1983), p. 27. Cf. Colin Spencer, *The Heretic's Feast: A History of Vegetarianism* (London: Fourth Estate, 1993; Hanover, NH, and London: University Press of New England, 1995), pp. 29ff.; and Dudley Giehl, *Vegetarianism: A Way of Life* (New York: Harper & Row: 1979), chap 12.

13. Spencer, *Heretic's Feast,* p. 180.

14. James Davidson, *Courtesans and Fishcakes: The Consuming Passions of Classical Athens* (London: Fontana Press, 1998), p. 291. I am grateful to Steve Leighton for making me aware of this work.

15. Frans de Waal, *Good Natured: The Origins of Right and Wrong in Humans and Other Animals* (Cambridge, MA, and London: Harvard University Press, 1996), pp. 138–39.

16. Ibid., p. 146.

17. Ibid.

18. Fiddes, *Meat: A Natural Symbol,* p. 5.

19. Ibid., p. 229.

20. Mary Douglas, "Deciphering a Meal," in *Implicit Meanings: Essays in Anthropology* (London and Boston: Routledge & Kegan Paul, 1975), p. 273.

21. This account draws upon the following sources: "Boycott Against lang," *Toronto Globe and Mail,* 5 July 1990, p. C6; "Beef Stew Boils Over," *Toronto Globe and Mail,* 7 July 1990, p. D1; "Anti-lang Feelings Harden," *Calgary Herald,* 10 July 1990, p. B3; "Cattlemen Running Scared, Group Says," *Vancouver Sun,* 17 July 1990, p. D8; "Farmers' Beef Cans k.d.'s Concert," *Toronto Star,* 14 June 1992, A18.

22. Sharon Bloyd-Peshkin, "Mumbling About Meat," *Vegetarian Times,* 170 (October 1991): 70.

23. Midgley, *Animals and Why They Matter*, p. 27. Cf. Donna Maurer, "Meat as a Social Problem: Rhetorical Strategies in the Contemporary Vegetarian Literature," in *Eating Agendas: Food and Nutrition as Social Problems,* ed. Donna Maurer and Jeffrey Sobal (New York: Aldine de Gruyter, 1995), pp. 155–56.

24. Carol J. Adams, *The Sexual Politics of Meat: A Feminist-Vegetarian Critical Theory* (New York: Continuum, 1991), p. 67.

25. Ibid., p. 149.

26. See Maurer, "Meat as a Social Problem," p. 156.

27. Adams, *The Sexual Politics of Meat*, p. 14.

28. Adams borrows the concept from French philosopher Jacques Derrida. See, for example, his *Limited Inc.*, trans. Samuel Weber and Jeffrey Mehlman (Evanston: Northwestern University Press, 1988).

29. Adams, *The Sexual Politics of Meat*, pp. 41–42.

30. Ibid., pp. 42–43.

31. Ibid., p. 47.

32. Ibid., esp. pp. 29–32, 44–45.

33. Mark Mathew Braunstein, *Radical Vegetarianism: A Dialectic of Diet and Ethic,* rev. ed. (Quaker Hill, CT: Panacea Press, 1993), p. 48.

Chapter 3: Compartmentalization of Thought and Feeling—and the Burden of Proof

1. Both stories appeared in *Kingston* (Ontario) *This Week,* 16 April 1997, p. 1.

2. The classic study, of course, is Stanley Milgram's *Obedience to Authority: An Experimental View* (New York: Harper & Row, 1974). See also Robert W. Gardiner, *The Cool Arm of Destruction: Modern Weapons and Moral Insensitivity* (Philadelphia: Westminster Press, 1974); Robert Jay Lifton and Richard Falk, *Indefensible Weapons: The Political and Psychological Case Against Nuclearism* (New York: Basic Books; Toronto: CBC Enterprises, 1982); Michael Allen Fox, "The Nuclear Mindset: Motivational Obstacles to Peace," in *Nuclear War: Philosophical Perspectives,* ed. Michael Allen Fox and Leo Groarke, 2nd ed. (New York: Peter Lang, 1987), pp. 113–29.

3. Hitler loved children and animals (Klaus P. Fischer, *Nazi Germany: A New History* [New York: Continuum, 1995], p. 299). He was himself a vegetarian, who "would often make fun of meat eaters" and refer to meat broth as "'corpse tea'" (Albert Speer, *Inside the Third Reich: Memoirs,* trans. Richard Winston and Clara Winston [New York: Macmillan, 1970], p. 301). For more detailed discussion, see Janet Barkas, *The Vegetable Passion: A History of the Vegetarian State of Mind* (London:

Routledge & Kegan Paul; New York: Scribner's, 1975), chap. 7. It is entirely possible that some of the American combat pilots in Vietnam were vegetarians as well. Vegetarians have no monopoly on morality, nor are they immune to compartmentalization.

4.   E. S. Turner, *All Heaven in a Rage* (London: Michael Joseph, 1964), pp. 20, 22.

5.   Richard D. Ryder, *Animal Revolution: Changing Attitudes Toward Speciesism* (Oxford: Blackwell, 1989), p. 309.

6.   Ibid., p. 84.

7.   Curt Meine, *Aldo Leopold: His Life and Work* (Madison: University of Wisconsin Press, 1988), p. 162.

8.   Cited in Paul R. Amato and Sonia A. Partridge, *The New Vegetarians: Promoting Health and Protecting Life* (New York and London: Plenum Press, 1989), pp. 83–84.

9.   Daniel A. Dombrowski, *The Philosophy of Vegetarianism* (Amherst: University of Massachusetts Press, 1984), p. 104.

10.   Les Brown, *Cruelty to Animals: The Moral Debt* (Houndmills, Basingstoke, Hampshire: Macmillan, 1988), p. 74.

11.   I am not endorsing the human tendency to designate whatever is different as inferior, merely describing it.

12.   Complex and interesting explanations have been offered for these sources of inconsistency that it is not my purpose to analyze in detail here. For further discussion the reader is referred to works in the Bibliography by Mary Midgley and Richard D. Ryder.

13.   Susan Sperling, *Animal Liberators: Research and Morality* (Berkeley and Los Angeles: University of California Press, 1988), pp. 200, 128.

14.   J. Baird Callicott, "Animal Liberation: A Triangular Affair," in his *In Defense of the Land Ethic: Essays in Environmental Philosophy* (Albany: State University of New York Press, 1989), pp. 17, 18. (Originally published in *Environmental Ethics,* 2 [1980]: 311–28.) In a later paper, in which Callicott reconsiders his views, he again rationalizes meat-eating ("Second Thoughts on 'A Triangular Affair,'" in his *Companion to "A Sand County Almanac": Interpretive and Critical Essays* [Madison: University of Wisconsin Press, 1987], pp. 186–214).

15.   Aldo Leopold, *A Sand County Almanac, with Essays on Conservation from Round River* (New York: Sierra Club/Ballantine, 1970), p. 240.

16.   Callicott, "Animal Liberation," p. 36.

17.   Holmes Rolston III, *Environmental Ethics: Duties to and Values in the Natural World* (Philadelphia: Temple University Press, 1988), p. 78.

18.   Ibid., p. 79.

19.   Ibid., p. 80.

20. Ibid., p. 79.

21. Ibid., pp. 79–80.

22. Ibid., p. 78.

23. Ibid., p. 80 (emphasis in original).

24. Ibid., p. 82.

25. For additional discussions of Rolston's musings on culture versus nature, see Ned Hettinger, "Valuing Predation in Rolston's Environmental Ethics: Bambi Lovers Versus Tree Huggers," *Environmental Ethics*, 16 (1994): 3–20; and Paul Veatch Moriarty and Mark Woods, "Hunting ≠ Predation," *Environmental Ethics*, 19 (1997): 391–404.

26. Rolston, *Environmental Ethics*, p. 82.

27. Carol J. Adams, *The Sexual Politics of Meat: A Feminist-Vegetation Critical Theory* (New York: Continuum, 1991), p. 47.

28. Ibid., chap. 3.

29. Ibid., p. 68.

30. For a general treatment of this interesting topic, see James Cargile, "On the Burden of Proof," *Philosophy*, 72 (1997): 59–83.

Chapter 4: Vegetarian Outlooks

1. Paul R. Amato and Sonia A. Partridge, *The New Vegetarians: Promoting Health and Protecting Life* (New York and London: Plenum Press, 1989), p. vii.

2. Ibid., 71, 132.

3. Anonymous interview subjects, cited in ibid., p. 71.

4. Alice Walker "Am I Blue?" in *Living by the Word: Selected Writings, 1973–1987* (San Diego: Harcourt Brace Jovanovich, 1988), p. 8.

5. Amato and Partridge, *The New Vegetarians*, p. 73.

6. Richard D. Ryder, *Animal Revolution: Changing Attitudes Toward Speciesism* (Oxford; Blackwell, 1989), pp. 319–20.

7. Ibid., p. 321 (emphasis in original).

8. For discussion of the association between meat-eating and war, see Carol J. Adams, *The Sexual Politics of Meat: A Feminist-Vegetarian Critical Theory* (New York: Continuum, 1991), chap. 7; and Kath Clements, *Why Vegan: The Ethics of Eating and the Need for Change*, 2nd ed. (London: Heretic Books, 1995), chap. 7.

9. Jon Wynne-Tyson, *Food for a Future: The Complete Case for Vegetarianism* (London: Centaur Press; New York: Universe Books, 1979), pp. 127–28.

10. Donna Maurer, "Meat as a Social Problem: Rhetorical Strategies in the Contemporary Vegetarian Literature," in *Eating Agendas: Food and*

Nutrition as Social Problems, ed. Donna Maurer and Jeffrey Sobal (New York: Aldine de Gruyter, 1995), p. 146.

11.   Ibid.

12.   Ibid., pp. 147–48.

13.   The cumulative force of vegetarian arguments has also been discussed by William O. Stephens, "Five Arguments for Vegetarianism," *Philosophy in the Contemporary World*, 1:4 (Winter 1994): 25–39.

14.   Some important books that argue for these claims are Donald R. Griffin, *Animal Minds* (Chicago and London: University of Chicago Press, 1992); Marian Stamp Dawkins, *Through Our Eyes Only? The Search for Animal Consciousness* (Oxford, New York, and Heidelberg: W. H. Freeman/Spektrum, 1993); Jeffrey Moussaieff Masson and Susan McCarthy, *When Elephants Weep: The Emotional Lives of Animals* (New York: Delacorte Press, 1995); and Frans de Waal, *Good Natured: The Origins of Right and Wrong in Humans and Other Animals* (Cambridge, MA, and London: Harvard University Press, 1996). For an overview of these discussions and their import, see Michael Allen Fox, "Nonhuman, All Too Human," *Queen's Quarterly*, 102 (1995): 182–96; and Michael Allen Fox, "Humans and Other Animals: Ethical Reflections on Their Future Relationship," *Island*, 70 (Autumn 1997): 31–47.

15.   Charles Darwin, *The Descent of Man and Selection in Relation to Sex*, 2nd ed. (New York: Appleton, 1898), p. 128.

16.   Griffin, *Animal Minds*, p. 18.

17.   Barbara Noske, *Beyond Boundaries: Humans and Animals* (Montreal/New York/London: Black Rose Books, 1997).

18.   Gary L. Francione, *Animals, Property, and the Law* (Philadelphia: Temple University Press, 1995); Gary L. Francione, *Rain Without Thunder: The Ideology of the Animal Rights Movement* (Philadelphia: Temple University Press, 1996).

19.   For a detailed discussion of this topic, see Roger A. Caras, *A Perfect Harmony: The Intertwining Lives of Animals and Humans Throughout History* (New York: Simon & Schuster, 1997).

20.   Mark Mathew Braunstein, *Radical Vegetarianism: A Dialectic of Diet and Ethic*, rev. ed. (Quaker Hill, CT: Panacea Press, 1993), p. 82.

Chapter 5: Arguments for Vegetarianism: I

1.   Paul R. Amato and Sonia A. Partridge, *The New Vegetarians: Promoting Health and Protecting Life* (New York and London: Plenum Press, 1989), p. 71.

2.   "Position of the American Dietetic Association: Vegetarian Diets," *Journal of the American Dietetic Association*, 3 (1988): 351–55; "The Vege-

tarian Advantage," *Health* (New York), 20 (October 1988): 18; Randall White and Erica Frank, "Health Effects and Prevalence of Vegetarianism," *Western Journal of Medicine,* 160 (1994): 465–71; Junshi Chen, *Diet, Lifestyle, and Mortality in China: A Study of the Characteristics of Sixty-five Chinese Counties,* ed. T. Colin Campbell, Li Junyao, and Richard Peto (Ithaca: Cornell University Press, 1990); Neal D. Barnard, *Food for Life: How the New Four Food Groups Can Save Your Life* (New York: Harmony, 1993); Vesanto Melina, Brenda Davis, and Victoria Harrison, *Becoming Vegetarian: The Complete Guide to Adopting a Healthy Vegetarian Diet* (Toronto: Macmillan Canada, 1994).

3. Alan R. White, *Rights* (Oxford: Clarendon Press, 1984), p. 27.

4. Immanuel Kant, *Groundwork of the Metaphysics of Morals,* 3rd ed., trans. H. J. Paton (London: Hutchinson University Library, 1956), p. 96. First published in 1785.

5. As we saw in Chapter 1, Kant did not ascribe any significant moral status to animals themselves, nor was he a vegetarian. However, it is his way of arguing with which we are concerned here, and this may in fact lead to conclusions other than he might have supposed. For discussions of Kant's views on animals, see A. Broadie and Elizabeth M. Pybus, "Kant's Treatment of Animals," *Philosophy,* 49 (1974): 375–83; and Mary Midgley, *Animals and Why They Matter: A Journey Around the Species Barrier* (Harmondsworth, Middlesex: Penguin, 1983), pp. 51–61. See also an intriguing recent article by Dan Egonsson on "Kant's Vegetarianism," *Journal of Value Inquiry,* 31 (1997): 473–83.

6. John Stuart Mill, "On Liberty," in *Utilitarianism, Liberty, and Representative Government* (New York: E. P. Dutton, 1951), p. 182. First published in 1859.

7. Marcus G. Singer, "On Duties to Oneself," *Ethics,* 69 (1958–59): 203.

8. Warner Wick, "More About Duties to Oneself," *Ethics,* 70 (1959–60): 163 (emphasis in original).

9. Ibid., pp. 161–62.

10. William Neblett, "Morality, Prudence, and Obligations to Oneself," *Ethics,* 80 (1969–70): 70–73.

11. Ibid., p. 72.

12. Ibid., p. 73.

13. John Stuart Mill, "Utilitarianism," in *Utilitarianism, Liberty and Representative Government,* p. 77. First published in 1861.

14. Mary Midgley, "Duties Concerning Islands," in *Environmental Philosophy: A Collection of Readings,* ed. Robert Elliot and Arran Gare (University Park and London: Pennsylvania State University Press; St. Lucia: University of Queensland Press, 1983), pp. 176, 177 (emphasis in original).

15.   The fact that we now know this developmental process is geneti-cally preprogrammed (at least in nonhuman species) does not render this idea superfluous. It remains legitimate to express the meaning, significance, or purposive character of biological development in a nonbiological idiom.

16.   Aristotle, like Kant, was not a vegetarian, and argued (perhaps in-consistently) that animals were quite different from and inferior to humans. But again our purpose is to learn from his way of arguing and see how it might be developed. For a discussion of Aristotle's views on animals and vegetarianism, see Daniel A. Dombrowski, *The Philosophy of Vegetarianism* (Amherst: University of Massachusetts Press, 1984), pp. 63–73.

17.   Aristotle, *Nicomachean Ethics*, bks. 1, 2, 7, 10.

18.   Ibid., bk. 2, sec. 6.

19.   Confucius, *The Analects of Confucius*, trans. Lao An (Jinan, Peo-ple's Republic of China: Shandong Friendship Press, 1992).

20.   See "The Buddha and the Middle Way," in Gary E. Kessler, *Voices of Wisdom: A Multicultural Philosophy Reader*, 3rd ed. (Belmont, CA: Wadsworth, 1998), pp. 21–27.

21.   Greg Pence, "Virtue Theory," in *A Companion to Ethics*, ed. Pe-ter Singer (Oxford: Blackwell, 1993), p. 249.

22.   Ibid., p. 250.

23.   See, for example, John Robbins, *Diet for a New America* (Wal-pole, NH: Stillpoint, 1987); National Research Council, *Diet and Health: Implications for Reducing Chronic Disease Risk* (Washington, DC: National Academy Press, 1989); Neal D. Barnard, *The Power of Your Plate: A Plan for Better Living* (Summertown, TN: Book Publishing, 1990); Nick Fiddes, *Meat: A Natural Symbol* (London and New York: Routledge, 1991); and Ananda Mitra, *Food for Thought: The Vegetarian Philosophy* (Willow Springs, MO: NUCLEUS, 1991).

24.   "Industry Forced Changes to Food Guide, Papers Show," *Toronto Star*, 15 January 1993, p. A2.

25.   See Bhiku Jethalal, "Prescription for Good Health," *Toronto Star*, 3 December 1994, pp. L1, L16; and Melina et al., *Becoming Vegetarian*. It is as-sumed in all such discussions—as I assume here—that the ideal vegetarian diet is adequate in protein and other essential nutrients, high in fiber, and low in fat.

26.   Based in part on Louis Vorhaus, "Parasitic Diseases," in *Encyclo-pedia Americana*, international ed. (Danbury, CT: Grolier, 1988), vol. 21, pp. 421–23. See, in relation to the problem of drug additives, Andrew Niki-foruk, "The Threat of Farmyard Pharmaceuticals," *Toronto Globe and Mail* 29 March 1997, p. D5.

27.   Government of Canada, *The State of Canada's Environment* (Ot-tawa: Ministry of Supply and Services Canada, 1991), p. 9–26.

28.   Ontario Egg Producers' Marketing Board, "Egg Farming in Ontario" (n.d.).

29.   See especially Jim Mason and Peter Singer, *Animal Factories,* rev. ed. (New York: Harmony, 1990); and Jeremy Rifkin, *Beyond Beef: The Rise and Fall of the Cattle Culture* (New York: Dutton, 1992). See also H. Gordon Green, "That Bacon You're Eating Is from a Pig Penitentiary," *Toronto Star,* 12 October 1991, p F2; Bob Hunter, "Warning: Reading This May Spoil Your Supper," *eye weekly* (Toronto), 25 August 1994, p. 11; Scott Kilman, "Animal Farm's Brave New World," *Toronto Globe and Mail,* 1 April 1994, p. A11; "Transportation Exposed: Truckers Speak Out," *Canadians for the Ethical Treatment of Food Animals Newsletter,* 13 (Summer 1994): 1–6.

30.   Animals slaughtered include cattle, calves, hogs, sheep, lambs, and poultry. Sources: *Livestock Market Review 1994* (Ottawa: Agriculture and Agri-Food Canada, Market and Industry Services Branch, Agricultural Industry Services Directorate, Livestock and Animal Products Section, 1995), Tables 7, 12, 17, 28, and 31; *Poultry Market Review 1994* (Ottawa Agriculture and Agri-Food Canada, Market and Industry Services Branch, Agricultural Industry Services Directorate, Poultry Division, 1995), Tables 27, 28, 29, and 30. Over 80 percent of these animals are chickens, 3 percent are pigs, and fewer than 1 percent are cattle.

31.   Rifkin, *Beyond Beef,* p. 154.

32.   "Animals Butchered Alive, Former USDA Inspectors Say," *Toronto Globe and Mail,* 4 April 1998, p. A16 (Reuters News Agency story). See also Stewart Bell, "Meat Inspection System Gets Failing Grade," *National Post,* 6 February 1999, pp. A1–2; and Gail A. Eisnitz, *Slaughterhouse* (Buffalo: Prometheus, 1997).

33.   The situation is a good deal more complicated than this, however. Peter Singer, the principal utilitarian theorist on animal issues today, argues that several conditions must be met in order for animals to be justifiably killed for food: (1) The animals concerned are not distinct individuals and are therefore fully replaceable; (2) they lack self-consciousness; (3) they have been raised in a free-range setting; (4) they can be killed painlessly; (5) surviving conspecifics are not negatively affected by their deaths; and (6) they would not have been alive in the first place were it not for humans' desire to eat them (see Peter Singer, *Practical Ethics,* 2nd ed. [Cambridge: Cambridge University Press, 1993], chap. 5; see also the extensive critique of this view in Evelyn Pluhar, *Beyond Prejudice: The Moral Significance of Human and Nonhuman Animals* [Durham and London: Duke University Press, 1995], Chap. 4).

34.   "Individuals are subjects-of-a-life if they have beliefs and desires; perception, memory, and a sense of the future, including their own future; an emotional life together with feelings of pleasure and pain; preference-

and welfare-interests; the ability to initiate action in pursuit of their desires and goals; a psychophysical identity over time; and an individual welfare in the sense that their experiential life fares well or ill for them, logically independently of their utility for others and logically independently of their being the object of anyone else's interests" (Tom Regan, *The Case for Animal Rights* [Berkeley and Los Angeles: University of California Press, 1983], p. 243).

35. For a detailed critical discussion of the contrasting claims of animal rights theory and modern utilitarianism in addressing these issues, see Gary L. Francione, *Rain Without Thunder: The Ideology of the Animal Rights Movement* (Philadelphia: Temple University Press, 1996), especially chaps. 1 and 3. Francione argues that both utilitarianism and the animal welfare movement (for which "the animal rights movement" is a common misnomer) lack the "analytical framework" needed to prevent common types of animal suffering, and that only animal rights theory proper can provide that framework.

36. For example, Peter Carruthers, *The Animals Issue: Moral Theory in Practice* (Cambridge: Cambridge University Press, 1992); Peter Harrison, "Theodicy and Animal Pain," *Philosophy*, 64 (1989): 79–92; Peter Harrison, "Do Animals Feel Pain?" *Philosophy*, 66 (1991): 25–40; and Peter Harrison, "The Neo-Cartesian Revival: A Response," *Between the Species*, 9 (1993): 71–76.

37. One contemporary philosopher *does* take them seriously and takes the trouble to refute them in detail: Evelyn Pluhar (see *Beyond Prejudice*, pp. 14–46). On the pain and suffering of animals and the scientific basis for discussing them, see Marian Stamp Dawkins, *Animal Suffering: The Science of Animal Welfare* (London and New York: Chapman and Hall, 1980); Bernard E. Rollin, *The Unheeded Cry: Animal Consciousness, Animal Pain, and Science* (Oxford and New York: Oxford University Press, 1990); and F. Barbara Orlans, *In the Name of Science: Issues in Responsible Animal Experimentation* (New York and Oxford: Oxford University Press, 1993).

38. Jeremy Bentham, *An Introduction to the Principles of Morals and Legislation* (London: T. Payne, 1789), chap. 19, sec. 1.

39. Carol J. Adams, *The Sexual Politics of Meat: A Feminist-Vegetarian Critical Theory* (New York: Continuum, 1990), p. 70.

40. Les Brown, *Cruelty to Animals: The Moral Debt* (Houndmills, Basingstoke, Hampshire: Macmillan, 1988).

41. Ibid., p. 39.
42. Ibid., p. 40.
43. Ibid., p. 39.
44. Ibid., p. 40.

Chapter 6: Arguments for Vegetarianism: II

1. It is for this reason that Paul B. Sears first labeled ecology "subversive." See his essay "Ecology—A Subversive Subject," *BioScience*, 14:7 (July 1964): 11–13.

2. John Robbins, *Diet for a New America* (Walpole, NH: Stillpoint, 1987), pt. 3.

3. See, for example, Nick Fiddes, *Meat: A Natural Symbol* (London and New York: Routledge, 1991), chap. 14; John Lawrence Hill, *The Case for Vegetarianism: Philosophy for a Small Planet* (Lanham, MD: Rowman & Littlefield, 1996), chap. 4; and Frances Moore Lappé, *Diet for a Small Planet*, 20th ed. (New York: Ballantine, 1992).

4. Sharon Bloyd-Peshkin, "Mumbling About Meat," *Vegetarian Times*, 170 (October 1991): 67.

5. Government of Canada, *The State of Canada's Environment* (Ottawa: Ministry of Supply and Services Canada, 1991), pp. 9–9, 9–15.

6. Ibid., pp. 26–6, 9–14.

7. Animal Alliance of Canada, "Enviro Facts About Livestock Production" (compiled from *Worldwatch Paper*, no. 103 [Washington, DC: Worldwatch Institute, 1991]; Government of Canada, *The State of Canada's Environment*; and Agriculture Canada, *Livestock Market Review, 1993* [Ottawa: Agriculture and Agri-Food Canada, 1994]).

8. David Pimentel, "Livestock Production: Energy Inputs and the Environment," in *Proceedings of the Canadian Society of Animal Science 47th Annual Meeting, 24–26 July 1997, Montreal*, ed. S. L. Scott and Xin Zho (Montreal: Canadian Society of Animal Science, 1997), pp. 16–26.

9. Government of Canada, *The State of Canada's Environment*, p. 9–26.

10. Pimentel, "Livestock Production."

11. Fiddes, *Meat: A Natural Symbol*, p. 215.

12. Large multinational corporations seek to control the commercial food production process, from feed grains to slaughter and meat packing. For discussion of these trends see Barbara Noske, *Beyond Boundaries: Humans and Animals* (Montreal, New York, and London: Black Rose Books, 1997); Jeremy Rifkin, *Beyond Beef: The Rise and Fall of the Cattle Culture* (New York: Dutton, 1992); Jim Mason and Peter Singer, *Animal Factories*, rev. ed. (New York: Harmony, 1990), chap. 7; Marty Strange, *Family Farming: A New Economic Vision* (San Francisco: Institute for Food and Development Policy, 1988); and Michael W. Fox, *Superpigs and Wondercorn: The Brave New World of Biotechnology and Where It All May Lead* (New York: Lyons & Burford, 1992), p. 70.

13. Animal Alliance of Canada, "Enviro Facts" (emphasis in original).

14.   Lester R. Brown et al., *State of the World 1997: A Worldwatch Institute Report on Progress Toward a Sustainable Society* (New York and London: W. W. Norton, 1997), pp. 40–41.

15.   Edward O. Wilson, *The Diversity of Life* (New York: W.W. Norton, 1993), p. 344.

16.   Ibid., p. 280.

17.   Anita Gordon and David Suzuki, *It's a Matter of Survival* (Toronto: Stoddart, 1990), p. 2.

18.   Richard Swift, "Who's Next?" *New Internationalist*, 288 (March 1997): 8.

19.   Wilson, *The Diversity of Life*, p. 280.

20.   William K. Stevens, "Plant Species Threats Cited," *Toronto Globe and Mail*, 9 April 1998, p. A15.

21.   Food and Agricultural Organization of the United Nations, *Dimensions of Need: An Atlas of Food and Agriculture* (Santa Barbara: ABC-CLIO, 1995), p. 54.

22.   Al Gore, *Earth in the Balance: Ecology and the Human Spirit* (New York: Plume, 1993), p. 23 (statistic attributed to Thomas Lovejoy).

23.   John Terborgh, *Diversity and the Tropical Rain Forest* (New York: Scientific American/W. H. Freeman, 1992), p. 75.

24.   Ibid., p. 58.

25.   Nicki McKisson and Linda MacRae-Campbell, *The Future of Our Tropical Rainforests* (Tucson: Zephyr Press, 1990), p. 25.

26.   Mark Collins, ed., *The Last Rain Forests: A World Conservation Atlas* (New York: Oxford University Press, 1990), pp. 30, 32, 186; Food and Agricultural Organization, *Dimensions of Need*, p. 60.

27.   The term comes from Arnold Newman, *Tropical Rainforest* (New York and Oxford: Facts on File, 1990), p. 126.

28.   Collins, ed., *The Last Rain Forests*, p. 96.

29.   Ibid., p. 32.

30.   Food and Agricultural Organization, *Dimensions of Need*, p. 62.

31.   Thomas E. Lovejoy, "Species Leave the Ark One by One," in *The Preservation of Species: The Value of Biological Diversity*, ed. Bryan G. Norton (Princeton: Princeton University Press, 1986), pp. 16–17.

32.   Wilson, *The Diversity of Life*, p. 281.

33.   Collins, ed., *The Last Rain Forests*, p. 32.

34.   Vandana Shiva, *Biopiracy: The Plunder of Nature and Knowledge* (Boston: South End Press, 1997), pp. 66, 120.

35.   For further discussion, see Michael Allen Fox, "Thinking Ethically About the Environment," *Dalhousie Review*, 73 (1993–94): 493–511; Michael Allen Fox, "Anthropocentrism," in *Encyclopedia of Animal Rights*

and Animal Welfare, ed. Marc Bekoff with Carron A. Meaney (Westport, CT: Greenwood Press, 1998), pp. 66–68; and Bryan D. Norton, "Commodity, Amenity, and Morality: The Limits of Quantification in Valuing Biodiversity," in *Biodiversity,* ed. E. O. Wilson (Washington, DC: National Academy Press, 1988), pp. 200–205.

36. Gore, *Earth in the Balance,* p. 119.

37. One factor that compounds the problem is that imported cattle meat is classified as "domestic beef" by the U.S. government once it enters the country, which obscures its point of origin. See Norman Myers, *The Primary Source: Tropical Forests and Our Future* (New York and London: W. W. Norton, 1984), p. 131.

38. Rifkin, *Beyond Beef,* p. 193.

39. Collins, ed., *The Last Rain Forests,* p. 42.

40. Myers, *The Primary Source,* p. 127.

41. Ibid., p. 128; Rifkin, *Beyond Beef,* p. 193.

42. Myers, *The Primary Source,* p. 129.

43. Ibid., p. 130.

44. Newman, *Tropical Rainforest,* p. 126. Some fast-food giants, notably Burger King and McDonald's, claim that they no longer use rain forest–grown beef; other chains have made no such statements.

45. Myers, *The Primary Source,* p. 142.

46. U.S. Congress, Office of Technology Assessment, *Technology, Public Policy, and the Changing Structure of American Agriculture: A Special Report for the 1985 Farm Bill* (Washington, DC: U.S. Government Printing Office, 1985), introduction.

47. Fox attributes this prediction to J. Mintz in *Superpigs and Wondercorn,* p. 104.

48. Ibid.

49. Pat Spallone, *Generation Games: Genetic Engineering and the Future for Our Lives* (London: The Women's Press; Philadelphia: Temple University Press, 1992), p. 116; British Medical Association, *Our Genetic Future: The Science and Ethics of Genetic Technology* (Oxford and New York: Oxford University Press, 1992), pp. 100–101.

50. Fox, *Superpigs and Wondercorn,* chap. 6.

51. David Concar, "The Organ Factory of the Future?" *New Scientist,* 142 (18 June 1994): 24–29.

52. Bernard E. Rollin, *The Frankenstein Syndrome: Ethical and Social Issues in the Genetic Engineering of Animals* (New York: Cambridge University Press, 1995), p. 174.

53. Mason and Singer, *Animal Factories,* p. 47.

54. Fox, *Superpigs and Wondercorn,* pp. 114–25.

55.   Spallone, *Generation Games,* p. 54.

56.   I have, and it is a profoundly disturbing experience. For readers who have strong stomachs and might be willing to "visit" a slaughterhouse through the pages of a book, I recommend Sue Coe, *Dead Meat* (New York and London: Four Walls Eight Windows, 1995); and Gail Eisnetz, *Slaughterhouse* (Buffalo: Prometheus, 1997).

57.   Frances Moore Lappé, *Diet for a Small Planet,* rev. ed. (New York: Ballantine, 1975), p. 11.

58.   Fiddes, *Meat: A Natural Symbol,* p. 211.

59.   Lappé, *Diet for a Small Planet,* 1975 rev ed., p. 3.

60.   World Commission on Environment and Development, *Our Common Future* (New York: Oxford University Press, 1987), pp. 119–20.

61.   Food and Agricultural Organization, *Dimensions of Need,* p. 78. See also Newman, *Tropical Rainforest,* pp. 106–7.

62.   Alan Durning, "Fat of the Land: Livestock's Resource Gluttony," *World Watch,* 4:3 (May-June 1991): 11–17.

63.   Mark Gold, "On the Meat-Hook," *New Internationalist,* 215 (January 1991): 9–10.

64.   Michael Redclift, *Sustainable Development: Exploring the Contradictions* (London: Routledge, 1987), p. 93.

65.   Fiddes, *Meat: A Natural Symbol,* p. 211.

66.   Food and Agricultural Organization, *Dimensions of Need,* p. 100.

67.   Andy Crump, *Dictionary of Environment and Development: People, Places, Ideas, and Organizations* (London: Earthscan, 1991), p. 127.

68.   Patricia L. Kutzner, *World Hunger: A Reference Book* (Santa Barbara: ABC-CLIO, 1991), p. 164.

69.   Newman, *Tropical Rainforest,* p. 106.

70.   Kutzner (citing UNICEF and WHO figures), *World Hunger,* p. 159.

71.   Cited in ibid., p. 2.

72.   Newman, *Tropical Rainforest,* p. 106.

73.   Scott Barbour, ed., *Hunger* (San Diego: Greenhaven Press, 1995), pp. 194–95; Kutzner, *World Hunger,* p. 3; Food and Agricultural Organization, *Dimensions of Need,* p. 78. In a crisis-ridden world food aid may be imperative, but many believe that by itself, and as administered today, it is not the answer to the world hunger problem because it creates dependency and perpetuates disempowerment among the poor of developing nations. For a brief overview, see Food and Agricultural Organization, *Dimensions of Need,* p. 79.

74.   Pimentel, "Environmental and Social Implications of Waste," p. 11.

75.   Robbins, *Diet for a New America,* p. 351.

76.   Ibid., p. 352.

77. Ibid.

78. Ibid., p. 353.

79. For detailed discussion of this issue, see Dan Morgan, *Merchants of Grain* (New York: Viking Press, 1979); Redclift, *Sustainable Development;* Gold, "On the Meat-Hook"; Fiddes, *Meat: A Natural Symbol;* and Hope Shand, "Bio-Meltdown," *New Internationalist,* 288 (March 1997): 22–23.

80. See, however, the references in nn. 12 and 79 above.

81. Kutzner, *World Hunger,* pp. 49, 50.

82. Ibid., p. 50.

83. The best brief treatment of most of these theories is Carolyn Merchant's *Radical Ecology: The Search for a Livable World* (New York and London: Routledge, 1992). For the environmental justice movement, see Wilmette Brown, *Roots: Black Ghetto Ecology* (London: Housewives in Dialogue, 1986); and Peter Wenz, *Environmental Justice* (Albany: State University of New York Press, 1988). The term "antidomination theories" was suggested by Karen J. Warren's important essay, "The Power and the Promise of Ecological Feminism," *Environmental Ethics,* 12 (1990): 125–46, in which she sketched and discussed what she calls "the logic of domination."

84. Huey-li Li, "A Cross-Cultural Critique of Ecofeminism," in *Ecofeminism: Women, Animals, Nature,* ed. Greta Gaard (Philadelphia: Temple University Press, 1993), pp. 290–91.

85. See Nel Noddings, *Caring: A Feminine Approach to Ethics and Moral Education* (Berkeley and Los Angeles: University of California Press, 1984), chap. 7. See also Josephine Donovan, "Animal Rights and Feminist Theory," *Signs,* 15 (1990): 350–75; Nel Noddings, "Comments on Donovan's 'Animal Rights and Feminist Theory,'" *Signs,* 16 (1991): 418–22; Josephine Donovan, "Reply to Noddings," *Signs,* 16 (1991): 423–25; and Gary L. Francione, "Ecofeminism and Animal Rights: A Review of *Beyond Animal Rights: A Feminist Caring Ethic for the Treatment of Animals,*" *Women's Rights Law Reporter,* 18 (1996): 95–106.

86. Jane Meyerding, "Feminist Criticism and Cultural Imperialism (Where Does One End and the Other Begin?)," *Animals' Agenda,* November–December 1982, pp. 22–23.

87. For a sensitive treatment of this issue, see Alice Walker, "Am I Blue?" in *Living by the Word: Selected Writings, 1973–1987* (San Diego: Harcourt Brace Jovanovich, 1988).

88. See Carol J. Adams, *The Sexual Politics of Meat: A Feminist-Vegetarian Critical Theory* (New York: Continuum, 1990), chap. 2.

89. Contrast, for example, Lynn White, Jr., "The Historical Roots of Our Ecologic Crisis," *Science,* 155 (10 March 1967): 1203–7, and John Passmore, *Man's Responsibility for Nature,* 2nd ed. (London: Duckworth,

1980), chap. 1, on the one hand, with Robin Attfield, *The Ethics of Environmental Concern* (Oxford: Blackwell, 1983), chap. 2, and Susan Power Bratton, "Christian Ecotheology and the Old Testament," *Environmental Ethics*, 6 (1986): 195–209, on the other.

90.   That at least some animals have these sorts of interests and that the interests are morally relevant have, I think, been sufficiently demonstrated in the literature. Animals can *have an interest* in something even if they (like infant, comatose, or seriously mentally deficient humans) cannot *take an interest* in it. For discussion see S. F. Sapontzis, *Morals, Reason, and Animals* (Philadelphia: Temple University Press, 1987), chap. 7.

91.   Peter Singer, *Animal Liberation*, new rev. ed. (New York: Avon, 1990), chap. 1. See also Marjorie Spiegel, *The Dreaded Comparison: Human and Animal Slavery*, rev. and enl. ed. (New York: Mirror Books, 1996).

92.   I once thought this view was unacceptable too. See Michael Allen Fox, *The Case for Animal Experimentation: An Evolutionary and Ethical Perspective* (Berkeley and Los Angeles: University of California Press, 1986), pp. 58–59. For a current example, see Kathleen Marquardt, with Herbert M. Levine and Mark LaRochelle, *AnimalScam: The Beastly Abuse of Human Rights* (Washington, DC: Regnery Gateway, 1993). It should be noted that Singer's position has been frequently misunderstood and widely misrepresented; he does not claim that the oppression of animals bears all the same features of racism and sexism, but rather that it arises from the same type of error, namely, discriminating on the basis of differences that are morally irrelevant.

93.   Allen W. Wood, "Exploitation," in *Exploitation*, ed. Kai Nielsen and Robert Ware (Atlantic Highlands, NJ: Humanities Press International, 1997), p. 15. Wood's essay originally appeared in *Social Philosophy and Policy*, 12 (1995): 135–58.

94.   Nielsen and Ware, eds., *Exploitation*, back cover. Animals are also omitted from Iris M. Young's substantial feminist piece "The Five Faces of Oppression," in *Throwing Like a Girl and Other Essays in Feminist Philosophy and Social Theory* (Bloomington: Indiana University Press, 1990), pp. 39–65.

95.   Beth A. Dixon, "The Feminist Connection Between Women and Animals," *Environmental Ethics*, 18 (1996): 187.

96.   Ibid., p. 191.

97.   Two excellent examples are Donald R. Griffin, *Animal Minds* (Chicago and London: University of Chicago Press, 1992); and Jeffrey Moussaieff Masson and Susan McCarthy, *When Elephants Weep: The Emotional Lives of Animals* (New York: Delacorte Press, 1995).

98.   Peter Singer, *Practical Ethics*, 2nd ed. (Cambridge: Cambridge University Press, 1993), chaps. 2, 3.

99.   Josephine Donovan, "Animal Rights and Feminist Theory," in

Ecofeminism: Women, Animals, Nature, ed. Gaard, p. 178; see also Keith Thomas, *Man and the Natural World: A History of the Modern Sensibility* (New York: Pantheon, 1983), pp. 128, 170, 173–74, 280, 293–94.

100.   Donovan, "Animal Rights and Feminist Theory," p. 173.

101.   Bonnie Kreps, *Authentic Passion: Loving Without Losing Your Self* (Toronto: M & S Paperbacks, 1990), p. 14 (emphasis in original).

102.   Genevieve Lloyd, *The Man of Reason: "Male" and "Female" in Western Philosophy* (Minneapolis: University of Minnesota Press, 1984), p. 2. The Plato reference is to *Menexenus,* 238a.

103.   Elizabeth Dodson Gray, *Green Paradise Lost* (Wellesley, MA: Roundtable Press, 1981), p. 19. First published in 1979 as *Why the Green Nigger?*

104.   Lloyd, *The Man of Reason,* p. 3.

105.   Val Plumwood, *Feminism and the Mastery of Nature* (London and New York: Routledge, 1993); Ariel Salleh, *Ecofeminism as Politics: Nature, Marx, and the Postmodern* (Atlantic Highlands, NJ: Humanities Press; London: Zed Books, 1996).

106.   Elizabeth Grosz, *Volatile Bodies: Toward a Corporeal Feminism* (Bloomington and Indianapolis: Indiana University Press, 1994).

107.   Carol J. Adams, *Neither Man Nor Beast: Feminism and the Defense of Animals* (New York: Continuum, 1995), pp. 78–80; Patricia Hill Collins, *Black Feminist Thought: Knowledge, Consciousness, and the Politics of Empowerment* (Boston: Unwin Hyman, 1990), p. 225.

108.   For an introduction to feminist ethics, see Claudia Card, ed., *Feminist Ethics* (Lawrence: University of Kansas Press, 1991); Eve Browning Cole and Susan Coultrap-McQuin, eds., *Explorations in Feminist Ethics: Theory and Practice* (Bloomington and Indianapolis: Indiana University Press, 1992); and Eve Browning Cole, *Philosophy and Feminist Criticism: An Introduction* (New York: Paragon House, 1993), chap. 5.

Chapter 7: Arguments for Vegetarianism: III

1.   Martin Palmer, *Genesis or Nemesis: Belief, Meaning, and Ecology* (London: Dryad Press, 1988), p. 110.

2.   Friedrich Nietzsche, *Daybreak: Thoughts on the Prejudices of Morality,* trans. R. J. Hollingdale, ed. Maudemarie Clark and Brian Leiter (Cambridge: Cambridge University Press, 1997), sec. 547, p. 548.

3.   Jim Nollman, *Spiritual Ecology: A Guide to Reconnecting with Nature* (New York: Bantam Books, 1990), p. 18.

4.   Tom Regan, "The Nature and Possibility of an Environmental Ethic," in *All That Dwell Therein: Essays on Animal Rights and Environmental Ethics* (Berkeley, Los Angeles, and London: University of California

Press, 1982), p. 188 (emphasis in original). First published in *Environmental Ethics,* 3 (1981): 19–34.

5.   Stephen R. Kellert, *Kinship to Mastery: Biophilia in Human Evolution and Development* (Washington, DC, and Covelo, CA: Island Press/Shearwater Books, 1997), p. 2.

6.   Ibid., p. 3.

7.   Arthur Schopenhauer, *On the Basis of Morality,* trans. E.F.J. Payne, Library of Liberal Arts ed. (New York: Bobbs-Merrill, 1965), sec. 16 (emphasis in original). First published in 1841.

8.   Ibid., sec. 19, point 4.

9.   Arthur Schopenhauer, *The World as Will and Representation,* trans. E.F.J. Payne (New York: Dover Publications, 1969), vol. 1, 4th bk., "The World as Will: Second Aspect," sec. 53.

10.   Louise Noble, personal communication.

11.   Albert Schweitzer, *Civilization and Ethics. The Philosophy of Civilization, pt. 2,* 2nd ed., trans. C. T. Campion (London: A. & C. Black, 1929), p. 264.

12.   Ibid., p. 246.

13.   Ibid., p. 247.

14.   Ibid., pp. 254–55, 264, 260.

15.   For an application of this principle, see Michael Allen Fox, "On the 'Necessary Suffering' of Nonhuman Animals," *Animal Law,* 3 (1997): 25–30. See also the discussion of Leonard Nelson's views on pp. 19–20.

16.   Paul W. Taylor, *Respect for Nature: A Theory of Environmental Ethics* (Princeton: Princeton University Press, 1986), p. 75.

17.   Ibid.

18.   Ibid., p. 44.

19.   Ibid., pp. 269–77.

20.   Thich Nhat Hanh, *Peace Is Every Step: The Path of Mindfulness in Everyday Life* (New York: Bantam Books, 1991), p. 98.

21.   Ibid., p. 118.

22.   Stephen Batchelor, *Buddhism Without Beliefs: A Contemporary Guide to Awakening* (New York: Riverhead Books, 1997), p. 87.

23.   For an excellent contemporary exposition, see His Holiness the XIV Dalai Lama, *The Four Noble Truths: Fundamentals of the Buddhist Teachings,* trans. Geshe Thupten and ed. Dominique Side (London: Thorsons, 1997).

24.   Roy C. Amore and Julia Ching, "The Buddhist Tradition," in *World Religions: Eastern Traditions,* ed. Willard G. Oxtoby (Toronto, New York, and Oxford: Oxford University Press, 1996), p. 234.

25.   Ibid., p. 243.

26.   Helena Norberg-Hodge, *Ancient Futures: Learning from Ladakh* (San Francisco: Sierra Club Books, 1991), p. 31.

27.   For more on these roots see Robert L. Holmes, ed., *Nonviolence in Theory and Practice* (Belmont, CA: Wadsworth, 1990).

28.   *Jaina Sutras, pt. 1,* trans. H. Jacobi (Oxford: Clarendon Press, 1884), p. 11.

29.   Vasudha Narayanan, "The Jain Tradition," in *World Religions: Eastern Traditions,* ed. Oxtoby, p. 158.

30.   See Chapter 1, n. 87.

31.   Mohandas Karamchand Gandhi, *"Ahimsa* or Love," in *The Moral and Political Writings of Mahatma Gandhi,* ed. Raghavan Iyer (Oxford: Clarendon Press, 1986–87), vol. 2, *Truth and Non-Violence,* p. 577.

32.   Mohandas Karamchand Gandhi, "Soul-Force and *Tapasya,*" in *Moral and Political Writings,* ed. Iyer, vol. 3, *Non-Violent Resistance and Social Transformation,* p. 46.

33.   Ibid., p. 45.

34.   Mohandas Karamchand Gandhi, "Non-Violence of the Strong and of the Weak," in *Moral and Political Writings,* vol. 2, p. 405.

35.   Mohandas Karamchand Gandhi, "After-Effects of War," in ibid., p. 460.

36.   Bhikhu Parekh, *Gandhi* (Oxford and New York: Oxford University Press, 1997), p. 54.

37.   Gandhi, "Non-Violence of the Strong and of the Weak," p. 406.

38.   Cited in Steven Rosen, *Diet for Transcendence: Vegetarianism and the World Religions* (Badger, CA: Torchlight, 1997), p. 121. First published as *Food for the Spirit: Vegetarianism and the World Religions* (New York: Bala, 1987).

39.   Gandhi, "Non-Violence of the Strong and of the Weak," p. 405.

40.   Gandhi, *"Ahimsa* or Love," p. 578.

41.   Gandhi, "Destruction of Life," in *Moral and Political Writings,* vol. 2, p. 267.

42.   On the Australian Aborigines, see Diane Bell, *Daughters of the Dreaming,* 2nd ed. (Minneapolis: University of Minnesota Press, 1993), pp. 54–56. Gathering, of course, is traditionally the activity of women. On the Mohawk Indians, see *Tyendinaga Tales,* collected by Rona Rustige, with illustrations by Jeri Maracle Van Der Vlag (Kingston, ON, and Montreal: McGill-Queen's University Press, 1988), p. xii.

43.   Nollman, *Spiritual Ecology.*

44.   Sean Kane, *Wisdom of the Mythtellers* (Peterborough, ON: Broadview Press, 1994), pp. 14, 16, 19.

45.   Bell, *Daughters of the Dreaming,* p. 91.

46.   Barbara Noske, "Speciesism, Anthropocentrism, and Non-Western Cultures," *Anthrozoös,* 10 (1997): 183–90; "Boomerang," in *Encyclopaedia Brittanica,* 15th ed. (Chicago: Encyclopaedia Brittanica, 1998),

vol. 2, p. 373; C.W.M. Hart et al., *The Tiwi of North Australia,* 3rd ed. (Fort Worth: Holt, Rinehart and Winston, 1988), pp. 46–47.

47.   Alice Walker, "Everything Is a Human Being," in *Living by the Word: Selected Writings, 1973–1987* (San Diego: Harcourt Brace Jovanovich, 1988), p. 150.

48.   Kane, *Wisdom of the Mythtellers,* pp. 34, 44.

49.   See n. 42 above. I am grateful to John Rowinski for bringing this collection to my attention.

50.   Audrey Shenandoah (Onondaga Indian), 1987, cited in *Native Wisdom,* ed. Joseph Bruchac (San Francisco: HarperSanFrancisco, 1995), p. 13. First published in *Indian Roots of American Democracy,* ed. José Barriero (Ithaca, NY: Akwe:kon Press, 1992).

51.   Rosen, *Diet for Transcendence,* p. 93.

52.   Vasudha Narayanan, "The Hindu Tradition," in *World Religions: Eastern Traditions,* ed. Oxtoby, p. 24.

53.   Rosen, *Diet for Transcendence,* p. 94; Narayanan, "The Hindu Tradition," p. 89.

54.   All quotations are from *The New Jerusalem Bible,* reader's ed. (Garden City, NY: Doubleday, 1990).

55.   Rosen, *Diet for Transcendence,* p. 20 (emphasis in original); cf. ibid., pp. 43–44.

56.   Josef Scharbert, "Paradise," in *Encyclopedia of Biblical Theology: The Complete* Sacramentum Verbi, ed. Johannes B. Bauer (New York: Crossroads Publishing, 1981), p. 631.

57.   Mawil Y. Izzi Deen (Samarrai), "Islamic Environmental Ethics, Law, and Society," in *Ethics of Environment and Development: Global Challenge, International Response,* ed. J. Ronald Engel and Joan Gibb Engel (Tucson: University of Arizona Press, 1990), p. 190.

58.   All quotations are from *The Koran,* trans. N. J. Dawood, 5th further rev. ed. (London: Penguin Books, 1997).

59.   Deen, "Islamic Environmental Ethics, Law, and Society," pp. 190–91; Iqtidar H. Zaidi, "On the Ethics of Man's Interaction with the Environment: An Islamic Approach," *Environmental Ethics,* 3 (1981): 35–47.

60.   Rosen, *Diet for Transcendence,* p. 60.

61.   Ibid., p. 67.

Chapter 8: Arguments Against Vegetarianism

1.   Some may contend that a different counterargument, focusing on the alleged unhealthiness of a vegetarian diet, is of more immediate interest. This may be so, but as I have argued (Chapter 5, Section 2), health concerns

do not normally mark out the territory of *philosophical* argument. For the vegetarian response to the claim that meatless diets are less healthy, see Chapter 5, n. 2.

2. R. G. Frey, *Rights, Killing, and Suffering: Moral Vegetarianism and Applied Ethics* (Oxford: Blackwell, 1983), pp. 197–203. See also Michael P. T. Leahy, *Against Liberation: Putting Animals in Perspective* (London and New York: Routledge, 1991), chap. 8.

3. See, for example, Lester W. Milbrath, *Envisioning a Sustainable Society: Learning Our Way Out* (Albany: State University of New York Press, 1989), esp. chap. 9.

4. Marjorie Spiegel, *The Dreaded Comparison: Human and Animal Slavery*, rev. and enl. ed. (New York: Mirror Books, 1996), pp. 27–28.

5. Gary L. Francione, *Rain Without Thunder: The Ideology of the Animal Rights Movement* (Philadelphia: Temple University Press, 1996), pp. 60, 152 (emphasis in original).

6. Spiegel, *Dreaded Comparison*, p. 30.

7. For the best comparison see Peter Cox, *The New Why You Don't Need Meat* (London: Bloomsbury Publishing, 1992), p. 30, table. See also Jon Wynne-Tyson, *Food for a Future: The Complete Case for Vegetarianism* (London: Centaur Press; New York: Universe Books, 1979), pp. 39–45.

8. Colin Spencer, *The Heretic's Feast: A History of Vegetarianism* (Hanover, NH: University Press of New England, 1995), p. 232.

9. Elizabeth Telfer, *Food for Thought: Philosophy and Food* (New York and London: Routledge, 1996), p. 78.

10. Robert Andrews (in *The Columbia Dictionary of Quotations* [New York: Columbia University Press, 1993], p. 92) states that Reagan was quoted by the *Sacramento Bee* of 12 March 1966 as saying, "A tree's a tree. How many more do you need to look at?" but that Reagan later denied making the statement. See also Susan R. Schrepfer, *The Fight to Save the Redwoods: A History of Environmental Reform, 1917–1978* (Madison: University of Wisconsin Press, 1983), pp. 146, 296 n. 96.

11. Evelyn Pluhar, *Beyond Prejudice: The Moral Significance of Human and Nonhuman Animals* (Durham and London: Duke University Press, 1995), p. 185.

12. Peter Singer, *Animal Liberation*, new rev. ed. (New York: Avon, 1990), p. 229.

13. Pluhar, *Beyond Prejudice*, p. 189. For a comprehensive critique of the replaceability argument, refer to chap. 4 of her book.

14. J. Baird Callicott, "Animal Liberation: A Triangular Affair," in *In Defense of the Land Ethic: Essays in Environmental Philosophy* (Albany: State University of New York Press, 1989), p. 35 (emphasis in original). See also

Patrick F. Scanlon, "Humans as Hunting Animals," in *Ethics and Animals,* ed. Harlan B. Miller and William B. Williams (Clifton, NJ: Humana Press), pp. 199–205.

15.   Ibid., p. 35.

16.   Kathryn Paxton George, "Should Feminists Be Vegetarians?" *Signs,* 19 (1994): 405–34.

17.   Kathryn Paxton George, "Discrimination and Bias in the Vegan Ideal," *Journal of Agricultural and Environmental Ethics,* 7 (1994): 19. George is not always clear about the kind of bias she wishes to single out for attention. In an earlier piece, for example, anyone who matches the following descriptors is a human whose biological welfare does not depend on eating (any) meat: "an adult male, non-allergic, healthy, well-educated, middle or upper class individual or a young adult non-allergic, healthy, well-educated, middle or upper class female unable to bear children" ("So Animal a Human . . . , or the Moral Relevance of Being an Omnivore," *Journal of Agricultural and Environmental Ethics,* 3 [1990]: 179). Why George does not expand the female criteria to include women who have *chosen* not to bear children is a mystery.

18.   Readers will find several references in the Bibliography to replies and counterreplies, all appearing in the *Journal of Agricultural and Environmental Ethics,* authored separately by George, Pluhar, and Gary E. Varner.

19.   George, "So Animal a Human," p. 172.

20.   Ibid., p. 175.

21.   Ibid., p. 179.

22.   George, "Should Feminists Be Vegetarians?" p. 407.

23.   Ibid., p. 408.

24.   Cited in Geoffrey York, "Where Reindeer Are a Way of Life," *Toronto Globe and Mail,* 15 March 1997, p. D1.

25.   Emanuel Lowi, "Track 'Em Down, Round 'Em Up, Herd 'Em In, Rawhide," *Canadian Geographic,* 117:3 (May–June 1997): 72–78.

26.   Margaret Munro, "Whale of a Dilemma in the Arctic," *Vancouver Sun,* 21 January 1998, p. A13.

27.   Richard C. Paddock, "'Fox Food' Whale Hunt Casts Doubt on Tradition," *Vancouver Sun,* 26 September 1997, p. A17.

28.   Jane Meyerding, "Feminist Criticism and Cultural Imperialism, (Where Does One End and the Other Begin?)," *Animals' Agenda,* November–December 1982, pp. 14, 15, 22, 23.

29.   For further related discussion, see George Wenzel, *Animal Rights, Human Rights* (Toronto: University of Toronto Press, 1991); and Wendy Donner, "Animal Rights and Native Hunters: A Critical Analysis of Wenzel's Defence," in *Canadian Issues in Environmental Ethics,* ed. Alex Wellington, Allan Greenbaum, and Wesley Cragg (Peterborough, ON: Broadview Press, 1998), pp. 153–84.

30.   John Benson, "Duty and the Beast," *Philosophy*, 53 (1978): 547.

31.   For further discussion of humans' obligation to prevent predation in nature, see S. F. Sapontzis, *Morals, Reason, and Animals* (Philadelphia: Temple University Press, 1987), chap. 13.

32.   Michael Martin, "A Critique of Moral Vegetarianism," *Reason Papers*, 3 (Fall 1976): 19–21.

33.   See Al Capp's cartoon book *The Life and Times of the Shmoo* (New York: Simon and Schuster, 1948).

34.   The fantasy that animals want to be eaten by us is an old one. Ben Jonson (1572–1637) gives expression to it in his poem "To Penshurst" (1616), in *The Norton Anthology of English Literature*, ed. M. H. Abrams, 6th ed., vol. 1 (New York: W. W. Norton, 1993), pp. 1223–25, where nature is portrayed as existing to fill human plates with food, wild birds display their willingness to be killed, and fish and eels eagerly leap into nets or onto land to be caught easily.

35.   Henri Bergson, *Creative Evolution*, trans. Arthur Mitchell (New York: Random House/Modern Library, 1944), p. 149.

36.   John Stuart Mill, "On Liberty," in *Utilitarianism, Liberty, and Representative Government* (New York: E. P. Dutton, 1951), p. 96. First published in 1859.

37.   In his play *Dirty Hands (Les Mains sales)*, one of the protagonists, the commander of an underground resistance unit named Hoederer, gives voice to Sartre's view of the human condition: "Purity is an idea for a yogi or a monk. . . . Well, I have dirty hands. Right up to the elbows. I've plunged them in filth and blood" (Jean-Paul Sartre, *Dirty Hands*, trans. Lionel Abel, in *No Exit and Three Other Plays* [New York: Vintage International, 1989], p. 218.)

38.   Rita Manning, "Just Caring," in *Explorations in Feminist Ethics: Theory and Practice*, ed. Eve Browning Cole and Susan Coultrap-McQuin (Bloomington and Indianapolis: Indiana University Press, 1992), p. 52.

39.   Susan Sperling, *Animal Liberators: Research and Morality* (Berkeley and Los Angeles: University of California Press, 1988), pp. 115–16.

40.   Carol J. Adams, *The Sexual Politics of Meat: A Feminist-Vegetarian Critical Theory* (New York: Continuum, 1991), p. 70.

41.   U.S. Department of Agriculture, "Consumption: Per Capita Consumption of Major Food Commodities, United States, 1986–94," in *Agricultural Statistics 1995–96* (Washington, DC: U.S. Government Printing Office, 1996), pp. XIII-5–6, table 653. "Red meats" include beef, veal, lamb and mutton, and pork. While beef consumption was on a downward trend during this period, that of pork was up and that of poultry was sharply up. Overall, consumption of meat, fish, and poultry combined showed a 4.6 percent decline.

42.   Telfer, *Food for Thought*, p. 80.

43.   Arthur Schopenhauer, *The World as Will and Representation*,

trans. E.F.J. Payne (New York: Dover Publications, 1969), vol. 1, 4th bk., "The World as Will: Second Aspect," sec. 68.

44.   Elise Boulding, "The Social Imagination and the Crisis of Human Futures: A North American Perspective," *Forum for Correspondence and Contact*, 13:2 (February 1983): 27.

Chapter 9: Conscience and Change

1.   For another use of this expression, see Harold Hillman, "The Vegetarian Conscience," *Philosophy and Social Action*, 15 (1989): 51–59.

2.   Lester R. Brown, "Struggling to Raise Cropland Productivity," in *State of the World, 1998: A Worldwatch Report on Progress Toward a Sustainable Society*, ed. Lester R. Brown et al. (New York and London: W. W. Norton, 1998), pp. 95, 89.

3.   Ibid., p. 79.

4.   Kathryn Paxton George, "So Animal a Human . . . , or the Moral Relevance of Being an Omnivore," *Journal of Agricultural and Environmental Ethics*, 3 (1990): 178.

5.   For a lucid development of this point, see Andrew Tardiff, "Simplifying the Case for Vegetarianism," *Social Theory and Practice*, 22 (1996): 299–314.

6.   George, "So Animal a Human," p. 181 (emphasis in original).

7.   National Anti-Vivisection Society, *Personal Care for People Who Care*, 8th ed. (Chicago: NAVS, 1996). Copies may be obtained by sending US$4.95 to National Anti-Vivisection Society, Dept. 530-0110W, P.O. Box 94020, Palatine, IL 60094-4020, or by calling 1-800-888-NAVS.

8.   Kath Clements, *Why Vegan: The Ethics of Eating and the Need for Change*, 2nd ed. (London: Heretic Books, 1995), pp. 26, 27.

9.   Vesanto Melina, Brenda Davis, and Victoria Harrison, *Becoming Vegetarian: The Complete Guide to Adopting a Healthy Vegetarian Diet* (Toronto: Macmillan Canada, 1994), Table 6.1, p. 103.

10.   Rackham Holt, *George Washington Carver: An American Biography* (Garden City, NY: Doubleday, 1956), p. 224.

11.   Ibid., pp. 228, 258, 229.

12.   Richard Manning, *Grasslands: The History, Biology, Politics, and Promise of the American Prairie* (New York: Penguin, 1997), p. 273.

13.   Ibid.

14.   Ibid., p. 274.

15.   David Pimentel, personal communication, March 1999.

Select Bibliography

This select bibliography contains references to works devoted in whole or in part to philosophical discussions of vegetarianism, supplementary works on vegetarian themes, and other relevant works of outstanding philosophical or general interest. Additional references relating to topics discussed in this book will be found in the notes, by chapter. Many vegetarian resources may now be found on the Internet as well.

Adams, Carol J. "Ecofeminism and the Eating of Animals." *Hypatia,* 6 (1991): 125–45.

———. *Neither Man Nor Beast: Feminism and the Defense of Animals.* New York: Continuum, 1995.

———. *The Sexual Politics of Meat: A Feminist-Vegetarian Critical Theory.* New York: Continuum, 1991.

Akers, Keith A. *A Vegetarian Sourcebook.* Arlington, VA: Vegetarian Press, 1983.

Altman, Nathaniel. *Eating for Life: The Ultimate Diet.* New York: Vegetus Books, 1986.

Amato, Paul R. and Partridge, Sonia A. *The New Vegetarians: Promoting Health and Protecting Life.* New York and London: Plenum Press, 1989.

American Vegan Society, ed. *Here's Harmlessness.* Malaga, NJ: American Vegan Society, 1973.

Auxter, Thomas. "The Right Not to Be Eaten." *Inquiry,* 22 (1979): 221–30.

Ballantine, R. *Transition to Vegetarianism: An Evolutionary Step.* Honesdale, PA: Himalayan Press, 1987.

Barbour, Scott, ed. *Hunger.* San Diego: Greenhaven Press, 1995.

Bargen, R. *The Vegetarian's Self-Defense Manual.* Wheaton, IL: Quest Books, 1979.

Barkas, Janet. *The Vegetable Passion: A History of the Vegetarian State of Mind.* London: Routledge & Kegan Paul; New York: Scribner's, 1975.

Barnard, Neal D. *Food for Life: How the New Four Food Groups Can Save Your Life.* New York: Harmony, 1993.

———. *The Power of Your Plate: A Plan for Better Living.* Summertown, TN: Book Publishing, 1990.

Becker, Lawrence C. "The Priority of Human Interests." In *Ethics and*

Animals. Ed. Harlan B. Miller and William H. Williams. Clifton, NJ: Humana Press, 1983. Pp. 225–42

Beckoff, Marc, with Carron A. Meaney, eds. *Encyclopedia of Animal Rights and Animal Welfare.* Westport, CT: Greenwood Press, 1998.

Berman, Louis A. *Vegetarianism and the Jewish Tradition.* New York: Ktav, 1982.

Berry, Rynn. *Famous Vegetarians and Their Favorite Recipes: Lives and Lore from Buddha to the Beatles.* Rev. ed. New York and Los Angeles: Pythagorean Publishers, 1996.

———. *Food for the Gods: Vegetarianism and the World's Religions.* New York and Los Angeles: Pythagorean Publishers, 1996.

———. *The Vegetarians.* Brookline, MA: Autumn Press, 1979.

Bloyd-Peshkin, Sharon. "Mumbling About Meat." *Vegetarian Times,* 170 (October 1991): 66–68, 70, 72–75.

Boonin-Vail, David. "The Vegetarian Savage: Rousseau's Critique of Meat Eating." *Environmental Ethics,* 15 (1993): 75–84.

Booth, Annie L. "Learning from Others: Ecophilosophy and Traditional Native American Women's Lives." *Environmental Ethics,* 20 (1998): 81–99.

Braunstein, Mark Mathew. *Radical Vegetarianism: A Dialectic of Diet and Ethic.* Rev. ed. Quaker Hill, CT: Panacea Press, 1993.

Brown, Les. *Cruelty to Animals: The Moral Debt.* Houndmills, Basingstoke, Hampshire: Macmillan, 1988.

Caras, Roger A. *A Perfect Harmony: The Intertwining Lives of Animals and Humans Throughout History.* New York: Simon & Schuster, 1997.

Cargile, James. "Comments on 'The Priority of Human Interests.'" In *Ethics and Animals.* Ed. Harlan B. Miller and William H. Williams. Clifton, NJ: Humana Press, 1983. Pp. 243–49.

———. "Postscript." In *Ethics and Animals.* Ed. Harlan B. Miller and William H. Williams. Clifton, NJ: Humana Press, 1983. Pp. 267–70.

Cerquetti, Giorgio. *The Vegetarian Revolution.* Badger, CA: Torchlight, 1997.

Chapple, Christopher K. *Nonviolence to Animals, Earth, and Self in Asian Traditions.* Albany: State University of New York Press, 1993.

Clark, Stephen R. L. *Animals and Their Moral Standing.* London and New York: Routledge, 1997.

———. *The Moral Status of Animals.* Oxford: Clarendon Press, 1977.

Clements, Kath. *Why Vegan: The Ethics of Eating and the Need for Change.* 2nd ed. London: Heretic Books, 1995.

Coats, C. D. *Old Macdonald's Factory Farm.* New York: Continuum, 1989.

Coe, Sue. *Dead Meat.* New York and London: Four Walls Eight Windows, 1995.

Comstock, Gary L. "Pigs and Piety: A Theocentric Perspective on Food Animals." *Between the Species*, 8 (1992): 121–35.

Concar, David. "The Organ Factory of the Future?" *New Scientist*, 142 (18 June 1994): 24–29.

Cox, Michael, and Crockett, Dresda. *The Subversive Vegetarian: Tactics, Information, and Recipes for the Conversion of Meat-Eaters*. Santa Barbara: Woodbridge Press, 1980.

Cox, Peter. *The New Why You Don't Need Meat*. London: Bloomsbury Publishing, 1992.

Crisp, Roger. "Utilitarianism and Vegetarianism." *International Journal of Applied Philosophy*, 4 (1988): 41–49.

Crosby, Ernest. "The Meat Fetish." *Humane Review*, 5 (1904–5): 199–216.

Curnutt, Jordan. "A New Argument for Vegetarianism." *Journal of Social Philosophy*, 28:3 (Winter 1997): 153–72.

Curtin, Deane W., and Heldke, Lisa M. *Cooking, Eating, Thinking: Transformative Philosophies of Food*. Bloomington and Indianapolis: Indiana University Press, 1992.

David, William H. "Man-Eating Aliens." *Journal of Value Inquiry*, 10 (1977): 178–85.

Dawkins, Marian Stamp. *Animal Suffering: The Science of Animal Welfare*. London and New York: Chapman and Hall, 1980.

DeGrazia, David. *Taking Animals Seriously: Mental Life and Moral Status*. Cambridge: Cambridge University Press, 1996.

Devine, Philip E. "The Moral Basis of Vegetarianism." *Philosophy*, 53 (1978): 481–505.

Diamond, Cora. "Eating Meat and Eating People." *Philosophy*, 53 (1978): 465–79.

Dixon, Beth A. "The Feminist Connection Between Women and Animals." *Environmental Ethics*, 18 (1996): 181–94.

Dixon, Nicholas. "Reply—Feminism and Utilitarian Arguments for Vegetarianism: A Note on Alex Wellington's 'Feminist Positions on Vegetarianism.'" *Between the Species*, 11 (1995): 105.

———. "A Utilitarian Argument for Vegetarianism." *Between the Species*, 11 (1995): 90–97.

Dombrowski, Daniel A. *The Philosophy of Vegetarianism*. Amherst: University of Massachusetts Press, 1984.

———. "Vegetarianism and the Argument from Marginal Cases in Porphyry." *Journal of the History of Ideas*, 45 (1984): 141–43.

———. "Was Plato a Vegetarian?" *Apeiron*, 18 (1984): 1–9.

Donovan, Josephine. "Animal Rights and Feminist Theory." In *Ecofeminism:*

Women, Animals, Nature. Ed. Greta Gaard. Philadelphia: Temple University Press, 1993. Pp. 167–94.

Douglas, Mary. "Deciphering a Meal." In *Implicit Meanings: Essays in Anthropology.* London and Boston: Routledge & Kegan Paul, 1975. Pp. 249–75.

Durning, Alan. "Fat of the Land: Livestock's Resource Gluttony." *World Watch,* 4:3 (May–June 1991): 11–17.

Dyer, Judith C. *Vegetarianism: An Annotated Bibliography.* Metuchen, NJ: Scarecrow Press, 1982.

Egonsson, Dan. "Kant's Vegetarianism." *Journal of Value Inquiry,* 31 (1997): 473–83.

Eisnetz, Gail. *Slaughterhouse.* Buffalo: Prometheus, 1997.

Epstein, Robert. "A Benefactor of His Race: Thoreau's 'Hybrid Laws' and the Heroics of Vegetarianism." *Between the Species,* 1 (1985): 23–34.

Ferré, Frederick. "Moderation, Morals, and Meat." *Inquiry,* 29 (1986): 391–406.

Fiddes, Nick. *Meat: A Natural Symbol.* London and New York: Routledge, 1991.

Food and Agricultural Organization of the United Nations. *Dimensions of Need: An Atlas of Food and Agriculture.* Santa Barbara: ABC-CLIO, 1995.

Fox, Michael Allen. "Anthropocentrism." In *Encyclopedia of Animal Rights and Animal Welfare.* Ed. Marc Bekoff with Carron A. Meaney. Westport, CT: Greenwood Press, 1998. Pp. 66–68.

———. "Arguments for Vegetarianism." In *Canadian Issues in Environmental Ethics.* Ed. Alex Wellington, Allan Greenbaum, and Wesley Cragg. Peterborough, ON: Broadview Press, 1997. Pp. 165–73.

———. "Environmental Ethics and the Ideology of Meat Eating." *Between the Species,* 9 (1993): 121–32.

———. "On the 'Necessary Suffering' of Nonhuman Animals." *Animal Law,* 3 (1997): 25–30.

———. "Vegetarianism, Arguments for." In *Encyclopedia of Animal Rights and Animal Welfare.* Ed. Marc Bekoff with Carron A. Meaney. Westport, CT: Greenwood Press, 1998. Pp. 349–51.

Fox, Michael W. *Superpigs and Wondercorn: The Brave New World of Biotechnology and Where It All May Lead.* New York: Lyons & Burford, 1992.

Francione, Gary L. *Animals, Property, and the Law.* Philadelphia: Temple University Press, 1995.

———. *Rain Without Thunder: The Ideology of the Animal Rights Movement.* Philadelphia: Temple University Press, 1996.

Francis, Leslie Pickering, and Norman, Richard. "Some Animals Are More Equal Than Others." *Philosophy,* 53 (1978): 507–27.

Frey, R. G. *Rights, Killing, and Suffering: Moral Vegetarianism and Applied Ethics.* Oxford: Blackwell, 1983.

Gandhi, Mohandas Karamchand. *The Moral Basis of Vegetarianism.* Comp. R. K. Prabhu. Ahmedabad: Navajivan, 1959.

George, Kathryn Paxton. "Discrimination and Bias in the Vegan Ideal." *Journal of Agricultural and Environmental Ethics,* 7 (1994): 19–28.

———. "So Animal a Human . . . , or the Moral Relevance of Being an Omnivore." *Journal of Agricultural Ethics,* 3 (1990): 172–86.

———. "The Use and Abuse of Scientific Studies: Reply." *Journal of Agricultural and Environmental Ethics,* 5 (1992): 217–33.

———. "Use and Abuse Revisited: Response to Pluhar and Varner." *Journal of Agricultural and Environmental Ethics,* 7 (1994): 41–76.

Giehl, Dudley. *Vegetarianism: A Way of Life.* New York: Harper & Row, 1979.

Gold, Mark. *Assault and Battery: What Factory Farming Means for Humans and Animals.* London: Pluto Press, 1983.

———. "On the Meat-Hook." *New Internationalist,* 215 (January 1991): 9–10.

Grant, Robert. "Dietary Laws Among Pythagoreans, Jews, and Christians." *Harvard Theological Review,* 73 (1980): 299–310.

Gregerson, Jon. *Vegetarianism: A History.* Fremont, CA: Jain Publishing, 1994.

Grose, Anouchka, with Ruth Jones. *The Teenage Vegetarian Survival Guide.* London: Red Fox, 1992.

Gruzalski, Bart. "The Case Against Raising and Killing Animals for Food." In *Ethics and Animals.* Ed. Harlan B. Miller and William H. Williams. Clifton, NJ: Humana Press, 1983. Pp. 251–65.

Gupta, Surinder Nath. *Vegetarianism: A Human Imperative.* Bombay: Bharatiya Vidya Bhavan, 1986.

Harris, John. "Killing for Food." In *Animals, Men, and Morals: An Enquiry into the Maltreatment of Non-Humans.* Ed. Stanley Godlovitch, Roslind Godlovitch, and John Harris. London: Victor Gollancz; New York: Taplinger, 1971. Pp. 97–110.

Haussleiter, Johannes. *Der Vegetarismus in der Antike.* Berlin: A. Töpelmann, 1935.

Hettinger, Ned. "Valuing Predation in Rolston's Environmental Ethics: Bambi Lovers Versus Tree Huggers." *Environmental Ethics,* 16 (1994): 3–20.

Hill, John Lawrence. *The Case for Vegetarianism: Philosophy for a Small Planet.* Lanham, MD: Rowman & Littlefield, 1996.

Hillman, Harold. "The Vegetarian Conscience." *Philosophy and Social Action,* 15 (1989): 51–59.

Hogshire, Jim. "Animals and Islam." *Animals' Agenda,* 11:8 (October 1991): 10–14.

Horigan, Stephen. *Nature and Culture in Western Discourses.* London and New York: Routledge, 1988.

Hudson, Hud. "Collective Responsibility and Moral Vegetarianism." *Journal of Social Philosophy,* 24:2 (Fall 1993): 89–104.

Irvine, William B. "Cannibalism, Vegetarianism, and Narcissism." *Between the Species,* 5 (1989): 11–17.

Jamieson, Dale. "Killing Persons and Other Beings." In *Ethics and Animals.* Ed. Harlan B. Miller and William H. Williams. Clifton, NJ: Humana Press, 1983. Pp. 135–46.

Johnson, Edward. "Life, Death, and Animals." In *Ethics and Animals.* Ed. Harlan B. Miller and William H. Williams. Clifton, NJ: Humana Press, 1983. Pp. 123–33.

Kaleschofsky, R. *Haggadah for the Liberated Lamb.* Marblehead, MA: Micah, 1985.

Kapleau, Philip. *To Cherish All Life: A Buddhist View of Animal Slaughter and Meat Eating.* Rochester: Zen Center, 1981.

Kellert, Stephen R. *Kinship to Mastery: Biophilia in Human Evolution and Development.* Washington, DC, and Covelo, CA: Island Press/Shearwater Books, 1997.

Kellogg, John Harvey. *The Natural Diet of Man.* Battle Creek, MI: Modern Medicine Publishing, 1923.

Khalik, M.I.A. *An Article on Islam and Vegetarianism.* Madras: Vegetarian Way, 1977.

Kingsford, Anna and Maitland, Edward. *Addresses and Essays on Vegetarianism, 1881–1893.* Ed. S. H. Hart. London: John M. Watkins, 1912.

Kuffner, Glenn J. *Vegetarianism: Index of Modern Information.* Washington, DC: ABBE Publishers Association, 1988.

Kutzner, Patricia L. *World Hunger: A Reference Book.* Santa Barbara: ABC-CLIO, 1991.

Lappé, Frances Moore. *Diet for a Small Planet.* 20th ed. New York: Ballantine, 1992.

Lehman, Hugh. "On the Moral Acceptability of Killing Animals." *Journal of Agricultural Ethics,* 1 (1988): 155–62.

Lockwood, Michael. "Singer on Killing and the Preference for Life." *Inquiry,* 22 (1979): 157–70.

Lyttelton, E. "Vegetarianism." In *Encyclopaedia of Religion and Ethics.* Ed. James Hastings. Edinburgh: T. & T. Clark, 1921. Vol. 12, pp. 618–23.

Magel, Charles R. *A Bibliography on Animal Rights and Related Matters.* Washington, DC: University Press of America, 1981.

———. *Keyguide to Information Sources in Animal Rights.* London: Mansell; Jefferson, NC: McFarland, 1989.

Martin, Michael. "A Critique of Moral Vegetarianism." *Reason Papers,* 3 (Fall 1976): 13–43.

Mason, Jim. "Brave New Farm?" In *In Defense of Animals.* Ed. Peter Singer. New York: Blackwell, 1985. Pp. 89–107.

———. *An Unnatural Order.* New York: Simon & Schuster, 1993.

———, and Peter Singer. *Animal Factories.* Rev. ed. New York: Harmony, 1990.

Masri, Al-Hafiz Basheer Ahmad. *Animals in Islam.* Petersfield, Hants: Athlene Trust, 1989.

———. *Islamic Concern for Animals.* Petersfield, Hants: Athlene Trust, 1987.

Maurer, Donna. "Meat as a Social Problem: Rhetorical Strategies in the Contemporary Vegetarian Literature." In *Eating Agendas: Food and Nutrition as Social Problems.* Ed. Donna Maurer and Jeffrey Sobal. New York: Aldine de Gruyter, 1995. Pp. 143–63.

McKenna, Erin. "Feminism and Vegetarianism: A Critique of Peter Singer." *Philosophy in the Contemporary World,* 1:3 (February 1994): 28–35.

———. "Women, Power, and Meat: Comparing *The Sexual Contract* and *The Sexual Politics of Meat." Journal of Social Philosophy,* 27 (1996): 47–64.

McLachlan, H. V. "The Moral Case of a Carnivore." *Contemporary Review,* 237 (1980): 19–24.

Melina, Vesanto, Brenda Davis, and Victoria Harrison. *Becoming Vegetarian: The Complete Guide to Adopting a Healthy Vegetarian Diet.* Toronto: Macmillan Canada, 1994.

Mendel, L. B. "Some Historical Aspects of Vegetarianism." *Popular Science Monthly,* 64 (1903–4): 457–65.

Michael, Emily. "Vegetarianism and Virtue: On Gassendi's Epicurean Defense." *Between the Species,* 7 (1991): 61–72.

Midgley, Mary. *Animals and Why They Matter: A Journey Around the Species Barrier.* Harmondsworth, Middlesex: Penguin, 1983.

Mitra, Ananda. *Food for Thought: The Vegetarian Philosophy.* Corona, NY: Ananda Marga; Willow Springs, MO: NUCLEUS, 1991.

Moran, Victoria. *Compassion, the Ultimate Ethic: An Exploration of Veganism.* Wellingborough, Northamptonshire: Thorsons, 1985.

Moriarty, Paul Veatch, and Mark Woods. "Hunting ≠ Predation." *Environmental Ethics,* 19 (1997): 391–404.

Nearing, H., and S. Nearing. *Continuing the Good Life.* New York: Schocken, 1979.

————. *Living the Good Life*. New York: Schocken, 1970.

Noske, Barbara. *Beyond Boundaries: Humans and Animals*. Montreal, New York, and London: Black Rose Books, 1997.

Oldfield, J. "Vegetarian Still: A Reply to Sir Henry Thompson." *Nineteenth Century*, 44 (1898): 246–52.

Parham, Barbara. *What's Wrong with Eating Meat?* Denver: Ananda Marga, 1979.

Pateman, Carole. "The Sexual Contract and the Animals." *Journal of Social Philosophy*, 27 (1996): 65–80.

Perrett, Roy W. "Moral Vegetarianism and the Indian Tradition." In *Ethical and Political Dilemmas of Modern India*. Ed. Ninian Smart and Shivesh Thakur. New York: St. Martin's Press, 1993. Pp. 82–99.

Perry, Clifton. "We Are What We Eat." *Environmental Ethics*, 3 (1981): 341–50.

Pimentel, David. "Environmental and Social Implications of Waste in U.S. Agriculture and Food Sectors." *Journal of Agricultural Ethics*, 3 (1990): 5–20.

————. *Food, Energy, and Society*. 2nd ed. Niwot: University Press of Colorado, 1996.

————. "Livestock Production: Energy Inputs and the Environment." In *Proceedings of the Canadian Society of Animal Science, 47th Annual Meeting, 24–26 July 1997, Montreal*. Ed. S. L. Scott and Xin Zho. Montreal: Canadian Society of Animal Science, 1997. Pp. 16–26.

Pluhar, Evelyn. *Beyond Prejudice: The Moral Significance of Human and Nonhuman Animals*. Durham and London: Duke University Press, 1995.

————. "On Vegetarianism, Morality, and Science: A Counter-Reply." *Journal of Agricultural and Environmental Ethics*, 6 (1993): 185–213.

————. "Vegetarianism, Morality, and Science Revisited." *Journal of Agricultural and Environmental Ethics*, 7 (1994): 77–82.

————. "Who Can Be Morally Obligated to Be a Vegetarian?" *Journal of Agricultural and Environmental Ethics*, 5 (1992): 189–215.

Porphyry. *On Abstinence from Animal Food*. Trans. Thomas Taylor. Ed. Esme Wynne-Tyson. London: Centaur; New York: Barnes & Noble, 1965. Reprint, Watchung, NJ: Albert Saifer, 1989.

Rachels, James. "Vegetarianism and 'The Other Weight Problem.'" In *World Hunger and Moral Obligation*. Ed. William Aiken and Hugh LaFollette. Englewood Cliffs, NJ: Prentice-Hall, 1977. Pp. 180–93.

Regan, Tom. *The Case for Animal Rights*. Berkeley and Los Angeles: University of California Press, 1983.

————. "Ethical Vegetarianism and Commercial Animal Farming." In *Agri-*

culture, Change, and Human Values. Ed. R. Haynes and R. Lanier. Gainesville, FL: Humanities and Agricultural Program, 1984. Pp. 279–94.

———. "The Moral Basis of Vegetarianism." *Canadian Journal of Philosophy,* 5 (1975): 181–214.

———. "Utilitarianism and Vegetarianism Again." *Ethics and Animals,* 2 (1981): 2–7.

———. "Utilitarianism, Vegetarianism, and Animal Rights." *Philosophy and Public Affairs,* 9 (1980): 305–24.

Richards, Stewart. "Forethoughts for Carnivores." *Philosophy,* 56 (1981): 73–88.

Rifkin, Jeremy. *Beyond Beef: The Rise and Fall of the Cattle Culture.* New York: Dutton, 1992.

Ritson, Joseph. *An Essay on Abstinence from Animal Food, as a Moral Duty.* London: Phillips, 1802.

Robbins, John. *Diet for a New America.* Walpole, NH: Stillpoint, 1987.

———. *May All Be Fed: Diet for a New World.* New York: Avon, 1992.

Rosen, Steven. *Diet for Transcendence: Vegetarianism and the World Religions.* Badger, CA: Torchlight, 1997. First published as *Food for the Spirit: Vegetarianism and the World Religions.* New York: Bala, 1987.

Rudd, Geoffrey L. *Why Kill for Food?* Madras: Indian Vegetarian Congress, 1956.

Ruegg, D. Seyfort. "*Ahimsa* and Vegetarianism in the History of Buddhism." In *Buddhist Studies in Honour of W. Rahula.* Ed. Somaratna Balasooriya. London: Roundtable, 1980. Pp. 234–41.

Ryder, Richard D. *Animal Revolution: Changing Attitudes Toward Speciesism.* Oxford: Blackwell, 1989.

Salt, Henry S. *Animals' Rights Considered in Relation to Social Progress.* London and New York: G. Bell, 1892; rev. ed., London: G. Bell, 1922. Reprint, Clarks Summit, PA: Society for Animal Rights, 1980.

———. *The Logic of Vegetarianism: Essays and Dialogues.* London: Ideal Publishing Union, 1899. 2nd rev. ed., London: G. Bell and Sons, 1906.

———. *A Plea for Vegetarianism and Other Essays.* Manchester: Vegetarian Society, 1886.

Sanehi, Swaran Singh. *Vegetarianism in Sikhism.* Madras: Vegetarian Way, 1977.

Sapontzis, S. F. *Morals, Reason, and Animals.* Philadelphia: Temple University Press, 1987.

———. "Reply to Weir: Unnecessary Fear, Nutrition, and Vegetarianism." *Between the Species,* 7 (1991): 27–32.

Satchidananda, S. S. *The Healthy Vegetarian.* Buckingham, VA: Integral Yoga, 1986.

Schleifer, Harriet. "Images of Death and Life: Food Animal Production and the Vegetarian Option." In *In Defense of Animals.* Ed. Peter Singer. New York: Blackwell, 1985. Pp. 63–73.

Schwartz, Richard H. *Judaism and Vegetarianism.* Marblehead, MA: Micah, 1988.

Shafer-Landau, Russ. "Vegetarianism, Causation, and Ethical Theory." *Public Affairs Quarterly,* 8 (1994): 85–100.

Shelley, Percy Bysshe."On the Vegetable System of Diet." In *The Complete Works of Percy Bysshe Shelley.* Vol. 6, *Prose.* Ed. Roger Ingpen and Walter E. Peck. New York: Gordian Press; London: Ernest Benn, 1965. Pp. 335–44.

———. "A Vindication of Natural Diet." In *The Complete Works of Percy Bysshe Shelley.* Vol. 6, *Prose.* Ed. Roger Ingpen and Walter E. Peck. New York: Gordian Press; London: Ernest Benn, 1965. Pp. 3–18.

Sheth, Tej, and Sheth, Tarang. *The Case for Vegetarianism.* Toronto: Amrit, 1991.

———. *Why Be a Vegetarian?* Fremont, CA: Jain Publishing, 1995.

Shiva, Vandana. *Biopiracy: The Plunder of Nature and Knowledge.* Boston: South End Press, 1997.

Silverstein, Brett. *Fed Up! The Food Forces That Make You Fat, Sick, and Poor.* Boston: South End, 1984.

Singer, Peter. *Animal Liberation.* New rev. ed. New York: Avon, 1990.

———. "Feminism and Vegetarianism: A Response." *Philosophy in the Contemporary World,* 1:3 (February 1994): 36–38.

———. "Killing Humans and Killing Animals." *Inquiry,* 22 (1979): 145–56.

———. *Practical Ethics.* 2nd ed. Cambridge: Cambridge University Press, 1993.

———. "Utilitarianism and Vegetarianism." *Philosophy and Public Affairs,* 9 (1980): 325–37.

Skriver, C. A. *The Forgotten Beginnings of Creation and Christianity.* Trans. and ed. A. Ingle et al. Arlington, VA: Vegetarian Press, 1987.

Spencer, Colin. *The Heretic's Feast: A History of Vegetarianism.* London: Fourth Estate, 1993; Hanover, NH: University Press of New England, 1995.

Spiegel, Marjorie. *The Dreaded Comparison: Human and Animal Slavery.* Rev. and enl. ed. New York: Mirror Books, 1996.

Stacey, Michelle. *Consumed: Why Americans Love, Hate, and Fear Food.* New York: Touchstone, 1994.

Stephens, William O. "Five Arguments for Vegetarianism." *Philosophy in the Contemporary World,* 1:4 (Winter 1994): 25–39.

Subramuniyaswami, Satguru Sivaya. "How to Win an Argument with a Meat

Eater." Concord, CA: Himalayan Academy, 1998. Published on the Internet at http://arrs.envirolink.org/ar-voices/virtues.html.

Sussman, Vic S. *The Vegetarian Alterative: A Guide to a Healthful and Humane Diet.* Emmaus, PA: Rodale Press, 1978.

Tannahill, Reay. *Food in History.* New York: Stein and Day, 1973.

Tardiff, Andrew. "A Catholic Case for Vegetarianism." *Faith and Philosophy,* 15 (1998): 210–22.

———. "Simplifying the Case for Vegetarianism." *Social Theory and Practice,* 22 (1996): 299–314.

Telfer, Elizabeth. *Food for Thought: Philosophy and Food.* London and New York: Routledge, 1996.

Thompson, H. "Why 'Vegetarian'?" *Nineteenth Century,* 43 (1898): 556–69, 966–76.

Tideman, T. Nicholas. "Deciding What to Kill." In *Ethics and Animals.* Ed. Harlan B. Miller and William H. Williams. Clifton, NJ: Humana Press, 1983. Pp. 317–22.

Townsend, Aubrey. "Radical Vegetarians." *Australasian Journal of Philosophy,* 57 (1979): 85–93.

Twigg, J. "Food for Thought: Purity and Vegetarianism." *Religion,* 9 (1979): 13–35.

———. "Vegetarianism and the Meanings of Meat." In *The Sociology of Food and Eating: Essays on the Sociological Significance of Food.* Ed. A. Murcott. Aldershot, Hampshire: Gower, 1983. Pp. 18–30.

Vaclavik, Charles. *The Vegetarianism of Jesus Christ: The Pacificism, Communalism, and Vegetarianism of Primitive Christianity.* Platteville, WI: Kaweah, 1988.

VanDeVeer, Donald. "Interspecific Justice and Animal Slaughter." In *Ethics and Animals.* Ed. Harlan B. Miller and William H. Williams. Clifton, NJ: Humana Press, 1983. Pp. 147–62.

Varner, Gary E. "In Defense of the Vegan Ideal: Rhetoric and Bias in the Nutrition Literature." *Journal of Agricultural and Environmental Ethics,* 7 (1994): 29–40.

———. "Rejoinder to Kathryn Paxton George." *Journal of Agricultural and Environmental Ethics,* 7 (1994): 83–86.

———. "What's Wrong with Animal *By-Products?*" *Journal of Agricultural and Environmental Ethics,* 7 (1994): 7–17.

Vedic Contemporary Library Series. *The Higher Taste.* Los Angeles: Bhaktivedanta Book Trust, 1983.

Vialles, Noëlie. *Animal to Edible.* Trans. J. A. Underwood. Cambridge: Cambridge University Press; Paris: Editions de la maison des sciences de l'homme, 1994.

Weir, Jack. "Response to Sapontzis's Reply." *Between the Species*, 7 (1991): 33–35.

———. "Unnecessary Pain, Nutrition, and Vegetarianism." *Between the Species*, 7 (1991): 13–26.

Wellington, Alex. "Response—Feminist Positions on Vegetarianism: Arguments for and Against and Otherwise." *Between the Species*, 11 (1995): 98–104.

Wenz, Peter S. "An Ecological Argument for Vegetarianism." *Ethics and Animals*, 5 (1984): 2–9.

Williams, Howard. *The Ethics of Diet: A Biographical History of the Literature of Humane Dietetics, from the Earliest Period to the Present Day*. Rev. and enl. ed. London: Sonnenschein, 1896.

Wynne-Tyson, Jon. "Dietethics: Its Influence on Future Farming Patterns." In *Animal Rights: A Symposium*. Ed. David Paterson and Richard Ryder. Fontwell, Sussex, and New York: Centaur, 1979. Pp. 135–42.

———. *Food for a Future: The Complete Case for Vegetarianism*. London: Centaur Press; New York: Universe Books, 1979.

Young, Thomas. "The Morality of Killing Animals." *Ethics and Animals*, 5 (1984): 88–101.

Index

aboriginal peoples. *See* indigenous peoples

Adams, Carol J., 20, 33–36, 37, 51, 79, 171

aggression. *See* violence and aggression

agribusiness, 76, 87, 95, 96. *See also* agriculture; cattle; eggs; farming, factory; livestock industry

agriculture, 49, 85–88, 154. *See also* agribusiness

ahimsa. See nonviolence

Alcott, Amos Bronson, 17

Alcott, Louisa May, 17

Alcott House Concordium, 17

Allah, 138

Amato, Paul R., 17, 43, 55, 56, 57, 65

Amazon, 90. *See also* rain forests, tropical

animal liberation, 48, 103, 152

Animal Liberation, 20

animal products, 169–73, 179

animal rights. *See* rights, of animals

animal welfare movement, 18, 46

animals: as "absent referent," 34 (*see also* Adams, Carol J.); ambivalence toward, 43; anthropomorphizing of, 47; as commodities, 94, 102; companion, 40, 42, 46, 56, 72, 95, 115, 147, 151, 164, 165, 169, 171; confinement of, 76, 77; as consenting to be eaten, 30, 164–68, 213n. 34; consumption of, 34–35, 51; as contributing to human culture, 28–29, 58, 63; cruelty toward (*see* cruelty); defined, 62; as different from humans, 10, 15, 45, 63, 82, 163, 206n. 92 (*see also* humans,

relationship to animals of); exploitation of, 58, 95, 104; farm, 40, 115, 147, 151, 155; as inferior, 44, 187n. 32; killing of, 8, 11, 15, 20, 26, 29, 32–33, 37, 40, 46, 47, 49, 50, 76–78, 111, 124, 125, 126, 134, 146, 152, 153, 158, 163, 171, 177, 199n. 33; and the law, 145; linguistic capacities of, 9–10, 17; mental capacities of, 9, 14, 16, 17, 49, 62–64, 105, 142; moral status of, 2, 20, 22, 61–64, 78, 103, 142 (*see also* rights, of animals); in myth, 131–32; oppression of women and, 20, 34; pain and suffering of, 9, 14, 17, 26, 37, 40, 47, 49, 50, 51, 52, 58, 62, 76–79, 82, 83, 112, 122, 125, 142, 152, 163, 173, 200n. 37; predatory, 147, 163–64; as property, 12, 15, 63; religious sacrifice of, 6, 9, 27, 185–86n. 12; replaceability of, 150–53, 199n. 33; respect for, 15, 49; as "subjects-of-a-life," 20, 77, 199n. 34; value of, 9, 20, 33, 45, 176

Animals, Men, and Morals: An Enquiry into the Maltreatment of Non-Humans, 20

anthropocentrism, 22, 104, 116. *See also* speciesism

antidominionist theories, 100, 205n. 83. *See also* ecofeminism

antimetaphysical views, 2–3

antivivisectionism, 18, 43, 46

apes, 62, 152

Aquinas, Saint Thomas, 13, 107

Aristotle, 7, 13, 72–73, 198n. 16

Aśoka, Emperor, 6, 124

Augustine, Saint, 107